A Reader's Guide to

ROBERT BROWNING

A Reader's Guide to ROBERT BROWNING

Norton B. Crowell

UNIVERSITY OF NEW MEXICO PRESS

Albuquerque

Manufactured in the United States of America.
Library of Congress Catalog Card No. 72-86825.
First Edition

To Ruthmary, Lawrence, Dring, Steven, and Donald

Acknowledgments

The author gratefully acknowledges the kindness of these authors and publishers in giving permission to reproduce material in this book. Anthony Sheil Associates Limited, for quoted material from *Robert Browning: A Study of His Poetry*, by Thomas Blackburn, Eyre and Spottiswoode, 1967. Appleton-Century-Crofts for quoted material from *A Browning Handbook*, by William C. DeVane, 2nd Edition Copyrighted © 1955 by Appleton-Century-Crofts, Inc., by permission of the publishers, Educational Division, Meredith Corporation. Barnes & Noble Publishers and Oliver and Boyd, the original publishers, for material adapted from Barbara Melchiori, *Browning's Poetry of Reticence*, Barnes & Noble Publishers, New York, New York, 1968. The Bobbs-Merrill Company, for quoted material from *Robert Browning*, by William Lyon Phelps, copyright 1932, by the Bobbs-Merrill Company, Inc., 1960, reprinted by permission of the publisher, and for quoted material from *Robert Browning: "Pippa Passes," and Shorter Poems*, edited by Joseph E. Baker, copyright, 1947, by The Odyssey Press, Inc., reprinted by permission of the Bobbs-Merrill Company, Inc. Bowes and Bowes Publishers, Ltd., for quoted material from *Amphibian, A Reconsideration of Browning*, by Henry Charles Duffin, 1956. *The Explicator*, for quoted material from "Browning's 'Johannes Agricola in Meditation,'" by John W. Willoughby, *The Explicator*, XXI (1962), Item 5; "Browning's 'The Bishop Orders His Tomb in Saint Praxed's Church,'" by Frances W. Bonner, *The Explicator*, XXII (1964), Item 57; "Browning's 'The Bishop Orders His Tomb in Saint Praxed's Church,'" by Vincent M. Milosevich, *The Explicator*, XXVII (1969), Item 67. E. M. Higgins, literary executor of the estate of Dallas Kenmare, for quoted material from *Ever a Fighter: A Modern Approach to the Work of Robert Browning*, by Dallas Kenmare, copyright 1952, Barrie and Jackson, Ltd. The University of Michigan Press, for quoted material from *The Bow and the Lyre*, by Roma A. King, Jr., 1964.

Contents

Preface

Since the end of World War II the critical attention devoted to Robert Browning has increased steadily both in scope and in depth. After a half century of relative neglect, Browning is being discussed and reexamined, in books, in journals, and in seminars, as no one would have predicted after World War I. More encouraging, the quality of scholarship shows signs of maturity and balance as the vogue of hostility to Browning and denigration of him seems to have passed its apex. After the heyday of the adulation of the Browning Societies, it was natural to have the pendulum swing to open hostility both to the man and to his poetry; but the critical climate now seems favorable for objective critical assessment.

The purpose of this *Guide* is to provide the serious student of Browning with close critical judgments of some of his major short poems, those frequently anthologized and, at the same time, most subject to a diversity of interpretation and commentary. Among the critical apparatus included are a bibliography of scholarly works on Browning from 1945 through 1969, bibliographies of Browning's published works by title and by date, and suggested readings on the poems discussed.

I owe a debt of gratitude to my colleagues and to my students, who have given me encouragement, counsel, and incentive. I am particularly indebted to my former colleagues, Professors Willis D. Jacobs, Dudley Wynn, and Katherine Simons, of the University of New Mexico, who read the manuscript and gave valuable advice for its improvement. I am grateful to my colleagues at Illinois State University for their help and understanding.

Norton B. Crowell
Illinois State University

INTRODUCTION

Brief Sketch of Browning's Life and Works

Robert Browning was born on May 7, 1812, in Camberwell, at that time a sylvan and unspoiled suburb of London, three miles south of the Strand, St. Paul's, and the Tower of London. To the south, a thirty-minute walk across pleasant fields, lay Dulwich, with its famous art gallery and the Dulwich wood nearby. The Brownings can be traced to the Dorsetshire of Henry VII, where they were substantial manor owners. Robert Browning, the grandfather of the poet, became a clerk in the Bank of England, at the recommendation of the Earl of Shaftesbury, in which capacity he served for fifty years. His faithful service was rewarded by his being appointed to a commanding position in the Bank Stock office, at a salary of £500 a year. He was a strong, dynamic, somewhat domineering man, with an uncertain temper when provoked. In 1778, at the age of twenty-nine, he married Margaret Tittle, who inherited a sugar plantation in St. Kitts in the West Indies.

His oldest son, the second Robert Browning (1782-1866) and father of the poet, was sent to St. Kitts to oversee the plantation. He gave up the post in revulsion against the system of slave labor which he was expected to administer, and in so doing he forfeited his inheritance and returned to England to make his way as best he could without the aid of his imperious father. Like his father he too became a clerk in the Bank of England, and in 1811, without the blessing of his estranged father, he married Sarah Anna Weidemann, the daughter of a Dundee shipowner. Mr. Weidemann, a German from Hamburg and the father of Sarah Anna, had married a Scots woman.

The poet's father was a bibliophile, with antiquarian and recondite leanings. He haunted the bookstalls of London and, later, of Paris in his quest for literary rarities. This penchant was to be absolutely formative in its influence on his son's character as man and poet, for Robert's schooling was substantially bounded by the confines of his father's remarkable library of six thousand books. His school life was negligible, and, except for his tutors, his formal education was little. In his father's library were the *Biographie Universelle,* in fifty volumes, which he read in their entirety; and *The Art of Painting in All Its Branches,* by Gerard de Lairesse, which the young Browning read with the greatest delight and more often than any other book in the library.

The young boy was not wholly bookish. He rode a pony and romped with his dogs and played with his other pets, which included monkeys, magpies, and an eagle. He was always vitally alive to his surroundings and peculiarly attentive to nature. When a mere child, Browning was as alive to nature and its minutiae as was Gerard Manley Hopkins. The sights and sounds and smells of nature were for him a source of endless delight.

In *Pauline,* Browning's first printed work, he remarked upon his abnormal awareness of his surroundings:

I am made up of an intensest life,
Of a most clear idea of consciousness
Of self, distinct from all its qualities,
From all affections, passions, feelings, powers;
And thus far it exists, if tracked, in all:
But linked, in me, to self-supremacy,
Existing as a centre to all things,
Most potent to create and rule and call
Upon all things to minister to it;
And to a principle of restlessness
Which would be all, have, see, know, taste, feel, all—
This is myself; and I should thus have been
Though gifted lower than the meanest soul.
(ll. 268-80)

Years later, in one of his most perfect portraits, he pictured his concept of a poet, who appears to be strikingly like Robert Browning, as a man chiefly notable for his vital interest in life in every passing moment:

He walked and tapped the pavement with his cane,
Scenting the world, looking it full in face,
An old dog, bald and blindish, at his heels.
They turned up, now, the alley by the church,
That leads nowhither; now, they breathed themselves
On the main promenade just at the wrong time:
You'd come upon his scrutinizing hat,
Making a peaked shade blacker than itself

> Against the single window spared some house
> Intact yet with its mouldered Moorish work,—. . . .
> ("How It Strikes a Contemporary," ll. 10-19)

As a boy Browning loved exotic and feral animals. One of his favorite haunts was the Royal Menagerie of Edward Cross, in the Strand, which included lions and tigers that fascinated the boy by their sinuous beauty and vitality and equally by their menace. Some years later the menagerie was moved south of the Thames, within easy walking distance of the residence of the Brownings in Southampton Street.

Browning's first volume, *Incondita,* remained unpublished in spite of the efforts of his parents. Of special interest is the influence of Byron on these juvenile poems. In later years he wrote to Elizabeth Barrett Browning:

> I always retained my first feeling for Byron in many respects, I would at any time have gone to Finchley to see a curl of his hair or one of his gloves, I am sure—while Heaven knows that I could not get up enthusiasm to cross the room if at the other end of it all Wordsworth, Coleridge, and Southey were condensed into the little china bottle yonder, after the Rosicrucian fashion.[1]

Perhaps his adulation of Byron accounts for the judgment of W. J. Fox, who, while generally approving of the collection, remarked that it showed "too great splendour of language and too little wealth of thought." Browning destroyed the manuscript, and only two poems remain: "The First-born of Egypt" and "Dance of Death," which were discovered by Bertram Dobell and printed in the *Cornhill Magazine* under the title "The Earliest Poems of Robert Browning" and later published by Sir F. G. Kenyon in *New Poems of R. and E. B. Browning* in 1914.

W. J. Fox, who became Browning's literary mentor and friend, shaped many of the poet's opinions. Although reared in the sabre-tooth tradition of Calvinism, he abandoned his position as pastor at the Congregational Chapel at Fareham in Hampshire, and became the leader of the Unitarians. His interest in social reform was keen, and he was in the vanguard of those who championed the right of free discussion of controversial social issues. He helped James Mill, the father of John Stuart Mill, to found the liberal *Westminster Review,* and he contributed to its pages. From him, Browning gained some measure of his interest in philosophical and social problems.

Browning did not attend a public school, a fact that for good or ill

1. *The Letters of Robert Browning and Elizabeth Barrett Browning, 1845-1846,* II (New York, 1898), 453.

shaped his development. He attended the school run by the Rev. Thomas Ready and was tutored in French by M. Loradoux. At this time he became acquainted with the works of John Donne, whose influence on his style is striking. The daring images, intellectual conceits, conversational quality, and intellectual toughness made an impression on the young poet and shaped his poetic vision.

Among Browning's close acquaintances were the Flower sisters, Eliza and Sarah, the one his senior by nine years, the other by seven. They were the intelligent and talented daughters of Benjamin Flower, the editor for seven years of the *Cambridge Intelligencer*, a journal devoted to liberal causes, political and religious. It was Eliza Flower who made a copy of *Incondita*, which W. J. Fox read. It has been suggested with considerable plausibility that Pauline, in Browning's first printed work, is in reality Eliza Flower.[2]

Browning's family being dissenters, the young poet was denied admission to Oxford and Cambridge. Until 1854 no dissenter was admitted to Oxford or could take a degree from Cambridge. When in 1825 a proposal for the founding of the University of London was circulated, the poet's father happily became a shareholder in the amount of £100, a contribution entitling him to send his son free to the University, and three years later, on June 30, 1828, Browning matriculated to study Latin, Greek, and German. Unluckily he was not used to conforming to a strict regimen of class attendance, and, homesick and miserable, he left after a half year, obliging his indulgent father to forfeit the rights accruing to him through his contribution.

The most pervasive influence upon the young Browning was exerted by Shelley, the "sun-treader" in *Pauline*. Browning first read Shelley in an edition of the lyrics pirated by Benbow (1826). The event was of the most formative character. Browning learned from Shelley the meaning of the committed life. The necessity of poetry to speak to the total condition of man, and the supreme worth and interest of the soul under stress he found in Shelley:

> Sun-treader, life and light be thine forever!
> Thou art gone from us; years go by and spring
> Gladdens and the young earth is beautiful,
> Yet thy songs come not, other bards arise,
> But none like thee. . . .
>
> . . . .
>
> Yet, sun-treader, all hail! From my heart's heart
> I bid thee hail! E'en in my wildest dreams,

2. See Mrs. Sutherland Orr, *Life and Letters of Robert Browning*, rev. F. G. Kenyon (London, 1908), p. 35.

I proudly feel I would have thrown to dust
The wreaths of fame which seemed o'erhanging me,
To see thee for a moment as thou art.
(*Pauline*, ll. 151-205)

Pauline was published in 1833 by Saunders and Otley at the expense of Browning's aunt, Mrs. Christiana Silverthorne, who supplied the necessary £30 for the venture. Browning sent twelve review copies to W. J. Fox to distribute, one of which went to John Stuart Mill, who annotated the volume liberally and judiciously. The journal to which Mill was to send his intended review anticipated him by printing a short and unflattering notice, and Mill, to show his good intentions, returned the annotated copy to Fox, who, strangely, returned it to Browning. Mill's remarks were in places harsh. He scribbled above the long Latin motto: "too much pretension in this motto." In the margin he wrote such comments as "obscurely expressed," "What does this mean?" "poor." But he also wrote generously: "Beautiful," "deeply true," "good descriptive writing." At the bottom of the last page he added, under the date, the stinging comment, "this transition from speaker to Pauline to writing a letter to the public with *place* and *date*, is quite horrible."

Mill appended his considered judgment of the work on two blank pages at the end of the volume, and these words which were of unique importance in shaping the course of Browning's poetic life began as follows:

> With considerable poetic powers, the writer seems to me possessed with a more intense and morbid self-consciousness than I ever knew in any sane human being.

The painful fact that not a single copy of the work was sold, coupled with Mill's crushing remarks, prompted Browning to write ruefully in the flyleaf of the volume words that reveal the impact of Mill's animadversions on his romantic confession:

> The following Poem was written in pursuance of a foolish plan which occupied me mightily for a time, and which had for its object the enabling me to assume & realize I know not how many different characters;—meanwhile, the world was never to guess that "Brown, Smith, Jones & Robinson" (as the spelling books have it) the respective authors of this poem, the other novel, such an opera, such a speech, etc. etc. were no other than one and the same individual. The present abortion was the first work of the *Poet* of the batch, who would have been more legitimately *myself* than most of the others; but I surrounded him with all manner of (to my then

notion) poetical accessories, and had planned quite a delightful life for him.

Only this crab remains of the shapely Tree of Life in this Fool's paradise of mine.—R.B.[3]

Pauline is a romantic account of a young man who is almost compulsively pouring out his confession of pride, sin, and moral confusion. Pauline remains throughout a silent two-dimensional figure, patiently stoical, or stricken dumb, one is not quite sure which. Mill is right in regarding her as a mere phantom, symbolizing imagination, poetry, love. The young poet, as Mill observes, does treat her *de haut en bas*. She is to love him eternally and unquestioningly, while he, old and burned out by imagined Byronic excesses, which remain nameless, can promise her, not love, but faith:

Thou lovest me;
And thou art to receive not love but faith,
For which thou wilt be mine, and smile and take
All shapes and shames, and veil without a fear
That form which music follows like a slave. . . .
(ll. 42-46)

The Byronic influence is seen in the young poet's world weariness and juvenile parade of dimly adumbrated sins. He is not unlike the young men in Tennyson's juvenilia who Byronically allude to their old and aching eyes and to their imminent damnation, both the fruits of wild excesses.

The spiritual history of the young poet recorded in *Pauline* is quite obviously the fictionalized history of the young Browning. We hear his posturing and self-conscious account of his egocentricity and his Faustian search for knowledge and power. He has been guilty, he feels, of hubris—the desire to be like God in knowledge and power:

Still I can lay my soul bare in its fall,
Since all the wandering and all the weakness
Will be a saddest comment on the song:
And if, that done, I can be young again,
I will give up all gained, as willingly
As one gives up a charm which shuts him out
From hope or part or care in human kind.
As life wanes, all its care and strife and toil
Seem strangely valueless, while the old trees
Which grew by our youth's home, the waving mass

3. Reproduced from a photostatic copy of the copy of *Pauline* annotated by John Stuart Mill, by courtesy of the Victoria and Albert Museum.

Of climbing plants heavy with bloom and dew,
The morning swallows with their songs like words,
All these seem clear and only worth our thoughts. . . .
(ll. 124-36)

Isolated from life and social responsibility, he has let life pass by as he "deeply mused." This is the earliest expression in Browning of what was to become one of the foundation stones of his whole poetic vision: life is to be lived first, to be thought about second, and being transcends essence. The young poet recognizes his selfish sin:

I deeply mused.

And suddenly without heart-wreck I awoke
As from a dream: I said " 'T was beautiful,
Yet but a dream, and so adieu to it!"
(ll. 447-50)

Pauline is the first and the last volume in which Browning exposed himself and his problems so directly to the gaze of the public, for Mill's remarks made him resolve never again to let the public see into his soul. He would be a dramatic poet, as he wrote in the poems "House" and "Shop."

In 1834 Browning accompanied the Chevalier George de Benkhausen, the Russian consul general, on a special mission to St. Petersburg. The journey included fifteen hundred miles by carriage, a grueling trip at top speed by day and by night. Browning's poetry is filled with his recollections of this three-month journey: the wild ride chronicled in "Through the Metidja to Abd-el-Kadr," the galloping of hooves heard in "How They Brought the Good News," the frantic race in "Muléykeh," the nightmarish ride through the forests of Russia in "Iván Ivánovitch," and others.

For a while Browning considered taking up a diplomatic career. Undoubtedly the drama, the intrigue, the dazzling courts seized his imagination, and his romantic fancies were stirred by his recent association with the Comte Amédée de Ripert-Monclar, who at the time was representing the French Royalists in London. Luckily the role of the Comte proved to lie, not in enticing the young poet into diplomacy, but into the writing of *Paracelsus*, the subject of which he suggested. In 1834 Browning began his labors on the poem, which was destined to be his first poem acknowledged favorably by the public. He had already begun composition upon *Sordello*, but he put it aside to complete the shorter and far simpler poem on the sixteenth-century physician.

Paracelsus, which was published in 1835 at the expense of the poet's father, continues the examination of the course of life one must follow, and especially examines the theme of hubris and the limitations set upon life. *Paracelsus* is dramatic and thus avoids the marked self-revelation which Mill found so alarming in *Pauline* and which Browning resolved to conceal thereafter. The sixteenth-century physician is not Browning, and the poem is in no literal sense autobiographical. Nevertheless, the problems facing the young Browning in his composition of *Pauline*, which remained unresolved, are those of Paracelsus: notably the problem of knowledge and its limits, the dangers of hubris, the role of love and wholeness in life, and the legitimate means of attaining the desired fusion of love and knowledge. Surely the problem facing the young man in *Pauline*—the proper limits to be set on self-indulgent reading in the isolation of a large and recondite library—weighed equally upon Paracelsus and the young Browning.

In the poetic drama are Aureolus Paracelsus, who represents the monomaniacal, hubristic seeker after knowledge at the expense of all else in life: love, human warmth and sympathy, and even joy itself. Paracelsus is not an unsympathetic character, for he is attempting to find the answer to a grand and imposing question: can man, by an effort of the will, involving sacrifice of all other aspects of life, attain to absolute knowledge, or to something closely resembling it? His error is threefold: he wants to attain godhead; in his impatience he wants to do so through forbidden means (black magic, conjuring, necromancy); and he renounces love and the whole emotional life in his monomania.

His foil in the poem is Aprile, a Shelleyan poet, who repudiates knowledge in his equally monomaniacal pursuit of love at the expense of knowledge. A married couple, Festus and Michal, represent the proper balance between mind and heart—a theme which Browning was to embrace during the rest of his life.

Paracelsus, impatient and proud, abjures traditional paths of study and scorns the established curricula—the regimen of pedants—even though he hears in his conscience a voice warning him of the fatal dangers of attempting to look upon absolute knowledge, "no veil between." Undeterred, he seeks

> . . . to comprehend the works of God,
> And God himself, and all God's intercourse
> With the human mind. . . .
>
> (Pt. I, ll. 533-35)

Paracelsus, as I have tried to show in my *Triple Soul: Browning's Theory of Knowledge* and *The Convex Glass: The Mind of Robert Browning*, is not an attack upon mind or knowledge, but rather upon imbalance and monomania. It is a drama of unmistakable power, with firm characterization and skill in invention and dialogue. Browning took considerable pride in the poem, and, although it did not become a best seller, it did bring Browning to the attention of the literary world of London. It was enthusiastically reviewed by John Forster in the *Examiner* and by W. J. Fox in *The Monthly Repository*, although other reviews were tepid. It was soon discovered that the poem owed much of its style and manner to Shelley. *Alastor*, with its theme of the pursuit of knowledge and the need of the leaven of love and warm communion with one's fellow men, seemed to be the principal source. In both poems alienation from one's fellows is fatal.

In a note appended to the poem, Browning enunciates the belief that the liberties he took with his subject were "very trifling," a belief that he later held and affirmed about *The Ring and the Book*. To the most casual reader it is clear that in both poems art has wrought substantive changes throughout, as indeed it must. Browning's assertion is puzzling until one understands that the poet held to the concept of the relativity of truth: each man sees fact through the filter of his own bias, self-interest, and, indeed, total context. What is "true" for one man may not be true for his neighbor. Absolute truth, unattainable by man in the mortal state, is reserved for the next world. He was far from being blind to the workings of his craft, but because he was Browning he saw Paracelsus as he did, and his vision was true for him.

The success of *Paracelsus* may be seen in the anecdote of the memorable evening, May 26, 1836, when at a party given by Sergeant Talfourd, Browning was included in a toast to the "Poets of England." The aging Wordsworth honored him signally by announcing: "I am proud to drink your health, Mr. Browning." During the same evening, William Charles Macready, the famous actor, said to the young poet, "Will you not write me a tragedy, and save me from going to America?"

Browning responded by writing *Strafford*, his first play. The topic was fresh in his mind, for Browning had recently completed a prose *Life of Strafford* which John Forster had begun but which he could not finish because of illness. The play was performed five times in May 1837, but was indifferently received, and Macready came to doubt the dramatic talents of the poet. Although the play was a failure on the stage, it served as an excellent discipline and reinforced Browning's lifelong passion for liberty of the people against tyrants.

For ten years Browning wrote for the stage, and he failed. His interest lying in historical dramas, he gave the world *King Victor and King Charles*, *The Return of the Druses*, *A Blot in the 'Scutcheon*, *A Soul's Tragedy*, and *Luria*, dramas which served to direct his interests toward the dramatic monologue, but it became apparent to Macready and later to all that as a playwright Browning was unsuccessful. The reason is not far to seek. In the preface to *Sordello,* Browning affirmed that his

> . . . stress lay on the incidents in the development of a soul: little else is worth study. I, at least, always thought so—you, with many known and unknown to me, think so—others may one day think so. . . .

In short, his interest lay in interior, psychological probing, not in action. His dramas, even though melodramatic, were essentially static, lacking in motion and action.

While he was struggling to write for the stage, he was writing other things as well, notably *Sordello* (1840), which he finished after a seven-year struggle. This work immediately passed into legend as the most tangled, incomprehensible, crabbed poem of the century. The stories associated with it are legion, including the sour note of Mrs. Thomas Carlyle, who affirmed she had not been able to determine whether Sordello was a person, a book, or a city; the familiar account of Douglas Jerrold, who, after reading the book during an illness without understanding a word, feared that he had lost his reason; and Tennyson's libelous assertion that he had understood only the first and the last lines of the poem ("Who will, may hear Sordello's story told" and "Who would has heard Sordello's story told"), and both were lies. Suffice it to say, the book put Browning's reputation under a cloud for nearly a quarter of a century and made his name a byword for willful obscurity. One of the many ironies in Browning scholarship is the fact that in our day sober and sound studies reveal the work to be a psychological probing many years ahead of its time.

Sordello is in a sense a rewriting of *Pauline*. The same themes appear: romantic isolation and social responsibility, the concept of wholeness through equipoise of mind and heart, and the demands of poet craft upon the young poet. Here as in *Pauline* the poet is trying to find the answer to the demands of his craft, the world, and God. It is always dangerous—and usually disastrous—to identify Browning with the creatures of his invention, and he is not to be identified with Sordello, but both poets shared the same problems and anxieties and frustrations, and to this extent they are similar. Both led withdrawn, sheltered lives, away from the demands of the world, Browning in his father's library and Sordello in Goito, an idyllic paradise far from the hustle and bustle of the world.

Browning made his first Italian journey in 1838 and visited Venice and Asolo, the locale of his *Pippa Passes* (1841). This work was the first of a series of eight pamphlets entitled *Bells and Pomegranates,* published between 1841 and 1846, under the following titles:

I. *Pippa Passes*, 1841
II. *King Victor and King Charles*, 1842
III. *Dramatic Lyrics*, 1842
IV. *The Return of the Druses*, 1843
V. *A Blot in the 'Scutcheon*, 1843
VI. *Colombe's Birthday*, 1844
VII. *Dramatic Romances and Lyrics*, 1845
VIII. *Luria and A Soul's Tragedy*, 1846

Browning's father defrayed the cost of the publishing venture, which, because of the fine type, double-column format, and paper covers, amounted to only about £16 per volume. When in 1846 the series was complete, Edward Moxon, the publisher, bound the unsold copies of the series singly in dark green cloth, royal octavo volumes and sold them under the title *Bells and Pomegranates*. Originally Browning had intended to include only plays in the pamphlet series, but Moxon persuaded him to include some of his shorter poems (*Bells* Nos. III and VII). The title of the series was taken from Exodus 28:33-34, where God is telling Moses what manner of tribute the Israelites must prepare for him:

> And *beneath* upon the hem of it [a robe] thou shalt make pomegranates *of* blue and *of* purple, and *of* scarlet, round about the hem thereof; and bells of gold between them round about:
> A golden bell and a pomegranate, a golden bell and a pomegranate, upon the hem of the robe round about.

Pippa Passes was the first substantial poem which clearly fused the lyrical and dramatic power of the poet with the psychological insight which marks his greatest works. The pamphlet, which sold for sixpence a copy, comprised a proem and four sections, entitled Morning, Noon, Evening, and Night, followed by an epilogue. The poem demonstrated unusual virtuosity, with the seven songs which Pippa sings, and prose passages interspersed among the predominantly blank verse lines. William C. DeVane finds *Pippa Passes* to be "the better spirit of *Sordello*," and discovers that it "seems to have been written in a spirit of revulsion from the larger poem." He notes that both Sordello and Pippa are stolen children, who are finally discovered to be children of wealthy parents: "Browning had grown tired of the fruitless life which Sordello lived; he even, towards the end of *Sordello*, called that life a 'sorry farce.' "[4] It is true that Pippa is unconscious of her dramatic effect upon the lives of the "happiest four" in Asolo, and it is also true, as DeVane observes, that Sordello was morbidly introspective and conscious of his effect on others,

4. William C. DeVane, *A Browning Handbook*, 2nd ed. (New York, 1955), p. 93.

but it is strange to find DeVane saying that Browning grew "tired" of Sordello's retiring, ivory-tower life, for one of the major themes of the work is the waste and folly of such a life. To demonstrate dramatically the fatality in such evasion was the reason for writing the poem. He did not tire of the theme; rather he was indignant from the beginning—if by the word one means that he held no sympathy with Sordello's false vision of the role of the artist. The poem from the beginning demonstrates the paralytic effect of such a life upon both life and art. If at the end he calls Sordello's life "a sorry farce," it is not because he failed to see it so in the beginning, for this was his artistic purpose.

Pippa Passes is connected with *Sordello* in that both grow out of his Italian journey in 1838. The colorful life in Asolo, the silk mills, with their pathetic laborers, often no more than children, the beautiful hills stirred Browning's artistic invention and gave it dramatic form. For the first time, he freed himself both from the rigorous demands of the drama written for stage production and from the exigencies of history. For the first time he could give free rein to his imagination and to his art.

Browning's dramas written for the stage need not occupy us here, but *Bell* No. III, *Dramatic Lyrics*, is worthy of notice by reason of six superior poems in it:

"Italy" [later entitled "My Last Duchess"]
"France" [later entitled "Count Gismond"]
"Cloister (Spanish)" [later entitled "Soliloquy of the Spanish Cloister"]
"There's Heaven above . . ." [later entitled "Johannes Agricola in Meditation"]
"The rain set early in tonight . . ." [later entitled "Porphyria's Lover"]
"In a Gondola"

All six of these poems reveal the emphasis which was to be Browning's throughout his literary life: psychological examination of souls under stress, probing into twisted minds and hearts, careful dissection of motive and act. "My Last Duchess" is everywhere recognized as the happiest fruit of Browning's early period. The last two, save one, are among the most striking of Browning's studies of madness. "In a Gondola" is the earliest study of adulterous, passionate love, which, though sinful, is nevertheless true love and thus less reprehensible than the lives of the wealthy hypocrites whose splendid homes the lovers pass in their gondola, and far less culpable than the savage and stunted lives of the cuckolded husband and his cohorts.

When Browning was in Italy in 1844, Elizabeth Barrett published her *Poems*, in which she, in linking Browning with Wordsworth and Tennyson, wrote:

Or from Browning some pomegranate which, if cut deep down the middle,
Shows a heart within blood-tinctured of a veined humanity.[5]

The story of his response to her has passed into the currency of literature and of romance as well. Without having seen the author of these lines, Browning wrote to her on January 10, 1845: "I love your verses with all my heart, dear Miss Barrett . . . and I love you too."

The epistolary romance prospered. She wrote to a friend, "I had a letter from Browning the poet last night which threw me into ecstasies—Browning the author of *Paracelsus*, and king of the mystics."[6] Browning soon decided that he would devote his life to the charming and intellectual invalid, even though it seemed unlikely that she would ever for long leave her couch. He visited her once or twice weekly, and their letters crossed in the mails. By summer she was able to leave her couch and to walk about the room and even to take a short drive. Mr. Barrett, her father, suspicious and alerted by the new relationship and determined to thwart all thought of marriage among his children, made clear his grave displeasure, terminating all favors and visits to her chamber. Upon the urgent recommendation of her doctor, she asked her father to permit her to spend the winter in Italy, where she might recover her strength in a hospitable climate, but he sternly refused his permission, saying that if she should make the journey she must bear his heaviest displeasure for her disobedience. Mr. Barrett, as everyone knows, has passed into legend as among the most brutally unenlightened of fathers, a veritable psychopath of possessiveness, but the evidence is clear that he loved his children in his demonic way.

By September Robert and Elizabeth were in love. She acknowledged her love in most gracious terms: "Henceforth I am yours for everything but to do you harm. It rests with God and with you—only in the meanwhile you are most absolutely free, unentangled, as they call it, by the breadth of a thread."[7] Mr. Barrett absolutely forbade all mention, let alone discussion of marriage, and it was hopeless to suppose that he would relent where his favorite daughter was concerned.

It became apparent that only through forthright action could the stalemate be broken, and accordingly on September 12, 1846, Elizabeth left her home and, with her maid Wilson, journeyed to St. Marylebone Church, where she and Robert were married in secrecy, the only witnesses

5. Ibid., p. 19.
6. W. Hall Griffin and Henry C. Minchin, *The Life of Robert Browning* (London, 1910), p. 148.
7. Ibid., p. 149.

being Wilson and Browning's cousin James Silverthorne. During the next five days Browning, with his usual delicacy, refused to call and ask to see Miss Barrett, now Mrs. Browning. On Saturday, September 19, the Brownings departed for Southampton and thence to Paris, where they stayed a week, and then they journeyed to Orleans and by boat on the Loire, Saône, and Rhone, to Avignon, Vaucluse, Marseilles, and by sea to Leghorn and the Riviera and Genoa and from there to Pisa, where they stayed, basking in the sun-drenched warmth of Italy.

Mr. Barrett never forgave his daughter or acknowledged her frequent letters to him. After five years, when the Brownings were again in London, both Browning and his wife appealed to him to forgive and forget, but he instead wrote in malignant anger to Browning and returned all of Elizabeth's letters, unopened, each tightly sealed.

In April 1847, the Brownings went to Florence, which was to be their home for fourteen years, until her death in June 1861. Since their marriage their finances had been rather straitened. Except for £100 borrowed from Robert Browning's father and £300 annually from Mrs. Browning's £8000 invested in the funds, there was no regular income, except from the sale of Mrs. Browning's books. Their financial concerns were relieved in 1856 by John Kenyon's bequest of £11,000 to his second cousin, Elizabeth. Freed of financial worry, the Brownings could indulge their taste for travel, and they journeyed thrice to Paris and London, and twice they spent the winter in Rome. Casa Guidi became the mecca of many friends, literary and otherwise, among whom may be mentioned Isa Blagden, William W. Story, W. S. Landor, and Mr. and Mrs. T. A. Trollope.

In 1849 Chapman and Hall published the first collected edition of Browning, in two volumes, which included all his published works except *Pauline*, *Strafford*, and *Sordello*, an augury of an improved literary future. In the same year a son was born to the Brownings, Robert Wiedemann Barrett Browning, bringing great joy into their hearts, but Browning's joy was moderated by the death of his mother in England at about the same time.

In 1850 Browning broke a long literary silence with the publication of *Christmas-Eve and Easter-Day*, paired poems of considerable interest for the light they throw on Browning's religious thinking at this time, but hardly to be classed among his most lyrical or dramatic works. Essentially they are a philosophical disquisition on Browning's views of the state of religion at mid-century and they are little admired by the general public, although they are important in understanding the mind of the poet. If the speaker in *Christmas-Eve* is not Browning, his character is so sketchy as hardly to constitute a persona distinguishable from the author. The whole tone of the poem is highly personal, as if Browning at last, for the first time since *Pauline*, had decided to speak out, as his wife had urged him to—in his own personality and with the voice which God made with such power and sweetness of speech. The poem has a compelling emotional urgency, for, as DeVane notes, both poems were probably prompted by the juxtaposition of the birth of his son and the death of his mother. Browning was unable to return to England for the funeral, and the loss weighed on his spirit for many months. The tone, as well as the substance of the poems—his exploration of the mystery of life and death in immediate juxtaposition, the form of worship and the creed best suited to man and his needs, and the great mystery of oblivion and immortality—bears the mark of profound and personal experience.

In 1855 appeared the book on which more than on any other work his reputation rests: *Men and Women* in two volumes. Here is the pure dramatic monologue, the zest for life and dramatic situation, which distinguish Browning at his best. It stands preeminent in the Browning canon partly because drama, vitality, and human character triumph over message. In this book life stands paramount above theme. Rarely, if ever, has the dramatic monologue been more perfectly realized than in the characters of Fra Lippo Lippi, Andrea del Sarto, Cleon, Karshish, Childe Roland, and Bishop Blougram. Here lies Browning's immortality as a poet; upon these pulsating, vital pictures of life his fame must rest—even more than upon his greatest opus, *The Ring and the Book*, which is relatively unknown outside the seminar and the study, superb as it is.

In June 1861, Elizabeth Barrett Browning died, and Browning found his philosophical view of evil as a test of the measure of a man put to a dreadful trial. After fifteen years of an incomparable marriage, Browning was alone, except for his son Robert Wiedemann Barrett, affectionately called Penini, or, later, Pen. Today it is increasingly *de rigueur* to find Browning's marriage unhappy, although there is no valid evidence to support the belief that it was so. Betty Miller's *Robert Browning, A Portrait* (1952) attempts to prove that Browning was too neurotic and undeveloped to be a mature man or husband, as may be seen in the fact that by marrying a woman six years his senior, he must have been symbolically marrying his mother, an infallible sign of immaturity. Richard Freedman also finds Browning's marriage to have been a burden:

> Elizabeth Barrett must have been, all told, quite a cross a bear, what with her spiritualism and her inexplicable devotion to Napoleon III, but we get no sense here [i.e., in Maisie Ward's *Robert Browning and His World*, which he is reviewing] of what Browning must have suffered from her.[8]

If in fifteen years of marriage only two subjects of disagreement can be advanced to support Browning's alleged unhappiness with his wife, the

8. *Book World, Chicago Tribune*, October 1, 1967, p. 20.

marriage hardly sounds like a disaster. In point of fact, another and far more potentially serious disagreement might be advanced: Elizabeth's rearing of Pen as a little Lord Fauntleroy. Pen was notorious throughout Florence for his silks, velvets, laces, and curly locks, to which Browning objected. Upon the death of Elizabeth, one of Browning's first acts was to take Pen to a barber and next, to supply him with more normal clothing—surely a symptom of unusual balance and mental health. But today the belief persists that it is a mark of scholarship to discover inflamed wounds of spirit behind the Victorian picture of Browning as a man sound and hale and imperturbably cheerful. Freedman voices the mood well:

> Miss Ward constantly attacks the psychological premises of the last book [Betty Miller's *Robert Browning: A Portrait*], claiming in her old fashioned way that a poet as great as Browning need not necessarily have borne the psychological wounds that Miss Miller—sometimes over-zealously, to be sure—ascribes to him.[9]

It is often suggested that Elizabeth's dependence on laudanum must have blighted his marriage, and it is true, as the letters prove, that he tried to encourage her to free herself from the drug, but his concern is a direct reflection of his love, not of frustration and bitterness.

There is no question of Browning's capacity to suffer or of his actual suffering. The question is whether his suffering twisted or diminished his psyche. Properly looked at, the whole matter is irrelevant, of course, for what is important is Browning's poetry, not his supposed psychiatric state, but in effect the issue assumes a considerable importance, for Browning spent his poetic life illustrating in characterization and precept that the function of life is to test one through adversity, pain, and evil. The corollary to this belief was that one should never weary in combat, never shirk the fight. The old Pope in *The Ring and the Book* asks

> Was the trial sore?
> Temptation sharp? Thank God a second time!
> Why comes temptation but for man to meet
> And master and make crouch beneath his foot,
> And so be pedestaled in triumph?
> (Bk. X, ll. 1178-82)

Old and tested and tired as he is, the Pope supplies the answer which is central in Browning:

> I am near the end; but still not at the end;
> All to the very end is trial in life:

9. Idem.

At this stage is the trial of my soul
Danger to face, or danger to refuse?
Shall I dare try the doubt now, or not dare?
(Bk. X, ll. 1299-1302)

If Browning's marriage was in fact unhappy, a trial to his soul, which proved to be beyond his endurance, if he was an inadequate man and husband, it is important that such facts be made known and documented fully, but if the evidence is lacking, it is equally important that such unsupported speculations be clearly labeled for what they are. The allegations are almost always founded on what he "must" have felt or been. Richard D. Altick says that Browning was insecure and timorous:

> This picture of the private Browning as a disappointed idealist, a man whose fear of betraying his own heart drove him to the perpetually unsatisfactory device of speaking obscurely through the mouths of others, scarcely accords with his friends' untroubled assumption that he was the definition of self-assurance. But the truth seems to be—and it goes a long way towards explaining his abnormal reticence—that he was basically a most insecure man.[10]

It might be noted that if the practice of writing dramatically—creating characters who speak—is a mark of psychiatric instability, Shakespeare, Ben Jonson, John Milton, and Euripides were desperately sick men. To many critics today, of whom Altick is a spokesman, Browning, because he was inhibited from speaking *in propria persona* after the embarrassment of *Pauline*, created puppets to speak for him. In short, his characters are not individuals, not artistic creations with independent lives and characters, but are all mouthpieces for the frustrated Browning. Nowhere is this better seen than in Altick's statement:

> It is by no means accidental that Andrea del Sarto, the frustrated artist, is the most profoundly and poignantly realized of all Browning's characters. No one who had not himself known the ashen flavor of failure could have written that moving poem, so filled with rationalizations which give but momentary solace. . . . [Browning's] fervent celebration of the glories of the incomplete, the imperfect, as being part of God's inscrutable but unquestionable plan for men, is far less the manifestation of an intellectual conviction than it is the result of Browning's growing need to salve his awareness of failure.[11]

Perhaps the most telling evidence of Browning's essential soundness

---

10. See Richard D. Altick, "The Private Life of Robert Browning," *Yale Review*, XLI (1951), 247-62.
11. Ibid.

is the productivity and character of the years following his wife's death. He left Florence, never to return, and went to London, where he became almost notorious as a social lion, widely dined and cultivated by the socially and artistically important people, but his work did not cease. In 1864 appeared *Dramatis Personae*, including some of his most vivid dramatic triumphs: "Abt Vogler," "Rabbi Ben Ezra," "A Death in the Desert," "Caliban," and "Mr. Sludge, 'The Medium.' "

The towering achievement of his life, *The Ring and the Book*, appeared in four volumes: the first on November 21, 1868; the second on December 26, 1868; the third on January 30, 1869; and the fourth on February 27, 1869.

When in June of 1860 Browning found the Old Yellow Book in a book stall in Florence and paid a lira, "eightpence English just," for it, he bought one of the treasures of his life. The old book in itself was of no great value or even interest, being a gathering of testimony and court records, compiled by Cencini, a Florentine lawyer, of a seventeenth-century murder trial; but Browning sensed that within its covers lay the germ of a great work. He had always been fascinated by accounts of celebrated murders and he knew the facts connected with both crimes and trials with a total recall that surprised his friends. His interest was not by any means morbid or unhealthy, for his great interest was in the study of souls under stress, personalities put into situations that tried their metal. The brutal murder was admirably fitted to his needs and only wanted shaping into a coherent and meaningful form.

In addition to the Old Yellow Book, Browning acquired from a Mrs. Baker, a friend of Isa Blagden, a pamphlet concerning the murder story, which is known as the Secondary Source. Professor Hodell included a translation of this pamphlet in his facsimile edition of the Old Yellow Book, under the title "The Death of the Wife-Murderer Guido Franceschini, by Beheading."

The story of the affair recounted in the Old Yellow Book is one of fraud, duplicity, cruelty, hatred, and maniacal violence. Elizabeth found the story repellent and thought it unsuitable for poetic treatment. Thomas Carlyle, later, dismissed it contemptuously, pronouncing it to be only an Old Bailey story that simply wanted forgetting. Certainly the facts do not suggest the very stuff of poetry.

The facts in the story are these: Count Guido Franceschini, of Arezzo, an impoverished nobleman remarkable for his avarice and hate, married Francesca Pompilia, supposed daughter of Pietro and Violante Comparini. The marriage was marked by duplicity on both sides: Guido misrepresented his financial condition to the Comparini, assuring them that he was a man of substance, the intimate of the wealthy nobility. Violante, in turn, neglected to inform Guido that Pompilia was not her child, but rather was the daughter of a strumpet who had sold the newborn baby to Violante, without the knowledge of old Pietro, in order that the Comparini might inherit a legacy which was to be theirs only if they had legitimate issue. A substantial dowry was given to Guido with the proviso that the Comparini be allowed to live with their daughter in Guido's palace in Arezzo, where they yearned for the good life that seemed assured to them. Their disillusionment was total and crushing. The food was inadequate and of poor quality; the palace, which Browning pronounced as vast as a quarry and as cold, was a standing humiliation; and the conduct of Guido and his two brothers was a calculated insult to drive the Comparini from the palace and back to Rome.

After four months of such ignominy, the Comparini left and instituted a suit against Guido to have the return of the dowry, on the grounds of Pompilia's illegitimacy. This action inflamed Guido to desperate acts of cruelty and revenge against his wife, and he, in turn, conceived of a plan to retain the dowry and get rid of Pompilia at a stroke. Knowing of her unhappiness and of her previous attempts to escape, he sought out a gallant who would run away with her in an adulterous affair. The man he decided upon was Giuseppe Caponsacchi, a young, worldly canon of some reputation with pretty women. Since Pompilia was illiterate, it was necessary to forge love letters supposedly from Pompilia to the canon and to get them delivered without arousing suspicion. The plot failed of its purpose to stir Caposacchi to an adulterous union, but it succeeded in gaining his acquiescence to Pompilia's desperate plea that he help her escape from her bondage.

On April 28, 1697, Pompilia and Caponsacchi fled by coach toward Rome, where she hoped to find shelter with the Comparini. Fifteen miles from Rome, at an inn in Castelnuovo, after a dreadful flight, Guido caught up with them, and after a clash in which Pompilia threatened Guido with a sword, the two fugitives were arrested and charged with adultery. The judgment of the court in Rome was that Caponsacchi was to be relegated to Civita Vecchia for three years for adultery and Pompilia was to be sent to a nunnery reserved for fallen women. Later, when it was discovered that she was pregnant, she was sent under bond to the home of the Comparini, where on December 18, 1697—eight months after her flight—she gave birth to a son, Gaetano.

On January 2, 1698, Guido, with four hired assassins, came to the house, and, after knocking and calling out, "Open to Caponsacchi," when Violante opened the door Guido and his cohorts rushed in and murdered the Comparini and stabbed Pompilia twenty-two times with a Genoese dagger—a three-bladed knife with tiny hooks along the edges to tear the flesh when the blade is withdrawn. Pompilia survived for four days. By good fortune Gaetano was not in the house at the time, for Pompilia had sent him away for fear that Guido might become violent. Guido and his men were caught and brought to trial, where the fact that Guido planned and executed the deed was never in question, but where the issue before the court was whether a husband had the right to kill an adulterous wife and be exonerated on the grounds of *honoris causa*. The weakness of Guido's case was that he could only with difficulty argue that he had acted in hot blood in defending his home and preserving his honor. If he had killed the two fugitives at Castelnuovo in a fit of rage, there is little doubt that he would have gone free, but a delay of eight months, it might be argued, gives the blood time to cool.

The court found Guido guilty and sentenced him to the block. The four henchmen were sentenced to be hanged. Guido, who held a minor church office, appealed to the old Pope Innocent XII to reverse the judgment of the court, but the Pope, after a lengthy review of the court record, sustained the judgment, and Guido and his men were executed on February 22, 1698.

In Browning's version of the story, the Monastery of the Convertites, where Browning mistakenly believed the court had sent Pompilia, instituted a suit to claim Pompilia's property under the law which gave the monastery ownership of the property of fallen women dying while in its custody. The court had found Guido guilty but had failed to find Pompilia innocent of adultery. In one of his most ironic passages, Browning pictures the Fisc, the prosecuting attorney who in the trial found Guido a monster of guilt and Pompilia innocent, agreeing to argue the case for the Convertites, even though to do so he would have to establish Pompilia's adulterous and vicious life:

> Wherefore the Monastery claims its due:
> And whose, pray, whose the office, but the Fisc's?
> Who but I institute procedure next
> Against the person of dishonest life,
> Pompilia whom last week I sainted so?
>
> (Bk. XII, ll. 703-07)

It was not until 1864, when Browning was on vacation in the Pyrenees that the great plan occurred to him. He would allow the principals in the drama to speak their own views of the facts in the case, and thus he would dramatically illustrate the relative nature of truth, which, Browning believed, is always shifting and changing, differing from man to man, for it takes on the colors of a man's life, his desires, character, and the total context that has shaped him from birth. No work of art in the language so fully examines the nature of the instability of truth. Not the principals only but the citizenry of Rome speak, and the disagreement is without limit.

The climax of the work, and the supreme philosophical utterance of the poet, is Book X, in which the old Pope examines the mass of evidence, the web of lies, distortions, and half truths, and arrives at his judgment. Uppermost in the Pope's mind is the terrible fact that in life it is impossible to gain absolute truth, and in every momentous decision there is the likelihood of error—error within the conflicting testimony of fallible and biased men, and error within the man who must judge. The pontiff is eighty-six years of age, "One of well-nigh decayed intelligence," but he must judge, "Life's business being just the terrible choice":

Through hard labor and good will,
And habitude that gives a blind man sight
At the practised finger-ends of him, I do
Discern, and dare decree in consequence,
Whatever prove the peril of mistake.
(Bk. X, ll. 1243-47)

The works following *The Ring and the Book* are somewhat less lyrical and dramatically alive than those before, and there is an increasing tendency toward what Browning called "my mere gray argument." Still it must not be supposed that the poetry is without merit or interest. Perhaps the most rewarding are the casuistical pieces *Prince Hohenstiel-Schwangau* (1871) and *Fifine at the Fair* (1872). *Red Cotton Night-Cap Country* (1873), a study in religious mania and its terrible resolution, is less successful, and *The Inn Album* (1875) is a somewhat repellent work with a peculiarly sordid and unattractive theme.

Pacchiarotto and How He Worked in Distemper: With Other Poems (1876), if it includes one of the worst poems of the age, "At the Mermaid," reveals in places a resurgence of lyricism and dramatic power, particularly in "Numpholeptos" and "St. Martin's Summer."

The volumes that appeared after *Pacchiarotto* tend to be somewhat knotty and crabbed, but here and there are poems with the old magic and the insight into souls of his earlier work: "Ixion," "Never the Time and the Place," and others. *La Saisiaz* (1878) is of interest chiefly because Browning once again speaks out *in propria persona* of death and the riddle of existence. It is in reality essentially a prose disquisition forced into verse, and as poetry it has not met with great favor.

Ferishtah's Fancies (1884) is, similarly, a series of philosophical parables illustrating Browning's views of evil, religion, God, pain, punishment, and the mystery of life. The value of the poems rests more on Browning's philosophical utterances than on the poems as poems. *Parleyings with Certain People of Importance in Their Day* is somewhat similar, except that a series of historical personages speak on the philosophical matters dear to the heart of the poet. As poetry, many critics believe, they represent a distinct falling off of lyricism, if not of poetical power.

Browning's last volume, *Asolando: Fancies and Facts* (1889), was published on December 12, 1889, the day of Browning's death at the Palazzo Rezzonico, the home of his son Pen, in Venice. The publisher dated the volume 1890, so that the volume would appear to be a current publication throughout the new year. It is heartening to note that the volume represents a return to lyricism, in such poems as "Summum Bonum," "Development," "Reverie," and the famous "Epilogue."

On December 12, 1889, at ten in the evening, Browning died. He was buried in Poets' Corner of Westminster Abbey. The Protestant cemetery where Elizabeth was buried long since had been filled and was closed to further burials. Dean Bradley of Westminster offered the poet's son the honor of placing the body of Elizabeth in Westminster Abbey beside her husband, but Pen refused, knowing that the Florentines treasured her memory and that she felt most at home in her beloved Florence.

Chronological Outline of Important Events in Browning's Life

1811, February 19

Marriage of Robert Browning, Senior (the second Robert Browning and the father of the poet) to Sarah Anna Wiedemann, in Camberwell, a suburb of London, without the sanction of his father, the first Robert Browning, who was angry with his son for refusing to remain as overseer of the family sugar plantation at St. Kitts, in the West Indies.

1812, May 7

Birth of Robert Browning, the poet, at Camberwell.

1826

Browning left the school of the Reverend Thomas Ready at Peckham, his only formal education except for a short period at the University of London. During the fourteen years his father instructed him in Latin and Greek, he was also tutored privately in French and in Italian. He studied music under John Relfe, musician-in-ordinary to the King and a pupil of the Abbé Vogler.

1826-1833

Profound influence of Shelley led to a period of atheism and vegetarianism until Browning's eyes suffered as a result.

1828, October

Browning enrolled at the newly formed University of London to study Greek, Latin, and German. He left after six months.

1832, October 22

After leaving Edmund Kean's performance of *Richard III*, Browning conceived the plan of writing a poem, an opera, and a novel under pen names, a plan leading to the composition of *Pauline*.

1833, March

Publication of *Pauline*, anonymously. The cost of £30 was defrayed by the poet's aunt, Mrs. Christiana Silverthorne.

October 30

Browning read the copy of *Pauline* annotated by John Stuart Mill, a harsh criticism of his morbid self-revelation, an event of a profoundly formative character, since Browning thereafter resolved to write dramatically.

1834, March and April

Accompanied the Chevalier George de Benkhausen, the Russian consul general, to St. Petersburg.

1835, August

Paracelsus published at the expense of his father, under Browning's name.

1836, May 26
Supper with Sergeant Talfourd celebrated the success of Talfourd's play *Ion*. Talfourd suggested a toast to the "Poets of England" and pointedly included Browning. Wordsworth leaned across the table and said, "I am proud to drink your health, Mr. Browning!" Later W. C. Macready, the actor, asked the young poet, "Will you not write me a tragedy, and save me from going to America?" Browning's efforts to oblige occupied his time substantially for the next ten years.

1837, May 1
Strafford, Browning's first play, performed at Covent Garden, was received with little enthusiasm, and was performed only five times.

1838, April-July
First Italian journey.

1840, January
The Brownings moved from Camberwell to New Cross, Hatcham, in Surrey.

March
Publication of *Sordello*, a poem whose alleged obscurity became a byword. For years after its publication Browning's reputation as a poet suffered.

1841, April
Publication of *Pippa Passes, Bells and Pomegranates*, No. I, a poem in which the genius of the mature Browning was first seen.

1842, March 12
Publication of *King Victor and King Charles, Bells and Pomegranates*, No. II.

November
Publication of *Dramatic Lyrics, Bells and Pomegranates*, No. III. Significant as including his first dramatic monologues.

1843, January
Publication of *The Return of the Druses, Bells and Pomegranates*, No. IV.

February 11
Publication of *A Blot in the 'Scutcheon, Bells and Pomegranates*, No. V.

1844
Second Italian journey.

April 20
Publication of *Colombe's Birthday, Bells and Pomegranates*, no. VI.

1845, January 10
Browning's first letter to Elizabeth Barrett.

May 20
First meeting of Browning and Miss Barrett.

November 6
Publication of *Dramatic Romances and Lyrics, Bells and Pomegranates*, No. VII.

1846, April 13
Publication of *Luria* and *A Soul's Tragedy, Bells and Pomegranates*, No. VIII.

September 12
Marriage of Browning and Miss Barrett, in secrecy, in St. Marylebone Church, London, with only two witnesses.

September 19
The married couple journeyed secretly to Italy via Southampton, Le Havre, Paris, Avignon, Marsailles, the Riviera, Leghorn, and Pisa.

1847, April
Arrival in Florence, where they lived until Mrs. Browning's death in June 1861.

1849, March 9
Birth of Robert Wiedemann Barrett Browning, called Penini or Pen for short, followed shortly after by the death of Browning's mother in England.

1850, April 1
Publication of *Christmas-Eve and Easter-Day*, two separate poems, always linked together in all the editions. The first of Browning's books, except for *Strafford*, to be printed at the expense of the publisher.

1852
Publication of "An Essay on Shelley," written at the request of Edward Moxon as an introduction to a volume of Shelley's letters, which proved to be spurious. Important for Browning's views of poetry and the two types of poets, subjective and objective.

1855, November 17
Publication of *Men and Women*, in two volumes, with twenty-seven poems in Volume I and twenty-four in Volume II. This is Browning's most distinguished achievement in the shorter poems, and in all his works is rivaled only by *The Ring and the Book*. In the distribution of poems in 1863, Browning assigned from *Men and Women* thirty poems to *Dramatic Lyrics* and twelve to *Dramatic Romances*, retaining only eight of the original poems in *Men and Women* and adding five poems selected from earlier volumes. But it is the original *Men and Women* that is the gem in Browning's coronal.

1856, December
Death of John Kenyon, second cousin to Elizabeth Barrett Browning, leaving the Brownings a bequest of £11,000.

1860, June
Discovery in Florence of the Old Yellow Book.

1861, June 29
Death of Elizabeth Barrett Browning.

August 1
Browning left Florence for London, never to return. Established residence at 19 Warwick Crescent, London.

1864, May 28
Publication of *Dramatis Personae*, with eighteen poems, which commanded the attention of the literary world and did much to restore the reputation that had been shattered by *Sordello*.

Summer and fall
Conceived the organization and method of *The Ring and the Book*.

1868, November 21
Publication of the first volume of *The Ring and the Book*, including the first three Books: "The Ring and the Book," "Half-Rome," "The Other Half-Rome."

December 26
Publication of the second volume of *The Ring and the Book*, including Books IV, V, VI, "Tertium Quid," "Count Guido Franceschini," "Giuseppe Caponsacchi."

1869, January 30
Publication of the third volume of *The Ring and the Book*, including Books VII, VIII, IX, "Pompilia," "Dominus de Archangelis, Pauperum Procurator," "Juris Doctor Johannes-Baptista Bottinius, Fisci et Rev. Cam. Apostol. Advocatus."

February 27
Publication of the fourth volume of *The Ring and the Book,* including Books X, XI, XII, "The Pope," "Guido," "The Book and the Ring."

September
Browning presumably proposed a marriage of convenience with Louisa Lady Ashburton, resulting in a bitter quarrel between the two.

1871, August 8
Publication of *Balaustion's Adventure, Including a Transcript from Euripides.*

December 16
Publication of *Prince Hohenstiel-Schwangau, Saviour of Society.*

1872, June 4
Publication of *Fifine at the Fair.*

1873, May
Publication of *Red Cotton Night-Cap Country, or Turf and Towers.*

1875, April 15
Publication of *Aristophanes' Apology.*

November
Publication of *The Inn Album.*

1876, July 18
Publication of *Of Pacchiarotto, and How He Worked in Distemper.*

1877, September 14
Death of Anne Egerton Smith, whose death prompted the composition of *La Saisiaz.*

October 15
Publication of *The Agamemnon of Aeschylus.*

1878, May 15
Publication of *La Saisiaz* and *The Two Poets of Croisic* in one volume.

1879, April 28
Publication of the first series of *Dramatic Idyls.*

1880, June 15
Publication of *Dramatic Idyls, Second Series.*

1881, October
Founding of the London Browning Society by F. J. Furnivall and Emily Hickey.

1883, March 9
Publication of *Jocoseria.*

1884, November 21
Publication of *Ferishtah's Fancies.*

1887, January 28
Publication of *Parleyings with Certain People of Importance in Their Day.*

1889, January 12
Death of Robert Browning at the home of his son, the Palazzo Rezzonico, in Venice. Publication of *Asolando: Fancies and Facts.*

Alphabetical Bibliography of Browning's Published Works

"Abt Vogler (After He Had Been Extemporizing upon the Musical Instrument of His Invention)"

First appearance: *Dramatis Personae* (1864), where it remains.

"Adam, Lilith, and Eve"

First appearance: *Jocoseria* (1883), where it remains.

"After"

First appearance: *Men and Women* (1855). In 1863, in *Dramatic Lyrics*. A companion poem to "Before."

Agamemnon of Aeschylus, The

Published by Smith, Elder and Co., London, October 15, 1877.

"Album Lines"

Ten lines, written in the album of Edith Longfellow, the daughter of the American poet, when she was visiting in Venice. The lines, bearing the subtitle "Comment on Epilogue of Dramatic Idyls," were written to explain the last ten lines of *Dramatic Idyls*, which had been misinterpreted. Appeared in *The Century*, XXV (February 1882), 159-60.

"Along the Beach"

Section IV of "James Lee's Wife," *q.v.*, in *Dramatis Personae* (1864).

"Among the Rocks"

Section VII of James Lee's Wife," *q.v.*, in *Dramatis Personae* (1864).

"Andrea del Sarto"

First appearance: *Men and Women* (1855), where it remains.

"Another Way of Love"

First appearance: *Men and Women* (1855), as a companion poem to "One Way of Love." In 1863, included in *Dramatic Lyrics*, where it remains.

"Any Wife to Any Husband"

First appearance: *Men and Women* (1855). In 1863, included in *Dramatic Lyrics*, where it remains.

"Apollo and the Fates"

Included in *Parleyings with Certain People of Importance in Their Day* (1887) as a prologue.

"Apparent Failure"

First appearance: *Dramatis Personae* (1864), where it remains.

"Appearances"

First appearance: *Pacchiarotto and How He Worked in Distemper: With Other Poems* (1876), where it remains.

"Arcades Ambo"
First appearance: *Asolando: Fancies and Facts* (1889), where it remains.

Aristophanes' Apology
Published by Smith, Elder and Co., London, April 15, 1875. Manuscript: Balliol College Library, Oxford.

"Artemis Prologizes"
First appearance: *Dramatic Lyrics* (1842), as "Artemis Prologuizes." In 1849, in *Dramatic Romances and Lyrics;* in 1863, in *Men and Women,* where it remains.

Asolando: Fancies and Facts
Published by Smith, Elder and Co., London, December 12, 1889, the day of Browning's death in Venice. The volume is dated 1890.

"At the 'Mermaid' "
Pacchiarotto and How He Worked in Distemper: With Other Poems (1876), where it remains.

"Bad Dreams. I"

"Bad Dreams. II"

"Bad Dreams. III"

"Bad Dreams. IV"
All four of the poems entitled "Bad Dreams" appeared in *Asolando: Fancies and Facts* (1889), where they remain.

Balaustion's Adventure, Including a Transcript from Euripides
Published by Smith, Elder and Co., London, August 8, 1871.

"Bean-Feast, The"
Asolando: Fancies and Facts (1889).

"Bean-Stripe, A: also, Apple-Eating"
Ferishtah's Fancies (1884). Poem number 12.

"Beatrice Signorini"
Asolando: Fancies and Facts (1889).

"Before"
First appearance: *Men and Women* (1855). In 1863, in *Dramatic Lyrics,* where it remains. A companion poem to "After."

Bells and Pomegranates
A series of eight pamphlets published between 1841 and 1846 as follows:
I. *Pippa Passes,* April 1841
II. *King Victor and King Charles,* March 12, 1842
III. *Dramatic Lyrics,* November 26, 1842
IV. *The Return of the Druses,* January 1843
V. *A Blot in the 'Scutcheon,* February 11, 1843
VI. *Colombe's Birthday,* April 20, 1844
VII. *Dramatic Romances and Lyrics,* November 6, 1845
VIII. *Luria* and *A Soul's Tragedy,* April 13, 1846

"Ben Karshook's Wisdom"
First appearance: in the literary annual *The Keepsake* for 1856. Browning did not include the poem in any of his collected editions. Reprinted in the *Browning Society's Papers* (I, 56) and in most editions of the poet's works after 1889.

"Beside the Drawing-Board"
Section VIII of *James Lee's Wife, q.v.,* in *Dramatis Personae* (1864).

"Bifurcation"
Pacchiarotto and How He Worked in Distemper: With Other Poems (1876), where it remains.

"Bishop Blougram's Apology"
Men and Women (1855), where it remains.

"Bishop Orders His Tomb at St. Praxed's Church, The"
First appearance: *Hood's Magazine,* III (March 1845), 237-39, under the title "The Tomb at St. Praxed's." In *Dramatic Romances* (1845), title unchanged. In *Dramatic Romances and Lyrics* in the collected edition of 1849, under its present title. In *Men and Women* in the collected edition of 1863.

"Blind Man to the Maiden, The"
Browning's contribution to *The Hour Will Come, A Tale of an Alpine Cloister* (1879), a translation by Clara Bell of a novel by Wilhelmine von Hillern. The twenty-line poem is a translation, included anonymously; but Mrs. Bell acknowledged her indebtedness to the kindness of a "friend" for the Englished version. Reprinted, as Browning's, in the *Whitehall Review,* March 1, 1883.

Blot in the 'Scutcheon, A
Bells and Pomegranates, No. V. Published by Edward Moxon, London, February 11, 1843.

"Boot and Saddle"
First appearance: *Dramatic Lyrics* (1842), under the title "My Wife Gertrude," one of three poems (with "Marching Along" and "Give a Rouse") making up "Cavalier Tunes." The title was altered to its present form in the collected edition of 1849. The poem remains in *Dramatic Lyrics.*

"Boy and the Angel, The"
First appearance: *Hood's Magazine,* II (August 1844), 140-42. In *Dramatic Romances* (1845); in *Dramatic Romances and Lyrics* in the collected edition of 1849; in *Dramatic Romances* in the edition of 1863, where it remains.

"By the Fire-Side"
First appearance: *Men and Women.* In *Dramatic Lyrics* in the edition of 1863.

"By the Fireside"
First appearance: *Dramatis Personae* (1864), as section II of "James Lee," later changed to the present title, "James Lee's Wife," in 1868. It remains in *Dramatis Personae.*

"Caliban upon Setebos; or, Natural Theology in the Island"
Dramatis Personae (1864), where it remains.

"Camel-Driver, A"
Ferishtah's Fancies (1884), where it remains. Poem number 7.

"Cardinal and the Dog, The"
Asolando: Fancies and Facts (1889), where it remains.

"Cavalier Tunes"
First appearance: *Dramatic Lyrics* (1842). Included under this title were three poems: "Marching Along," "Give a Rouse," and "My Wife Gertrude" (retitled in the 1849 edition to the present title, "Boot and Saddle"). The poem remains in *Dramatic Lyrics.*

"Cenciaja"
Pacchiarotto and How He Worked in Distemper: With Other Poems (1876), where it remains.

"Cherries"
Ferishtah's Fancies (1884). Poem number 9.

" 'Childe Roland to the Dark Tower Came' "
First appearance: *Men and Women* (1855). In *Dramatic Romances* in the edition of 1863, where it remains.

Christmas-Eve and Easter-Day
Published by Chapman and Hall, London, April 1, 1850.

"Cleon"
First appearance: *Men and Women* (1855), where it remains.

"Clive"
First appearance: *Dramatic Idyls, Second Series* (1880), where it remains.

Colombe's Birthday
Published by Edward Moxon, London, April 20, 1844.

"Confessional, The"
First appearance: *Dramatic Romances* (1845), along with "The Laboratory," under the general title *France and Spain*. In 1849 it was included in *Dramatic Romances and Lyrics* as a separate poem, unconnected with its twin. In 1863 it became one of the *Dramatic Lyrics*, where it remains.

"Confessions"
Dramatis Personae (1864), where it remains.

"Count Gismond. Aix in Provence"
First appearance: *Dramatic Lyrics* (1842), as "II. France," under the general title "Italy and France." In the collected edition of 1849 the poem was given its present title and was separated from "Italy," which was given the present title, "My Last Duchess." In 1863 both poems were included in *Dramatic Romances*, where they remain.

"Cristina"
First appearance: *Dramatic Lyrics* (1982), *Bells and Pomegranates*, No. III. The poem, together with "Rudel and the Lady of Tripoli" (renamed later "Rudel to the Lady of Tripoli"), appeared under the general title "Queen-Worship." In 1849, in *Dramatic Romances and Lyrics*, it lost its association with "Rudel." In 1863 it was one of the *Dramatic Lyrics*, where it remains.

"Cristina and Monaldeschi"
Jocoseria (1883), where it remains.

"Deaf and Dumb; A Group by Woolner"
First appearance: *Dramatis Personae*, in the collected edition of Browning's poems of 1868, where it remains.

"Death in the Desert, A"
First appearance: *Dramatis Personae* (1864), where it remains.

"De Gustibus—"
First appearance: *Men and Women* (1855). In 1863, in *Dramatic Lyrics*, where it remains.

"Development"
Asolando: Fancies and Facts (1889), where it remains.

"Dîs Aliter Visum; or, Le Byron de nos Jours"
Dramatis Personae (1864), where it remains.

"Doctor—"
Dramatic Idyls, Second Series (1880), where it remains.

"Donald"
Jocoseria (1883), where it remains.

Dramatic Idyls [First Series]
Published by Smith, Elder and Co., London, April 28, 1879.

Dramatic Idyls, Second Series
Published by Smith, Elder and Co., London, June 15, 1880.

Dramatic Lyrics, Bells and Pomegranates, No. III
Published by Edward Moxon, London, November 1842.
Cavalier Tunes
I. Marching Along
II. Give a Rouse
III. My Wife Gertrude [in 1849 called "Boot and Saddle"]

Italy and France
I. Italy [in 1849 called "My Last Duchess"]
II. France [in 1849 called "Count Gismond"]
Camp and Cloister
I. Camp (French) [in 1849 called "Incident of the French Camp"]
II. Cloister (Spanish) [in 1849 called "Soliloquy of the Spanish Cloister"]
In a Gondola
Artemis Prologuizes [in 1863 spelled "Prologizes"]
Waring
Queen-Worship
I. Rudel and the Lady of Tripoli [in 1849 called "Rudel to the Lady of Tripoli"]
II. Cristina
Madhouse Cells
I. "There's Heaven above . . ." [in 1849 called "Johannes Agricola in Meditation"]
II. "The rain set early in to-night . . ." [in 1849 called "Porphyria's Lover"]
Through the Metidja to Abd-el-Kadr.—1842
The Pied Piper of Hamelin; A Child's Story

Dramatic Romances and Lyrics, Bells and Pomegranates, No. VII
Published by Edward Moxon, London, November 6, 1845.
How They brought the Good News from Ghent to Aix (16—)
Pictor Ignotus. Florence, 15—
Italy in England [called in 1849 "The Italian in England"]
England in Italy [called in 1849 "The Englishman in Italy"]
The Lost Leader
The Lost Mistress
Home-Thoughts, from Abroad
The Tomb at St. Praxed's [called in 1849 "The Bishop Orders his Tomb at St. Praxed's Church"]
Garden Fancies
I. The Flower's Name
II. Sibrandus Schafnaburgensis
France and Spain
I. The Laboratory
II. The Confessional
The Flight of the Duchess
Earth's Immortalities
Song ["Nay, but you, who do not love her"]
The Boy and the Angel
Night and Morning [called in 1849 "Meeting at Night and Parting at Morning"]
Claret and Tokay [called in 1863 "Nationality in Drinks"]
Saul [the first nine sections]
Time's Revenges
The Glove

Dramatis Personae
Published by Chapman and Hall, London, May 28, 1864.
James Lee
Gold Hair: A Legend of Pornic
The Worst of It
Dîs Aliter Visum; or, Le Byron de nos Jours
Too Late
Abt Vogler
Rabbi Ben Ezra
A Death in the Desert
Caliban upon Setebos; or, Natural Theology in the Island
Confessions

May and Death
Prospice
Youth and Art
A Face
A Likeness
Mr. Sludge, "The Medium"
Apparent Failure
Epilogue

"Dubiety"
Asolando: Fancies and Facts (1889), where it remains.

"Eagle, The"
Ferishtah's Fancies (1884). Poem number 1.

"Earth's Immortalities"
First appearance: *Dramatic Romances, Bells and Pomegranates,* No. VII (1845). In two parts, untitled; but in the 1849 collected edition given the present titles, "Fame" and "Love" and included in *Dramatic Romances and Lyrics,* still under the general title "Earth's Immortalities." In the 1863 collected edition the poem was included in *Dramatic Lyrics,* where it remains.

Easter-Day
The second poem of *Christmas-Eve and Easter-Day.* Published by Chapman and Hall, London, April 1, 1850.

"Echetlos"
Dramatic Idyls, Second Series (1880), where it remains.

"Englishman in Italy, The"
First appearance: *Dramatic Romances* (1845), under the title "England in Italy." In 1849 in *Dramatic Romances and Lyrics,* where it remains.

Epilogue [to *Asolando*]
Asolando: Fancies and Facts (1889), where it remains.

Epilogue [to *Dramatis Personae*]
Dramatis Personae (1864), where it remains.

Epilogue [to *Ferishtah's Fancies*]
Ferishtah's Fancies (1884), where it remains.

Epilogue [to *Fifine at the Fair*]
Fifine at the Fair (1872), where it remains.

Epilogue [to *Pacchiarotto*]
Pacchiarotto and How He Worked in Distemper: With Other Poems (1876), where it remains.

"Epistle Containing the Strange Medical Experience of Karshish, the Arab Physician, An"
Men and Women (1855), where it remains.

"Epitaph on Levi Lincoln Thaxter"
A lapidary inscription above the grave of an early American admirer of Browning's verse (Februray 1, 1824—May 31, 1884). Uncollected by the poet. In *Fugitive Pieces,* in the Porter and Clarke edition, 1898, XII, 280.

"Eurydice to Orpheus; A Picture by Leighton"
First appearance: The Royal Academy Exhibition Catalogue (1864). In 1865, included in a volume of selections of the poet, under the title "Orpheus and Eurydice." In 1868 included in *Dramatis Personae* under its present title, where it remains.

"Evelyn Hope"
First appearance: *Men and Women* (1855). In 1863 it became one of the *Dramatic Lyrics,* where it remains.

"Eyes, calm beside thee (Lady, couldst thou know?)"
Sonnet. *The Monthly Repository,* VIII, N.S. (1834). Signed "Z." Not reprinted by Browning. Appears in "Fugitive Poems," in the Camberwell Browning.

"Face, A"
Dramatis Personae (1864), where it remains.

"Fame"
First appearance: *Dramatic Romances, Bells and Pomegranates,* No. VII. Untitled, the poem was linked with "Love," also untitled, under the general title "Earth's Immortalities." In the 1849 collected edition the two poems were given their present titles, still under the same general title, in *Dramatic Romances and Lyrics.* In 1863 both poems under "Earth's Immortalities" were included in *Dramatic Lyrics,* where they remain.

"Family, The"
Ferishtah's Fancies (1884), where it remains. Poem number 4.

"Fears and Scruples"
Pacchiarotto and How He Worked in Distemper: With Other Poems (1876), where it remains.

Ferishtah's Fancies
Published by Smith, Elder and Co., London, November 21, 1884.
Prologue
The Eagle
The Melon-Seller
Shah Abbas
The Family
The Sun
Mihrab Shah
A Camel-Driver
Two Camels
Cherries
Plot-Culture
A Pillar at Sebzevah [later titled "A Pillar at Sebzevar"]
A Bean-Stripe: also Apple-Eating

Fifine at the Fair
Published by Smith, Elder and Co., London, June 4, 1872.

"Filippo Baldinucci on the Privilege of Burial. A Reminiscence of A.D. 1676"
Pacchiarotto and How He Worked in Distemper: With Other Poems (1876), where it remains.

"*Flight of the Duchess, The*"
First appearance: The first nine sections appeared in *Hood's Magazine,* III (April 1845), 313-18. The completed work appeared in *Dramatic Romances* (1845). In 1849 it was included in *Dramatic Romances and Lyrics,* and in 1863 it became one of *Dramatic Romances,* where it remains.

"Flower's Name, The"
Under the general title "Garden Fancies," two poems, "The Flower's Name" and "Sibrandus Schafnaburgensis," appeared in *Hood's Magazine* II (July 1844), 45-48. Included in *Dramatic Romances* in 1845, and in *Dramatic Romances and Lyrics* in 1849. In 1863 both poems were included in *Dramatic Lyrics,* together with "Soliloquy of the Spanish Cloister," listed as "Garden Fancies III." In the collected edition of 1868, the "Soliloquy" was removed from "Garden Fancies."

"Flute-Music, with an Accompaniment"
Asolando: Fancies and Facts (1889), where it remains.

"Forgiveness, A"

Pacchiarotto and How He Worked in Distemper: With Other Poems (1876), where it remains.

"Founder of the Feast, The"

First appearance: In an album presented to Arthur Chappell, in recognition of the Popular Concerts which he organized for biweekly presentation at St. James's Hall, London. Dated by the poet April 5, 1884. Appeared in *The World*, April 16, 1884. The poem was not collected by Browning but appeared in various places, including the Porter and Clarke edition, F. G. Kenyon's *New Poems of Robert Browning* (1914), and the *Macmillan Edition.*

"Fra Lippo Lippi"

Men and Women (1855), where it remains.

"Fust and His Friends, An Epilogue"

Parleyings with Certain People of Importance in Their Day (1887), where it remains.

"Garden Fancies"

First appearance: *Hood's Magazine,* II (July 1844), 45-48. Under the general title of "Garden Fancies," two poems, "Garden Fancies I. The Flower's Name" and "Garden Fancies II. Sibrandus Schafnaburgensis," were grouped. They appeared in *Dramatic Romances* in 1845; they were included in *Dramatic Romances and Lyrics* in 1849; and they appeared in *Dramatic Lyrics* in 1863, where the "Soliloquy of the Spanish Cloister" was attached to them as "Garden Fancies III." In 1868 the "Soliloquy" was removed from the group, leaving the original two together under "Garden Fancies."

"Give a Rouse"

Dramatic Lyrics, Bells and Pomegranates, No. III (1842). The poem, together with "Marching Along" and "My Wife Gertrude" (in 1849 retitled "Boot and Saddle"), was grouped under the general title "Cavalier Tunes." In 1863 all three of the "Cavalier Tunes" remained in *Dramatic Lyrics,* where they are today.

"Glove, The"

First appearance: *Dramatic Romances* (1845); in 1849 it remained in *Dramatic Romances and Lyrics,* and in 1863 it was included in *Dramatic Romances,* where it remains.

"Gold Hair: A Legend of Pornic"

First appearance: the *Atlantic Monthly,* XIII (May 1864), 596-99. Included in *Dramatis Personae* (1864), where it remains.

"Goldoni"

First appearance: *Pall Mall Gazette,* December 8, 1883. Browning did not include this poem in any of his volumes, but it has appeared in several collected editions published after 1889.

"Grammarian's Funeral, A, Shortly After the Revival of Learning in Europe"

First appearance: *Men and Women* (1855). In 1863 included in *Dramatic Romances,* where it remains.

"Guardian-Angel, The: A Picture at Fano"

First appearance: *Men and Women* (1855). In 1863 included in *Dramatic Lyrics,* where it remains.

"Halbert and Hob"

Dramatic Idyls (1879), first series, where it remains.

"Helen's Tower"

First appearance: *Pall Mall Gazette,* December 28, 1883. The Earl of Dufferin asked Tennyson and Browning to contribute poems about a tower he built in memory of his mother, Helen, Countess of Gifford, on his estate at Clandeboye, Ireland. Browning compiled with this sonnet.

"Heretic's Tragedy, The. A Middle-Age Interlude"
First appearance: *Men and Women* (1855). In 1863 the poem was included in *Dramatic Romances*, where it remains.

"Hervé Riel"
First appearance: *Cornhill Magazine*, March 1871. Included in *Pacchiarotto and How He Worked in Distemper: With Other Poems* (1876), where it remains.

"Holy-Cross Day. (On which the Jews were Forced to Attend an Annual Christian Sermon in Rome)"
First appearance: *Men and Women* (1855). Included in 1863 in *Dramatic Romances*, where it remains.

"Home-Thoughts, from Abroad"
First appearance: *Dramatic Romances* (1845). Under this general title appeared, as Parts I, II, and III, three poems: "Oh, to be in England . . . ," "Here's to Nelson's Memory . . . ," and "Nobly, nobly Cape St. Vincent. . . ." In 1849 included in *Dramatic Romances and Lyrics*, where the first poem became independent of the others and was given its present title, "Home-Thoughts, from Abroad." In 1863 it became one of the *Dramatic Lyrics*, where it remains. "Here's to Nelson's memory . . ." (which was omitted from the 1849 collection) was included in the 1863 collection among the *Dramatic Lyrics* as the last poem of the three under the general title "Nationality in Drinks," where it was called "Beer (Nelson)." It is still included among the *Dramatic Lyrics*. The last of the three, "Nobly, nobly Cape St. Vincent . . ." was included in *Dramatic Romances and Lyrics* under the title "Home-Thoughts, from the Sea." In 1863 it became one of the *Dramatic Lyrics*, where it remains.

"Home-Thoughts, from the Sea"
First appearance: *Dramatic Romances* (1845), as Part III, untitled, of "Home-Thoughts, from Abroad." In 1849 "Nobly, nobly Cape St. Vincent . . ." was detached from the other two poems ("Oh, to be in England . . ." and "Here's to Nelson's Memory . . .") and was entitled "Home-Thoughts, from the Sea," in *Dramatic Romances and Lyrics*. In 1863 it was included in *Dramatic Lyrics*, where it remains.

"House"
Pacchiarotto and How He Worked in Distemper: With Other Poems (1876), where it remains.

"How It Strikes a Contemporary"
Men and Women (1855), where it remains.

"How They Brought the Good News from Ghent to Aix"
First appearance: *Dramatic Romances* (1845). In 1849, included in *Dramatic Romances and Lyrics*, and in 1863 it became one of the *Dramatic Lyrics*, where it remains.

"Humility"
Asolando: Fancies and Facts (1889), where it remains.

" 'Imperante Augusto Natus Est—' "
Asolando: Fancies and Facts (1889), where it remains.

"Impromptu"
Pall Mall Gazette, December 13, 1883. Uncollected by the poet. Included in the *Macmillan Edition* and in the Porter and Clarke edition among the *Fugitive Pieces*. DeVane in the *Browning Handbook* discusses the poem under the title "On Singers." The poem is a translation of Horace's First Book of *Satires*, III, 1-3.

"In a Balcony"
First appearance: *Men and Women* (1855). In 1863, included in *Tragedies and Other Plays*. In the collected edition of 1868 it was made independent and was placed between *Men and Women* and *Dramatis Personae*. In the Porter and Clarke edition, it still occupies this position.

"In a Gondola"

First appearance: *Dramatic Lyrics. Bells and Pomegranates,* No. III (1842). In 1863, included in *Dramatic Romances,* where it remains.

"Inapprehensiveness"

Asolando: Fancies and Facts (1889), where it remains.

"In a Year"

First appearance: *Men and Women* (1855), along with its companion poem, "In Three Days." In 1863 both poems were included in *Dramatic Lyrics,* where they remain.

"Incident of the French Camp"

First appearance: *Dramatic Lyrics. Bells and Pomegranates,* No. III (November 1842); under the general title "Camp and Cloister," the poem was entitled "Camp (French)." The other poem linked with it was entitled "Cloister (Spanish)." In the collected edition of 1849, the two poems were made separate poems and the general title "Camp and Cloister" disappeared. In the collected edition of 1863 the poem, under its permanent title, "Incident of the French Camp," was included in *Dramatic Romances.*

Inn Album, The

Published by Smith, Elder and Co., London, November 1875. During the same month, on November 14, 21, and 28, the poem was published in the *New York Times.*

"Instans Tyrannus"

First appearance: *Men and Women* (1855). In 1863 included in *Dramatic Romances,* where it remains.

"In the Doorway"

Part III of "James Lee" (in 1868 renamed "James Lee's Wife") in *Dramatis Personae* (1864), where it remains.

"In Three Days"

First appearance: *Men and Women* (1855), together with "In a Year," with which it was linked. In 1863 both poems were included in *Dramatic Lyrics,* where they remain.

"Italian in England, The"

First appearance: *Dramatic Romances* (1845), under the title "Italy in England." In 1849 it was included in *Dramatic Romances and Lyrics,* and in the collected edition of 1863 it was one of the *Dramatic Romances,* where it remains.

"Ivàn Ivànovitch"

Dramatic Idyls (1879), where it remains.

"Ixion"

Jocoseria (1883), where it remains.

"James Lee's Wife"

First appearance: *Dramatis Personae* (1864), under the title "James Lee." In the collected edition of 1868, the title now changed to "James Lee's Wife," the poem was kept in *Dramatis Personae,* where it remains. The poem comprises nine sections. The first six stanzas of section VI, beginning " 'Still ailing, Wind?' " appeared in the *Monthly Repository,* X, N.S. (May 1836), 270-71, signed "Z."

"Jochanan Hakkadosh"

Jocoseria (1883), where it remains.

Jocoseria

Published by Smith, Elder and Co., London, March 9, 1883.
Wanting is—what?
Donald

Solomon and Balkis
Cristina and Monaldeschi
Mary Wollstonecraft and Fuseli
Adam, Lilith, and Eve
Ixion
Jochanan Hakkadosh
Never the Time and the Place
Pambo

"Johannes Agricola in Meditation"

First appearance: *The Monthly Repository,* January 1836, under the title "Johannes Agricola." Included with it was "Porphyria," later called "Porphyria's Lover," but they were not linked under the later general title "Madhouse Cells." Each poem was signed "Z." Included in *Dramatic Lyrics, Bells and Pomegranates,* No. III (1842), where both poems, untitled, appeared under the general title "Madhouse Cells." In 1849 the present title, "Johannes Agricola in Meditation," was given to "Madhouse Cells, No. I," and the present title, "Porphyria's Lover," was given as a subtitle to the other, which still bore the title "Madhouse Cells, No. II." In the collected edition of 1863 "Johannes Agricola in Meditation" was included in *Dramatic Romances,* as was "Porphyria's Lover," but the title "Madhouse Cells" was omitted and thus also the connection between the two poems. In 1868 "Porphyria's Lover" became one of the poems in *Dramatic Romances;* "Porphyria's Lover" was included in *Men and Women.* They so remain.

"Jubilee Memorial Lines"

Four lines, appearing in the *Pall Mall Gazette.* Written for a jubilee window to be placed in St. Margaret's, Westminster, in celebration of the fiftieth anniversary of Queen Victoria's reign.

King Victor and King Charles

Bells and Pomegranates, No. II. Published by Edward Moxon, London, March 12, 1842.

"Laboratory, The (Ancien Régime)"

First appearance: *Hood's Magazine,* I (June 1844), 513-14. Included in *Dramatic Romances, Bells and Pomegranates,* No. VII (1845), under the general title "France and Spain," together with "The Confessional." In 1849 the two poems appeared in *Dramatic Romances and Lyrics,* where the connection was ended between the two poems, and the general title was abandoned. In 1863 both poems, still unconnected, appeared in *Dramatic Lyrics,* where they remain.

"Lady and the Painter, The"

Asolando: Fancies and Facts (1889), where it remains.

La Saisiaz

Included in the volume *La Saisiaz* and *The Two Poets of Croisic.* Published by Smith, Elder and Co., London, May 15, 1878.

"Last Ride Together, The"

First appearance: *Men and Women* (1855). In 1863 included in *Dramatic Romances,* where it remains.

"Life in a Love"

First appearance: *Men and Women* (1855). In 1863 included in *Dramatic Lyrics,* where it remains.

"Light Woman, A"

First appearance: *Men and Women* (1855). In 1863 included in *Dramatic Romances,* where it remains.

"Likeness, A"

Dramatis Personae (1864), where it remains.

"Lost Leader, The"

First appearance: *Dramatic Romances* (1845). In 1849 it was included in *Dramatic Romances and Lyrics;* in the collected edition of 1863 it became one of the *Dramatic Lyrics,* where it remains.

"Lost Mistress, The"

First appearance: *Dramatic Romances* (1845). In the edition of 1849 it was included in *Dramatic Romances and Lyrics,* and in the edition of 1863 it became one of the *Dramatic Lyrics,* where it remains.

"Love"

The second of two untitled poems (the other later called "Fame") under the general title "Earth's Immortalities" included in *Dramatic Romances* (1845). In the collected edition of 1849, included in *Dramatic Romances and Lyrics.* The present titles "Love" and "Fame" appeared under the general title "Earth's Immortalities." In the collected edition of 1863, the two poems, still under the general title, were included in *Dramatic Lyrics.*

"Love among the Ruins"

First appearance: *Men and Women* (1855). In 1863 the poem was included in *Dramatic Lyrics,* where it remains.

"Love in a Life"

First appearance: *Men and Women* (1855). In 1863 included in *Dramatic Lyrics,* where it remains.

"Lovers' Quarrel, A"

First appearance: *Men and Women* (1855). In 1863 the poem was included in *Dramatic Lyrics,* where it remains.

Luria

Bells and Pomegranates, No. VIII. *Luria; and A Soul's Tragedy.* Published by Edward Moxon, London, April 13, 1846.

"Magical Nature"

Pacchiarotto and How He Worked in Distemper: With Other Poems (1876), a companion poem to "Natural Magic." Both poems have remained in this volume.

"Marching Along"

The first of three poems (followed by "Give a Rouse" and "My Wife Gertrude," the latter retitled in the 1849 edition "Boot and Saddle"), under the general title "Cavalier Tunes," in *Dramatic Lyrics, Bells and Pomegranates,* No. III (November 1842). In the 1863 edition "Cavalier Tunes" was kept in *Dramatic Lyrics,* where it remains.

"Martin Relph"

Dramatic Idyls [First Series] (1879), where it remains.

"Mary Wollstonecraft and Fuseli"

Jocoseria (1883), where it remains.

"Master Hugues of Saxe-Gotha"

First appearance: *Men and Women* (1855). In 1863 the poem was included in *Dramatic Lyrics,* where it remains.

"May and Death"

First appearance: in the literary annual *The Keepsake* (1857). Included in *Dramatis Personae* (1864), where it remains.

"Meeting at Night"

First appearance: *Dramatic Romances* (1845), under the title "Night and Morning, I. Night and II. Morning." In the collected edition of 1849 the poems, which were included in *Dramatic Romances and Lyrics,* received their present titles, "Meeting at Night" and "Parting at Morning," and lost the general title "Night and Morning." In the collected edition of 1863 they were included in *Dramatic Lyrics,* where they remain.

"Melon-Seller, The"
Ferishtah's Fancies (1884), where it remains. Poem number 2.

"Memorabilia"
First appearance: *Men and Women* (1855). In the 1863 collection it was grouped with *Dramatic Lyrics*, where it remains.

Men and Women
Published by Chapman and Hall, London, November 17, 1855, in two volumes.

Volume I

Love Among the Ruins
A Lovers' Quarrel
Evelyn Hope
Up at a Villa—Down in the City
(As Distinguished by an Italian Person of Quality)
A Woman's Last Word
Fra Lippo Lippi
A Toccata of Galuppi's
By the Fire-Side
Any Wife to Any Husband
An Epistle containing the Strange Medical Experience of Karshish, the Arab Physician
Mesmerism
A Serenade at the Villa
My Star
Instans Tyrannus
A Pretty Woman
"Childe Roland to the Dark Tower Came"
Respectability
A Light Woman
The Statue and the Bust
Love in a Life
Life in a Love
How it Strikes a Contemporary
The Last Ride Together
The Patriot—An Old Story
Master Hugues of Saxe-Gotha
Bishop Blougram's Apology
Memorabilia

Volume II

Andrea del Sarto (Called "The Faultless Painter")
Before
After
In Three Days
In a Year
Old Pictures in Florence
In a Balcony—First Part
In a Balcony—Second Part
In a Balcony—Third Part
Saul
"De Gustibus—"
Women and Roses
Protus
Holy-Cross Day. (On which the Jews were Forced to Attend an Annual Christian Sermon in Rome)
The Guardian-Angel: A Picture at Fano
Cleon
The Twins

Popularity
The Heretic's Tragedy. A Middle-Age Interlude
Two in the Campagna
A Grammarian's Funeral
One Way of Love
Another Way of Love
"Transcendentalism:" A Poem in Twelve Books
Misconceptions
One Word More. To E. B. B.

"Mesmerism"
First appearance: *Men and Women* (1855). In 1863 it became one of the *Dramatic Romances,* where it remains.

"Mihrab Shah"
Ferishtah's Fancies (1884), where it remains. Poem number 6.

"Misconceptions"
First appearance: *Men and Women* (1855). In the 1863 edition the poem was included in *Dramatic Lyrics,* where it remains.

"Mr. Sludge, 'the Medium' "
Dramatis Personae (1864), where it remains.

"Muckle-Mouth Meg"
Asolando: Fancies and Facts (1889), where it remains.

"Muleykéh"
Dramatic Idyls, Second Series (1880), where it remains.

"My Last Duchess. Ferrara"
First appearance: *Dramatic Lyrics, Bells and Pomegranates,* No. III (November 1842), entitled "I. Italy" under the general title "Italy and France," which included "II. France," later called "Count Gismond." In the collected edition of 1849 the poem under its present title, "My Last Duchess," was included in *Dramatic Romances and Lyrics,* along with "Count Gismond." In 1863 both poems were included in *Dramatic Romances,* where they remain.

"My Star"
First appearance: *Men and Women* (1855). In the 1863 collected edition the poem was placed among the *Dramatic Lyrics,* where it remains.

"Names, The"
First appearance: *The Shakespearean Show-Book* (May 1884), upon the occasion of a Shakespearean show, held in London, May 29-31, 1884, to help pay the debt on the Hospital for Women. Browning did not collect the work in any of his editions, but it has been printed in various places, including the *Pall Mall Gazette,* May 29, 1884.

"Nationality in Drinks"
First appearance: *Hood's Magazine,* June 1844, under the title "Claret and Tokay." Both poems were included in *Dramatic Romances* (1845). Omitted in the collected edition of 1849, they were included in *Dramatic Lyrics* in the edition of 1863, linked with "Here's to Nelson's Memory" (in 1845 printed as the second poem of "Home-Thoughts from Abroad"), now entitled "Beer (Nelson)," the three poems coming under the general title "Nationality in Drinks." The poems remain in *Dramatic Lyrics.*

"Natural Magic"
Pacchiarotto and How He Worked in Distemper: With Other Poems (1876), where it was linked with "Magical Nature." Both poems remain in the *Pacchiarotto* volume.

"Ned Bratts"
Dramatic Idyls [First Series] (1879), where it remains.

"Never the Time and the Place"
Jocoseria (1883), where it remains.

"Now"
Asolando: Fancies and Facts (1889), where it remains.

"Numpholeptos"
Pacchiarotto and How He Worked in Distemper: With Other Poems (1876), where it remains.

"Old Pictures in Florence"
First appearance: *Men and Women* (1855). In 1863 and 1868, included in *Dramatic Lyrics*, where it remains.

"O Love! Love!"
An uncollected poem of nine lines, a translation of part of a chorus from the *Hippolytus* of Euripides, done at the request of J. P. Mahaffy.

"On Deck"
Part IX of "James Lee" in *Dramatis Personae* (1864). In the collected edition of 1868 the poem was entitled "James Lee's Wife." The poem remains in *Dramatis Personae*.

"On the Cliff"
Part V of "James Lee" in *Dramatis Personae* (1864). In the collected edition of 1868 the title was changed to "James Lee's Wife." The poem remains in *Dramatis Personae*.

"One Way of Love"
First appearance: *Men and Women* (1855). In the 1863 collected edition it was included, along with its companion poem "Another Way of Love," in *Dramatic Lyrics*, where they remain.

"One Word More. To E. B. B."
Men and Women (1855), where it remains.

Pacchiarotto and How He Worked in Distemper: With Other Poems
Published by Smith, Elder and Co., London, July 18, 1876.
Prologue
Of Pacchiarotto, and How He Worked in Distemper
At the "Mermaid"
House
Shop
Pisgah Sights. 1.
Pisgah Sights. 2.
Fears and Scruples
Natural Magic
Magical Nature
Bifurcation
Numpholeptos
Appearances
St. Martin's Summer
Hervè Riel
A Forgiveness
Cenciaja
Filippo Baldinucci on the Privilege of Burial
Epilogue

"Pambo"
Jocoseria (1883), where it served as an epilogue. It remains in *Jocoseria*.

"Pan and Luna"
Dramatic Idyls, Second Series (1880), where it remains.

Paracelsus
Published by Effingham Wilson, London, August 15, 1835.

"Parleying with Bernard de Mandeville"
Parleying with Certain People of Importance in Their Day. Published by Smith, Elder and Co., London, January 28, 1887.

"Parleying with Christopher Smart"
Parleying with Certain People of Importance in Their Day. Published by Smith, Elder and Co., London, January 28, 1887.

"Parleying with Daniel Bartoli"
Parleying with Certain People of Importance in Their Day. Published by Smith, Elder and Co., London, January 28, 1887.

"Parleying with Francis Furini"
Parleying with Certain People of Importance in Their Day. Published by Smith, Elder and Co., London, January 28, 1887.

"Parleying with George Bubb Dodington"
Parleying with Certain People of Importance in Their Day. Published by Smith, Elder and Co., London, January 28, 1887.

"Parleying with Gerard de Lairesse"
Parleying with Certain People of Importance in Their Day. Published by Smith, Elder and Co., London, January 28, 1887.

Parleyings with Certain People of Importance in Their Day
Published by Smith, Elder and Co., London, January 28, 1887.

"Parting at Morning"
Dramatic Romances (1845), the second of two parts entitled: "Night and Morning, I. Night and II. Morning." In the collected edition of 1849, among *Dramatic Romances and Lyrics*, the two poems, which were no longer linked by title, were renamed "Meeting at Night" and "Parting at Morning." In 1863 they were included in *Dramatic Lyrics*, where they remain.

"Patriot, The.—An Old Story"
First appearance: *Men and Women* (1855). In 1863 included in *Dramatic Romances*, where it remains.

Pauline
Published by Saunders and Otley, London, March 1833.

"Pearl, A Girl, A"
Asolando: Fancies and Facts (1889), where it remains.

"Pheidippides"
Dramatic Idyls [First Series] (1879), where it remains.

"Pictor Ignotus, Florence, 15—"
First appearance: *Dramatic Romances* (1845). In the edition of 1849 it was included in the *Dramatic Romances and Lyrics*, and in 1863 it became one of *Men and Women*, where it remains.

"Pied Piper of Hamelin, The; A Child's Story"
Dramatic Lyrics; Bells and Pomegranates, No. III (November 1842). In the collected edition of 1849 it became one of the *Dramatic Romances and Lyrics*, and in 1863 it was included in *Dramatic Romances*, where it remains.

"Pietro of Abano"
Dramatic Idyls, Second Series (1880), where it remains.

"Pillar at Sebzevah, A"
Ferishtah's Fancies (1884), later changed to "A Pillar at Sebzevar." Poem number 11.

"Pillar at Sebzevar, A"
Ferishtah's Fancies (1884), originally entitled "A Pillar at Sebzevah." Poem number 11.

Pippa Passes
Published by Edward Moxon, London, April 1841. The first pamphlet publication in *Bells and Pomegranates.*

"Pisgah-Sights"
Pacchiarotto and How He Worked in Distemper: With Other Poems (1876).

"Plot-Culture"
Ferishtah's Fancies (1884). Poem number 10.

"Poetics"
Asolando: Fancies and Facts (1889).

"Ponte dell' Angelo, Venice"
Asolando: Fancies and Facts (1889).

"Pope and the Net, The"
Asolando: Fancies and Facts (1889).

"Popularity"
First appearance: *Men and Women* (1855). In the collected edition of 1863 the poem was included in *Dramatic Lyrics* (1842), where it remains.

"Porphyria's Lover"
First appearance: *The Monthly Repository*, January 1836, under the title "Porphyria," along with its companion poem "Johannes Agricola." In *Dramatic Lyrics* (1842), both poems appeared under the general title "Madhouse Cells," the poems themselves being untitled. In the collected edition of 1863 the link was severed, and the two poems were included in *Dramatic Romances*, where they remain, and were given their present titles: "Porphyria's Lover" and "Johannes Agricola in Meditation."

"Pretty Woman, A"
First appearance: *Men and Women* (1855). In the collected edition of 1863 the poem was included in *Dramatic Lyrics*, where it remains.

Prince Hohenstiel-Schwangau, Saviour of Society
Published by Smith, Elder and Co., London, December 16, 1871.

Prologue [to *Asolando*]
Asolando: Fancies and Facts (1889).

Prologue [to *Ferishtah's Fancies*]
Ferishtah's Fancies (1884).

Prologue [to *Fifine at the Fair*]
Fifine at the Fair (1872).

Prologue [to *Pacchiarotto*]
Pacchiarotto and How He Worked in Distemper: With Other Poems (1876).

"Prospice"
First appearance: the *Atlantic Monthly*, XIII (June 1864), 694. In 1864 in *Dramatis Personae*, where it remains.

"Protus"
First appearance: *Men and Women* (1855). In 1863 it became one of the *Dramatic Romances*, where it remains.

"Rabbi Ben Ezra"
Dramatis Personae (1864), where it remains.

"Rawdon Brown"
First appearance: *Century Magazine*, XXVII (February 1884), 640. A poem written at the request of Mrs. Katherine Bronson, a friend of the poet who lived in Venice and with whom Browning visited. The poem was never collected by the poet, but it appears in a number of editions published after his death, including the Porter and Clarke and the Macmillan editions. The motto—a Venetian saying—" 'Tutti ga i so gusti, e mi go i mii!" means: Everyone follows his taste, and I follow mine."

"Reading a Book, under the Cliff"
Poem VI of "James Lee" in *Dramatis Personae* (1864). In the collected edition of 1868 the title was changed to "James Lee's Wife." The poem remains in *Dramatis Personae*.

Red Cotton Night-Cap Country, or Turf and Towers
Published by Smith, Elder and Co., London, May 1873.

"Rephan"
Asolando: Fancies and Facts (1889), where it remains.

"Respectability"
First appearance: *Men and Women* (1855). In the collected edition of 1863 the poem became one of the *Dramatic Lyrics*, where it remains.

Return of the Druses, The
Bells and Pomegranates, No. IV, January 1843.

"Reverie"
Asolando: Fancies and Facts (1889).

Ring and the Book, The
Published by Smith, Elder and Co., London, four volumes: I, November 21, 1868; II, December 26, 1868; III, January 30, 1869; and IV, February 27, 1869.

"Rosny"
Asolando: Fancies and Facts (1889), where it remains.

"Rudel to the Lady of Tripoli"
First appearance: *Dramatic Lyrics, Bells and Pomegranates*, No. III (November 1842), where under the name "Rudel and the Lady of Tripoli" it was a companion poem to "Cristina," under the general title "Queen-Worship." In 1849 it was included, under its present title, in *Dramatic Romances and Lyrics*, as was "Cristina," but the general title was dropped and the somewhat tenuous connection between the two poems was absent. In the collected edition of 1863 it was included in *Men and Women*. "Cristina" was placed among the *Dramatic Lyrics*. Neither poem has been reassigned since.

"Saul"
First appearance: the first nine sections of "Saul" were included in *Dramatic Romances* (1845). In the collected edition of 1849 these nine sections appeared in *Dramatic Romances and Lyrics*. The completed poem appeared in *Men and Women* (1855). In the collected edition of 1863 "Saul" was included in *Dramatic Lyrics*, where it remains.

"Serenade at the Villa, A"
First appearance: *Men and Women* (1855). In the edition of 1863 it was included in *Dramatic Lyrics*, where it remains.

"Shah Abbas"
Ferishtah's Fancies (1884), where it remains. Poem number 3.

"Shop"
Pacchiarotto and How He Worked in Distemper: With Other Poems (1876), where it remains.

"Sibrandus Schafnaburgensis"
First appearance: *Hood's Magazine*, II (July 1844), 46-48, as the second poem under the general title "Garden Fancies," along with its mate "The Flower's Name." Both poems were included in *Dramatic Romances* (1845), under the general title "Garden Fancies." In the collected edition of 1849 they were included in *Dramatic Romances and Lyrics*, and in 1863 they became part of *Dramatic Lyrics*, where a third poem, "Soliloquy of the Spanish Cloister," was added to the pair as "Garden Fancies III." In the collected edition of 1868 the "Soliloquy" was separated from the two, although the three were kept in *Dramatic Lyrics*, where they remain.

"Soliloquy of the Spanish Cloister"
First appearance: *Dramatic Lyrics, Bells and Pomegranates,* No. III (November 1842), under the title "II. Cloister (Spanish)," the second of two poems under the general title "Camp and Cloister." The first poem was entitled "I. Camp (French)," later entitled "Incident of the French Camp." In the edition of 1849 the second poem was called by its present title "Soliloquy of the Spanish Cloister" and was no longer linked with the "Incident of the French Camp." In 1863 it was included in *Dramatic Lyrics* as number III of the "Garden Fancies," along with "The Flower's Name" and "Sibrandus Schafnaburgensis." In 1868 the "Soliloquy was withdrawn from the "Garden Fancies," but was included in *Dramatic Lyrics* with the other two poems of the erstwhile triumvirate.

"Solomon and Balkis"
Jocoseria (1883), where it remains.

"Song: 'Nay but you, who Do Not Love Her' "
First appearance: *Dramatic Romances* (1845). In 1849 it was included in *Dramatic Romances and Lyrics,* and in 1863 it was included in *Dramatic Lyrics,* where it remains.

"Sonnet: 'Eyes, calm beside thee. . . .' "
First appearance: *The Monthly Repository,* VIII, N.S. (October 1834), 712, signed "Z." The poem was not collected by the poet, but has appeared in various places, especially in collected editions made after 1889.

Sordello, a Poem in Six Books
February 29, 1840, was the publication date announced by Edward Moxon, publisher (London) but in fact the book was published during the first week of March.

Soul's Tragedy, A
Published as *Bells and Pomegranates,* No. VIII *and Last, Luria;* and *A Soul's Tragedy,* by Edward Moxon, London, April 13, 1846.

"Speculative"
Asolando: Fancies and Facts (1889), where it remains.

"Statue and the Bust, The"
First appearance: *Men and Women* (1855). In the collected edition of 1863 the poem was included in *Dramatic Romances,* where it remains.

"St. Martin's Summer"
Pacchiarotto and How He Worked in Distemper: With Other Poems (1876), where it remains.

Strafford: An Historical Tragedy
Published by Longman, Rees, Orme, Brown, Green, and Longman, London, May 1, 1837. Omitted in the collected edition of 1849, but restored in the edition of 1863 and in subsequent editions.

"Summum Bonum"
Asolando: Fancies and Facts (1889), where it remains.

"Sun, The"
Ferishtah's Fancies (1884). Poem number 5.

"Through the Metidja to Abd-el-Kadr"
First appearance: *Dramatic Lyrics, Bells and Pomegranates,* No. III (November 1842). In 1849 it was included in *Dramatic Romances and Lyrics* and in 1863 it became one of the *Dramatic Lyrics,* where it remains.

"Time's Revenges"
Dramatic Romances (1845). In 1849 it was included in *Dramatic Romances and Lyrics,* and in 1863 it became one of the *Dramatic Romances,* where it remains.

"Toccata of Galuppi's, A"

First appearance: *Men and Women* (1855). In the collected edition of 1863 the poem was included in *Dramatic Lyrics,* where it remains.

"To Edward FitzGerald"

The Athenaeum, July 13, 1889. The poem was dated July 8, 1889. The occasion of the poem was Browning's reading in the *New Letters of Edward FitzGerald,* edited by W. Aldin Wright, the following passage:

> Mrs. Browning's death is rather a relief to me, I must say: no more Aurora Leighs, thank God! A woman of real genius, I know; but what is the upshot of it all? She and her sex had better mind the kitchen and the children; and perhaps the poor. Except in such things as little novels, they only devote themselves to what men do much better, leaving that which men do worse or not at all.

Browning apparently sent the sonnet to *The Athenaeum* in anger, but his repentance is seen in his vain efforts to have the poem returned unprinted. Although FitzGerald died in 1883 and did not see the offending lines, Browning was much shaken by having his wrath displayed before the world. He, of course, never collected the poem. It has variously appeared, especially in collected editions since his death.

"Too Late"

Dramatis Personae (1864), where it remains.

"Touch him ne'er so lightly"

The epilogue to *Dramatic Idyls, Second Series* (1880), where it remains.

" 'Transcendentalism:' A Poem in Twelve Books"

Men and Women (1855), where it remains.

"Tray"

Dramatic Idyls [First Series] (1879), where it remains.

"Twins, The"

First appearance: *Two Poems, by Elizabeth Barrett and Robert Browning,* April or May 1854, a pamphlet written to be sold for sixpence at a bazaar to raise funds for "Refuge for young destitute girls," being established by Arabel Barrett, Elizabeth's sister. "The Twins" was Browning's contribution to the pamphlet. It carried the motto: "*Give* and *It-shall-be-given-unto-you.*" Mrs. Browning's contribution was the poem "A Plea for the ragged Schools of London." "The Twins" appeared in *Men and Women* (1855). In the collected edition of 1863 the poem was included in *Dramatic Romances,* where it remains.

"Two Camels"

Ferishtah's Fancies (1884), where it remains. Poem number 8.

"Two in the Campagna"

First appearance: *Men and Women* (1855). In 1863 it was included in *Dramatic Lyrics,* where it remains.

Two Poets of Croisic, The; La Saisiaz

Published by Smith, Elder and Co., London, May 15, 1878.

Prologue	Prologue
La Saisiaz	The Two Poets of Croisic

Epilogue

"Up at a Villa—Down in the City (As Distinguished by an Italian Person of Quality)"

First appearance: *Men and Women* (1855). In 1863 included in *Dramatic Lyrics,* where it remains.

"Wanting is—What?

Jocoseria (1883), where it remains.

"Waring"

First appearance: *Dramatic Lyrics, Bells and Pomegranates,* No. III. In the collected edition of 1849 it was included in *Dramatic Romances and Lyrics,* and in 1863 it became one of the *Dramatic Romances,* where it remains.

"Which?"

Asolando: Fancies and Facts (1889), where it remains.

"White Witchcraft"

Asolando: Fancies and Facts (1889), where it remains

"Why I am a Liberal"

Printed in a volume entitled *Why I Am a Liberal,* edited by Andrew Reid, 1885. Browning did not include the sonnet in any of his collected editions, but it has appeared frequently in collected editions published after his death.

"Woman's Last Word, A"

First appearance: *Men and Women* (1855). In 1863 it was included in *Dramatic Lyrics,* where it remains.

"Women and Roses"

First appearance: *Men and Women* (1855). In 1863 it was included in *Dramatic Lyrics,* where it remains.

"Worst of It, The"

Dramatis Personae (1864), where it remains.

"Youth and Art"

Dramatis Personae (1864), where it remains.

Chronological Bibliography of Browning's Published Works

1833, March

Pauline; A Fragment of a Confession. Published by Saunders and Otley. Octavo. Anonymous. Cost of publication defrayed by a gift of £30 to the poet. Not one copy was sold. Browning suppressed the work, which was forgotten until Dante G. Rossetti on October 17, 1847, discovered the work in the British Museum, surmised shrewdly that Browning must have been the author, and wrote to him of his suspicion. Browning included it in the collected edition "with extreme repugnance" in order to forestall piracy.

1834

"Eyes calm beside thee (Lady, couldst thou know!)" Sonnet. *The Monthly Repository*, VIII, N.S. (1834), 712. Signed "Z." Not reprinted by Browning. Appears in "Fugitive Poems," the Camberwell Browning.

1835, August 15

Paracelsus. Published by Effingham Wilson. Cost of publication borne by Robert Browning, Senior.

November

"A king lived long ago." *The Monthly Repository*, IX, N.S. (November 1835), 707-08. A song of fifty-four lines, later reprinted (much altered and expanded to sixty lines) in Part III of *Pippa Passes*.

1836

Lines beginning: "Still Ailing, Wind?" *The Monthly Repository*, X, N.S. (1836), 270-71. The poem, signed "Z," comprising six stanzas, was apparently composed to stand alone, but was included in part VI of "James Lee," in *Dramatis Personae* (1864). The whole of part VI appeared in the *Atlantic Monthly* in June 1864, under the title "Under the Cliff." In the collected edition of 1868 the title of the poem was changed to its present form, "James Lee's Wife," shifting the interest and focus, characteristically, upon the woman and her bereavement. Minor changes in punctuation and diction appeared in the transition.

January

"Porphyria." *The Monthly Repository*, X, N.S. (January 1836), 43-44. Signed "Z." Title later changed to "Porphyria's Lover" and reprinted under the title of "Madhouse Cells" as "Madhouse Cells, No. II," in *Dramatic Lyrics*. "Madhouse Cells, No. I" was "Johannes Agricola in Meditation."

January

"Johannes Agricola." *The Monthly Repository*, X, N.S. (January 1836), 45-46. As "Madhouse Cells, No. I" in *Dramatic Lyrics*, the poem is untitled. In the collected edition of 1849, the title was expanded to "Johannes Agricola in Meditation."

1837, May 1
Strafford: An Historical Tragedy. Published by Longman, Rees, Orme, Brown, Green, and Longman, London. Not included in the collected edition of 1849, perhaps because of Elizabeth Barrett's poor opinion of the play, but included in the edition of 1863 and in subsequent editions.

1840, February 29
The announced date of publication of *Sordello*, which was actually published the following week by Edward Moxon, London. Not included in the collected edition of 1849, undoubtedly because of the hostile reception which blighted both the book and the author, but included in the edition of 1863, much altered, though Browning emphatically denied that it had been rewritten.

1841, April
Pippa *Passes*. *Bells and Pomegranates*, No. I. Published by Edward Moxon, London.

1842, March 12
King Victor and King Charles. Published by Edward Moxon, London.

November 26
Dramatic Lyrics. *Bells and Pomegranates*, No. III. Published by Edward Moxon, London. A pamphlet of sixteen pages, including the following poems:

Cavalier Tunes
I. Marching Along
II. Give a Rouse
III. My Wife Gertrude" [in 1849 called "Boot and Saddle"]

Italy and France
I. Italy [in 1849 called "My Last Duchess"]
II. France [in 1849 called "Count Gismond"]

Camp and Cloister
I. Camp (French) [in 1849 called "Incident of the French Camp"]
II. Cloister (Spanish) [in 1849 called "Soliloquy of the Spanish Cloister"]

In a Gondola

Artemis Prologuizes
[in 1863 spelled "Artemis Prologizes"]

Waring

Queen-Worship
I. Rudel and the Lady of Tipoli [in 1849 called "Rudel to the Lady of Tripoli"]
II. Cristina

Madhouse Cells
I. "There's Heaven above . . ." [in 1849 called "Johannes Agricola in Meditation"]
II. "The rain set early in to-night . . ." [in 1849 called "Porphyria's Lover"]

Through the Metidja to Abd-el-Kadr—1842

The Pied Piper of Hamelin; A Child's Story

Of the poems only the two poems under "Madhouse Cells" had appeared earlier. Under the names "Porphyria" and "Johannes Agricola," the two poems had appeared in *The Monthly Repository* in 1836 (q.v.), signed "Z." In *Dramatic Lyrics* the titles of the individual poems were dropped, and the general title "Madhouse Cells" was substituted.

1843, January
The Return of the Druses. A Tragedy. In Five Acts. Bells and Pomegranates, No. IV. Published by Edward Moxon, London.

February 11
A Blot in the 'Scutcheon. A Tragedy. In Three Acts. Bells and Pomegranates, No. V. Published by Edward Moxon, London.

April

Colombe's Birthday. A Play. In Five Acts. Bells and Pomegranates, No. VI.

1844, June

"The Laboratory, Ancien Régime." *Hood's Magazine,* I, No. VI (June 1844), 513-14. Included in *Dramatic Romances* (1845), linked with "The Confessional" under the title "France and Spain." The link was broken in 1849, and the poem was dissociated from "The Confessional" in *Dramatic Romances and Lyrics.*

June

"Claret and Tokay." *Hood's Magazine,* I, No. VI (June 1844), 525. Included in *Dramatic Romances* (1845), but not in the collected edition of 1849. In the collected edition of 1863, the poem was linked with "Here's to Nelson's memory" (in the 1845 volume printed as No. II of "Home-Thoughts from Abroad"), and a third section entitled "Beer" was added, the three sections assuming the title "Nationality in Drinks."

July

"Garden Fancies: I. The Flower's Name. II. Sibrandus Schafnaburgensis." *Hood's Magazine,* II, No. VII (July 1844), 45-48. Included in *Dramatic Romances and Lyrics* (1845). In 1863 the poems were included in *Dramatic Lyrics,* where "Soliloquy of the Spanish Cloister" was added to form "Garden Fancies III." In 1868 the three poems were no longer united under the title "Garden Fancies."

August

"The Boy and the Angel." *Hood's Magazine,* II, No. VIII (August 1844), 140-42. Included in *Dramatic Romances and Lyrics* (1845), expanded and altered, and in *Dramatic Romances and Lyrics* in the 1849 edition. In 1863 it was one of the *Dramatic Romances,* and one couplet was added. The poem is wholly imaginary. No Pope was called Theocrite.

1845

"The Flight of the Duchess." Appeared in two parts. The first part, consisting of the first nine sections of the poem, appeared in *Hood's Magazine,* III, No. IV (April 1845), 313-18. Publication of the magazine ended after the death of Thomas Hood on May 3, 1845, and the completed poem with the final seven sections was published in *Dramatic Romances* (1845) and was included in *Dramatic Romances and Lyrics* (1849) and in *Dramatic Romances* (1863).

March

"The Tomb at St. Praxed's (Rome, 15—)." *Hood's Magazine,* III, No. VI (March 1845), 237-39. Included in *Dramatic Romances* (1845). In 1849 the poem was included in *Dramatic Romances and Lyrics* under its present title, "The Bishop Orders His Tomb at St. Praxed's Church, Rome, 15—." In the collected edition of 1863, it became one of the poems in *Men and Women.*

November 6

Dramatic Romances and Lyrics. Bells and Pomegranates, No. VII. Published by Edward Moxon, London.

How They brought the Good News from Ghent to Aix (16—)
Pictor Ignotus. Florence, 15—
Italy in England [called in 1849 "The Italian in England"]
England in Italy [called in 1849 "The Englishman in Italy"]
The Lost Leader
The Lost Mistress
Home-Thoughts, from Abroad
The Tomb at St. Praxed's [called in 1849 "The Bishop Orders his Tomb at St. Praxed's Church"]
Garden Fancies
I. The Flower's Name

II. Sibrandus Schafnaburgensis
France and Spain
I. The Laboratory
II. The Confessional
The Flight of the Duchess
Earth's Immortalities
Song ["Nay, but you, who do not love her"]
The Boy and the Angel
Night and Morning [called in 1849 "Meeting at Night and Parting at Morning"]
Claret and Tokay [called in 1863 "Nationality in Drinks"]
Saul [the first nine sections]
Time's Revenges
The Glove

1846, April 13

Luria and *A Soul's Tragedy*. *Bells and Pomegranates, No. VIII and Last*. Published by Edward Moxon, London.

1849

Poems: A New Edition in Two Volumes. First collected edition. In this first collected edition appeared *Paracelsus* and the *Bells and Pomegranates*, omitting *Pauline, Sordello*, and *Strafford*.

1850, April 1

Christmas-Eve and Easter-Day. Published by Chapman and Hall, London.

1852

"Introductory Essay" to the *Letters of Percy Bysshe Shelley*. Published by Edward Moxon, London. The "Essay" was signed "R. B." Before completion of the volume, the letters were discovered to be spurious, and the book was suppressed. Browning consented to publication of the "Essay" by Furnivall in *The Browning Society Papers* (1881). Browning did not reprint the work or include it in his collected editions, but it was reprinted by the Shelley Society and has appeared in the Camberwell Browning, the Cambridge Edition, and many other collections.

1854

"The Twins," with the subheading "*Give* and *It-shall-be-given-unto-you*," appeared in a pamphlet entitled *Two Poems, by Elizabeth Barrett and Robert Browning*. Published by Chapman and Hall, London, 1854. Mrs. Browning's contribution to the pamphlet was "A Plea for the Ragged Schools of London." "The Twins" was included in *Men and Women* (1855), and in the collected edition of 1863 it was grouped under *Dramatic Romances*.

1855, November 17

Men and Women. Published by Chapman and Hall, London. The two volumes included fifty-one poems: twenty-seven in volume I and twenty-four in volume II; the last poem, "One Word More. To E. B. B.," served as an epilogue to the entire work.

Volume I

Love Among the Ruins
A Lovers' Quarrel
Evelyn Hope
Up at a Villa—Down in the City (As Distinguished by an Italian Person of Quality)
A Woman's Last Word
Fra Lippo Lippi
A Toccata of Galuppi's
By the Fire-Side
Any Wife to Any Husband
An Epistle containing the Strange Medical Experience of Karshish, the Arab Physician

Mesmerism
A Serenade at the Villa
My Star
Instans Tyrannus
A Pretty Woman
"Childe Roland to the Dark Tower Came"
Respectability
A Light Woman
The Statue and the Bust
Love in a Life
Life in a Love
How it Strikes a Contemporary
The Last Ride Together
The Patriot—An Old Story
Master Hugues of Saxe-Gotha
Bishop Blougram's Apology
Memorabilia

Volume II

Andrea del Sarto (called "The Faultless Painter")
Before
After
In Three Days
In a Year
Old Pictures in Florence
In a Balcony—First Part
In a Balcony—Second Part
In a Balcony—Third Part
Saul
"De Gustibus—"
Women and Roses
Protus
Holy-Cross Day. (On which the Jews were Forced to Attend an Annual Christian Sermon in Rome)
The Guardian-Angel: A Picture at Fano
Cleon
The Twins
Popularity
The Heretic's Tragedy. A Middle-Age Interlude
Two in the Campagna
A Grammarian's Funeral
One Way of Love
Another Way of Love
"Transcendentalism:" A Poem in Twelve Books
Misconceptions
One Word More. To. E. B. B.

Since *Men and Women* is widely considered to be Browning's masterwork (rivaled only by *The Ring and the Book*), it is especially important to understand that this judgment applies most fittingly to the original state of the splendid collection. When one turns to *Men and Women* as it appears in later collected editions, one is likely to be perplexed by the thinness of the volume, with its thirteen poems, and most particularly by the apparent discrepancy of Browning's lines in "One Word More": "There they are, my fifty men and women/ Naming me the fifty poems finished!" In the collected edition of 1863, Browning retained under the title *Men and Women* only eight of the poems originally included under that title, and he added five poems from the three collections of short poems previously printed. Of the poems removed from *Men and Women* in 1863 thirty were included under *Dramatic Lyrics* and twelve under *Dramatic Romances*. "In a Balcony" became part of *Tragedies and Other Plays* in the 1863 distribution. In the Porter and Clarke edition, "Cleon" and "The Statue and the Bust" are alleged to have appeared in pamphlet form in 1855. Both pamphlets are now considered to be forgeries. See John Carter and Graham Pollard, *An Enquiry into the Nature of Certain Nineteenth Century Pamphlets*, London, 1934.

1856

"Ben Karshook's Wisdom." *The Keepsake* (an annual publication), p. 16. Browning did not include the poem in any of his collected editions, apparently disliking it, but it is commonly included in collected editions appearing after his death.

1857

"May and Death." *The Keepsake* (an annual publication), p. 164. Collected, somewhat altered, in *Dramatis Personae* (1864).

1863

The Poetical Works of Robert Browning. Third Edition. In three volumes. In fact, this was the second collected edition, the first having appeared in 1849. Browning meant that in this third edition the poems appeared in print for the third time, not thrice in collected editions. In 1865 this edition was reissued as a "Fourth Edition."

1864, May

"Gold Hair: A Legend of Pornic." *Atlantic Monthly*, XIII (May 1864), 596-99. The poem was included in *Dramatis Personae* (1864), where it remains. The poem appears in a pamphlet, supposedly privately printed by W. Clowes and Sons, London, but *An Enquiry into the Nature of Certain Nineteenth Century Pamphlets*, by John Carter and Graham Pollard, establishes beyond a reasonable doubt that the pamphlet is spurious.

May

Dramatis Personae. Published by Chapman and Hall, London.
James Lee
Gold Hair: A Legend of Pornic
The Worst of It
Dîs Aliter Visum; or, Le Byron de nos Jours
Too Late
Abt Vogler
Rabbi Ben Ezra
A Death in the Desert
Caliban upon Setebos; or, Natural Theology in the Island
Confessions
May and Death
Prospice
Youth and Art
A Face
A Likeness
Mr. Sludge, "The Medium"
Apparent Failure
Epilogue
Most of the poems in *Dramatis Personae* had not appeared previously. The first six stanzas of "James Lee" had appeared in *The Monthly Repository*, X, N.S. (May 1836), 270-71.
"Prospice" had appeared in the *Atlantic Monthly*, XIII (June 1864), 694.
"Gold Hair" had appeared in the *Atlantic Monthly*, XIII (May 1864), 596-99.
"May and Death" had appeared in *The Keepsake* in 1857, p. 164.

June

"Under the Cliff." *Atlantic Monthly*, XIII (June 1864), 737-38.

June
"Prospice." *Atlantic Monthly,* XIII (June 1864), 694.

1868
The Poetical Works of Robert Browning. Six volumes. Third Collected Edition.

November 21
The Ring and the Book, Volume I. Published by Smith, Elder and Co., London.

December 26
The Ring and the Book, Volume II. Published by Smith, Elder and Co., London.

1869, January 30
The Ring and the Book, Volume III. Published by Smith, Elder and Co., London.

February 27
The Ring and the Book, Volume IV. Published by Smith, Elder and Co., London.

1871, March
"Hervé Riel." *Cornhill Magazine,* XXIII (March 1871), 257-60. Reprinted in 1876 in *Pacchiarotto and How He Worked in Distemper: With Other Poems.*

August 8
Balaustion's Adventure. Published by Smith, Elder and Co., London.

December 16
Prince Hohenstiel-Schwangau, Saviour of Society. Published by Smith, Elder and Co., London.

1872, June 4
Fifine at the Fair. Published by Smith, Elder and Co., London.

1873, May
Red Cotton Night-Cap Country, or Turf and Towers. Published by Smith, Elder and Co., London

1875, April 15
Aristophanes' Apology: Including a Transcript from Euripides, Being the Last Adventure of Balaustion. Published by Smith, Elder and Co., London.

November
The Inn Album. Published by Smith, Elder and Co., London. The poem appeared in the *New York Times* simultaneously, on three successive Sundays, November 14, 21, and 28.

1876, July 18
Pacchiarotto and How He Worked in Distemper: With Other Poems. Published by Smith, Elder and Co., London.
Prologue
Of Pacchiarotto, and How He Worked in Distemper
At the "Mermaid"
House
Shop
Pisgah Sights. 1.
Pisgah Sights. 2.
Fears and Scruples
Natural Magic
Magical Nature
Bifurcation
Numpholeptos
Appearances
St. Martin's Summer
Hervé Riel
A Forgiveness

Cenciaja
Filippo Baldinucci on the Privilege of Burial
Epilogue

1877, October 15
The Agamemnon of Aeschylus. Published by Smith, Elder and Co., London.

1878, May 15
La Saisiaz and the Two Poets of Croisic. Published by Smith, Elder and Co., London.

1879
"The Blind Man to the Maiden Said." In *The Hour Will Come, A Tale of an Alpine Cloister*, by Wilhelmine von Hillern, translated by Clara Bell. At the request of Mrs. Bell, Browning translated this poem, and Mrs. Bell included it in her translation of the novel, acknowledging only that the poem was translated by a friend. Reprinted in the *Whitehall Review*, March 1, 1883.

1879
" 'Oh Love! Love! thou that from the eyes diffusest.' " In *Euripides*, by J. P. Mahaffy. The poem is a translation at the request of Mahaffy, of a strophe of a chorus from Euripides' *Hippolytus* (ll. 525-44).

April 28
Dramatic Idyls. Published by Smith, Elder and Co., London.
Martin Relph
Pheidippides
Halbert and Hob
Ivàn Ivànovitch
Tray
Ned Bratts

1880, June
Dramatic Idyls, Second Series. Published by Smith, Elder and Co., London.
Echetlos
Clive
Muléykeh
Pietro of Abano
Doctor—
Pan and Luna

1882, February
"Album Lines." *The Century*, XXV (February 1882), 159-60.

1883, March 9
Jocoseria. Published by Smith, Elder and Co., London.
Wanting is—what?
Donald
Solomon and Balkis
Cristina and Monaldeschi
Mary Wollstonecraft and Fuseli
Adam, Lilith, and Eve
Ixion
Jochanan Hakkadosh
Never the Time and the Place
Pambo

December 8
"Goldoni." *Pall Mall Gazette*, December 8, 1883.

December 28
"Helen's Tower." *Pall Mall Gazette*, December 28, 1883.

1884, February
"Rawdon Brown." *Century Magazine*, XXVI (February 1884), 640.

April 16
"The Founder of the Feast." *The World*, April 16, 1884.

May 29
"The Names." *The Shakespearean Show-Book*. Reprinted in the *Pall Mall Gazette*, May 29, 1884. Not included by Browning in any of his volumes, but frequently included in editions of his works.

November 21
Ferishtah's Fancies. Published by Smith, Elder and Co., London.
The Eagle
The Melon-Seller
Shah Abbas
The Family
The Sun
Mihrab Shah
A Camel-Driver
Two Camels
Cherries
Plot-Culture
A Pillar at Sebzevah [later titled "A Pillar at Sebzevar"]
A Bean-Stripe: also Apple-Eating

1885
"Why I am a Liberal." In *Why I am a Liberal*, edited by Andrew Reid. Not included by Browning in any of his volumes, but frequently included in editions of his works.

1886
"A Spring Song." In *The New Amphion*, "The Book of the Edinburgh University Union Fancy Fair," 1886. Reprinted, untitled, at the end of "Parleying with Gerard de Lairesse."

1887
"Jubilee Memorial Lines." Four lines, appearing in the *Pall Mall Gazette* December, 1887. Written for a jubilee window to be placed in St. Margaret's, Westminster, in celebration of the fiftieth anniversary of Queen Victoria's reign.

1887, January 28
Parleyings with Certain People of Importance in Their Day. Published by Smith, Elder and Co., London. The title page bore the words: "Parleyings with Certain People of Importance in Their Day: To Wit: Bernard de Mandeville, Daniel Bartoli, Christopher Smart, George Bubb Dodington, Francis Furini, Gerard de Lairesse, and Charles Avison. Introduced by A Dialogue between Apollo and the Fates; Concluded by Another between John Fust and his Friends."

1888-89
The Poetical Works of Robert Browning. Sixteen volumes. The author's last revised edition.

July 13
"To Edward FitzGerald." *The Athenaeum*, p. 64.

1889, August
"Epitaph of Levi Lincoln Thaxter." *Poet-Lore*, I, viii, 398.

December 12
Asolando: Fancies and Facts. Published by Smith, Elder and Co., London.
Prologue
Rosny
Dubiety
Now
Humility
Poetics
Summum Bonum

A Pearl, A Girl
Speculative
White Witchcraft
Bad Dreams I
Bad Dreams II
Bad Dreams III
Bad Dreams IV
Inapprehensiveness
Which?
The Cardinal and the Dog
The Pope and the Net
The Bean-Feast
Muckle-Mouth Meg
Arcades Ambo
The Lady and the Painter
Ponte dell' Angelo, Venice
Beatrice Signorini
Flute-Music, with an Accompaniment
"Imperante Augusto Natus Est—"
Development
Rephan
Reverie
Epilogue

1

"My Last Duchess"

"My Last Duchess," an exquisite dramatic monologue, is one of Browning's most vivid examinations of an extraordinarily complex Renaissance nobleman. The poem has stirred lively controversy and critical contention. Traditionally the poem has been seen as a study in Renaissance pride and cruelty, which it certainly is, but it is more.

In 1957 B. R. Jerman opened an attack on the established position that the Duke is a clever man, giving "instructions as to the sort of behavior he expects of his next wife."[1] His thesis is that the Duke is in reality a "witless" fellow, an art collector of the third rank who is preoccupied with "pointing out his own stature as an art collector." He is not shrewd and he is not directly or indirectly lessoning the visiting envoy of the Count, for whose daughter's hand he is suing, in the conduct he expects of his next wife.

Laurence Perrine replied to Jerman two years later, contending that the Duke is in fact "a shrewd bargainer and a master diplomat who, while exposing himself fully to the reader, not improbably obtains high commendation from the emissary in his report to the Count. . . . The Duke is vain but he is no fool."[2]

I fancy that the Duke is rather more complex and less easily labeled than Jerman or Perrine supposes. He is at once an intelligent and shrewd bargainer and a fool as well. He is a collector of *objets d'art*, and at the same time he is blind to beauty. His tragic flaw is overweening pride, which blinds him to his moral and esthetic poverty and drives him to unconscious self-revelation which, we feel certain, must prove destructive to his matrimonial plans.

I agree with Jerman that the Duke is not *consciously* warning the emissary that the Count's daughter had better be more dutiful to his wishes

1. B. R. Jerman, "Browning's Witless Duke," *PMLA*, LXXII (1957), 488-93.
2. Laurence Perrine, "Browning's Shrewd Duke," *PMLA*, LXXIV (1959), 157-59.

than the last Duchess. To do that he would indeed be a fool, for his discourse makes it unmistakable that the penalty for his wife's noncompliance is death. It is unlikely that a suitor, even an imperious Duke, would threaten his intended wife with death before the startled eyes of the emissary who has come for the express purpose of finding out whether the proposed match is likely to be advantageous. It must not be forgotten that the woman for whom he is negotiating is the daughter of a Count, who is undoubtedly almost as imperious as the Duke himself. The Count has carefully selected a trusted man to negotiate the terms of the wedding, with particular attention to be paid to the dowry the Count must pay and the advantages that are likely to accrue to him.

Certainly the character of the Duke is of supreme importance in this negotiation, and we may be sure that this is a point about which the Count is more than casually interested, for he obviously knows that the last Duchess is dead. He may even know that she is murdered, but of this we cannot be sure. The puzzling words "This grew; I gave commands;/ Then all smiles stopped together" may be interpreted in wholly opposite ways. They may imply that the news of her murder has become common knowledge and the Duke assumes that there is nothing to be gained by an attempt at concealment; on the other hand, they may imply that the Duke is trying to convey the false impression that she died of natural causes, as his candid and unevasive reference suggests.

The evidence points toward the latter interpretation, for if it were common knowledge that the Duke murdered his last Duchess, it is unlikely that the Count would be considering the marriage at all, if not from humanitarian reasons, at least from reasons of prestige and property. If he hopes to gain in worldly power and place by the alliance, the homicidal character of the Duke bodes ill. It simply is impossible to believe that a reasonably sane man would openly confess to murdering his last wife while he is negotiating for a replacement. It is far more acceptable to believe that he is trapped in his recital of jealousy and hate and in a moment of inadvertence almost confesses his final villainy and certainly is understood by the envoy as equivocally making the dreadful admission.

Just as it is impossible to believe that the Duke is freely confessing to murder, it is impossible to believe that he is warning the envoy of the summary justice that he metes out to erring wives, for he pictures the life of his last Duchess as being so pathetic as to make death seem a release. He is not warning anyone. He is merely speaking of what became so intolerable to his pride and hauteur that he has been half demented with hate. It seems likely that he has had no one until this moment to pour out his story to, and when he starts, there is no stopping. He is totally blind to the fact that he is revealing himself, not as a cultivated Italian nobleman, but as a Bluebeard.

Perrine is right in saying that the visit of the envoy is a horse-trading deal. Both men are shrewd and sharp, and they play their roles as best they can, but the Duke's pride and arrogance and paranoid jealousy have blurred his wits and blinded him to the mounting horror in the eyes of the envoy. The Duke knows that his interlocutor is the shrewdest man the Count could find to send on the important mission, and it is equally certain that he knows he is being studied with absolute attention, and this knowledge makes it most difficult to explain his mad and ruinous self-revelation. It can be explained only if one understands his ruinous mental state.

The envoy has spent a substantial part of the day with the Duke, we may assume, exploring his art gallery, the spacious grounds, and the marble statues, and he has been taking careful note of the man and his estate. This is probably the most important task he has ever performed for his master, and he is alert to every nuance and detail that may prove useful to the Count in assessing the worth of the proposed marriage and the proper size of the dowry. It is clear that the dowry has not been agreed upon:

> I repeat,
> The Count your master's known munificence
> Is ample warrant that no just pretence
> Of mine for dowry will be disallowed. . . .

Indeed the dowry has hardly been discussed, for it is clear the proceedings are in their initial state, and the reader is confident that they will go no further, once the envoy makes his report.

As the poem opens, the Duke and the envoy are touring the palace. They come upon a covered picture, and as the Duke draws back the curtain he says:

> That's my last Duchess painted on the wall,
> Looking as if she were alive. I call
> That piece a wonder, now: Frà Pandolf's hands
> Worked busily a day, and there she stands.
> Will 't please you to sit and look at her?

The reader (and presumably the envoy) immediately wonders why he keeps the picture covered. Is it out of touching delicacy? Loving sentiment? Or is it out of revulsion and guilt? Is it out of possessiveness? It soon becomes clear that the paranoid Duke, who could never achieve exclusive possession of the Duchess, fancies that he has done so on canvas. His twisted soul is similar to that of Porphyria's lover, who kills his woman whom he cannot possess and holds her dead body in a moment he hopes to make infinite—beyond time, beyond change, beyond life. Both men have in effect found sick means of stopping time. They trade life for death and find it good.

The Duke utters no syllable of love or pity or remorse. It would not have occurred to him to do so, for his Duchess is beyond change now, beyond the irritating annoyances that she in her innocence brought upon him. Art is greater than life, he believes, for art can be purged of annoyance, whim, and mutability—a belief among the most repugnant to Browning. Life, he knew, must come first, before art or all the arts together. But the Duke cannot understand this, for he denies life. His words, "That's my last Duchess painted on the wall/ Looking as if she were alive," are perilously close to the words of Porphyria's insane lover:

> That moment she was mine, mine, fair,
>   Perfectly pure and good; I found
> A thing to do, and all her hair
>   In one long yellow string I wound
> Three times her little throat around,
> And strangled her.

But the picture frustrates the Duke with the "depth and passion of its earnest glance," for he cannot forget that " 't was not/ Her husband's presence only, called that spot/ Of joy into the Duchess' cheek. . . ."

Jerman discovers that the painting must have been an artistic failure: "a mechanically reproduced realistic picture of a photogenic woman, a dilettante's trophy." I do not think it possible to pass on the artistic worth of the picture. The only clue we have is the words of the Duke, and he is blind with pride, malice, and spite. All strangers who see the painting seem to be impressed, especially with the color and the glance of the striking woman. It is impossible to say whether the Duke's demand that the picture be painted in a day ("Frà Pandolf's hands/ Worked busily a day . . .") affords much evidence of the picture's quality, but it ably substantiates the Duke's jealousy, which was stronger than his desire that the picture be painted slowly and painstakingly. It is clear that his reason for demanding haste was not eagerness for the picture or an unreasonable insistence upon a nearly impossible performance, but rather was a ready stratagem for guaranteeing that the hands of the artist be fully engaged in painting, not in amorous dalliance. Whether the picture is in fact a masterpiece is doubtful, but the Duke thinks it is, for it represents, though imperfectly, his solution to the problem of possession, which in turn represents his sick view of life and art.

Perrine argues that the Duke's shrewdness may be seen in his skill in speech, and he is quite right. His disclaimer of skill in speech ("Even had you skill/ In speech—[which I have not]—. . .") is a simple bid for contradiction, a transparent ploy he finds useful. In his pride, he probably has never confessed to any kind of weakness, for he chooses "never to stoop."

Perrine maintains that the wily Duke has three goals:

> He wishes (1) to stipulate politely but clearly exactly what he expects for his share in the bargain, both as to dowry and as to daughter, (2) to impress the envoy with his position, his power, and his importance, and (3) to flatter the envoy so as to ensure a favorable report on the envoy's return to his master. He accomplishes all three purposes.[3]

It appears to me, on the contrary, that he has much less success than Perrine suggests. Assuming that he is consciously attempting to spell out "exactly" the nature of the wife and dowry he wants (which I doubt), does he in fact do so? No one would argue against the conclusion that his heartless account of his dissatisfaction with his last Duchess may properly instruct the envoy in what he cannot abide in a wife, but his purpose is not to instruct, certainly not to instruct the envoy that he demands a wife who is neurotically obedient, a virtual slave. As for dowry there is nothing more exact than the hastily bundled up flattery of the Count's generosity. Regarding the second point, it appears unlikely that he is impressing the envoy with his importance, but it is clear that he is impressing him with his psychopathic arrogance, pride, contempt for the common human values, and heartless brutality. If the Duke succeeds in flattering the envoy sufficiently to win a favorable report from him, the envoy is a master of either imperception or duplicity, of which there is no suggestion in the poem.

The character of the Duchess is of interest second only to that of the Duke. Jerman implies that she was apparently an insipid, shallow young woman, indifferent to the demands of her position in life and impervious to the wishes of her husband. There is no evidence in the poem to support this judgment. She undoubtedly was a woman of simple tastes and unusual capacity for joy. She had the *joie de vivre* in uncommon measure, and she loved the elemental beauty of life. Flowers, sunsets, and cherry blossoms delighted her heart, and she thanked men in heartfelt sincerity for small acts of kindness. It is significant that people rather habitually conferred small favors upon her, knowing that she was delighted and grateful for all signs of human warmth. Only to an imperious Duke, jealous of his name and lineage and morbidly eager for unchallenged possession, could such sweet simplicity and unaffected joy appear to be shallow insipidity.

She smiled when the Duke passed, but she smiled at others as well, and it is certain that in her smile for the Duke, there were fear and unnatural strain, missing from her smile for others. This the Duke could not fail to observe, and he was driven to murderous jealousy.

3. Ibid., p. 159.

Evidence that the sick Duke becomes aware of the rashness of his self-revelation may be seen in the gesture of camaraderie and bonhomie he affects as the envoy steps back to allow the great man to proceed down the stairs: "Nay, we'll go/ Together down, sir." He is hastily mending fences, hoping that by such unusual deference and egalitarianism he may counteract the dreadful confession he has made. I do not suppose he has a sense that he has lost all he has been seeking, for he is too vain and arrogant to believe that he could be weighed in the balance and found wanting, but he is aware that he has all but admitted the murder of his wife—and to the very man who is judging his potential as a husband. The envoy is surely not deceived or distracted by the transparently dishonest and hasty affirmation "Though his fair daughter's self, as I avowed/ At starting is my object."

The final words of the Duke, as he calls attention to the statue of Neptune "Taming a sea-horse," have an effect on the reader which the envoy must share. In the Duke's bad heart, all is one: the portrait of the woman he has tamed and finally killed, the statue of Neptune similarly taming a helpless creature, and the memory of the Duchess when she was alive. Women to him are *objets d'art,* whether in flesh or on canvas, and the incongruous juxtaposition of his hollow protestation of desire for the fair daughter of the Count, together with his wonderfully insensitive reference to a prized piece of sculpture, is a fitting indication of the nature of the report the envoy will bring to the Count.

SUGGESTED READINGS

Assad, Thomas J., "Browning's 'My Last Duchess,'" *Tulane Studies in English,* X (1960), 117-28.

Fleissner, R. F., "Browning's Last Lost Duchess: A Purview," *Victorian Poetry,* V (1967), 217-19.

Questions the usual view that the Duchess was killed or sent to a convent, suggesting rather that she might very well have been "out of her wits, that she smiled a bit too much and thus had to be confined for the benefit of society in a madhouse" (p. 217). Mr. Fleissner points out that the inhuman conditions prevailing in Renaissance lunatic asylums might be depended upon to make the life of an inmate not only miserable but short.

Friedland, Louis S., "Ferrara and *My Last Duchess,*" *Studies in Philology,* XXXIII (1936), 656-84.

Irvine, William, "Four Monologues in Browning's *Men and Women,*" *Victorian Poetry,* II (1964), 155-64.

"'My Last Duchess' (1842), set in the Renaissance, introduces in a highly paradoxical manner the ideas of the gentleman and of *noblesse oblige*. Negotiating with an ambassador for a second marriage, an Italian duke discloses in a gesture of splendid insolence that he murdered his innocent first wife in the name of a fantastic decorum—and at a financial profit" (p. 155).

Millet, Stanton, "Art and Reality in 'My Last Duchess,' " *Victorian Newsletter*, No. 17 (1960), pp. 25-27.

Nathanson, Leonard, "Browning's 'My Last Duchess,' " *Explicator*, Vol. XIX (1961), Item 68.

Pipes, B. N., Jr., "The Portrait of 'My Last Duchess,' " *Victorian Studies*, III (1960), 381-86.

Rea, John D., " 'My Last Duchess,' " *Studies in Philology*, XXIX (1932), 120-22.

Argues that the Duke in "My Last Duchess" and the Bishop in "The Bishop Orders His Tomb" may have been suggested from the picture of Vespasiano Gonzaga presented in his biography by Ireneo Affó, published in Parma in 1780, or in an earlier biography by Alessandro Lisca, Verona, 1592—"just such out-of-the-way volumes as Browning and his father delighted in" (p. 120).

Shaw, W. David, "Browning's Duke as Theatrical Producer," *Victorian Newsletter*, No. 29 (1966), pp. 18-22.

Maintains that "My Last Duchess" "occupies the same position in Browning's canon as *Hamlet* does in Shakespeare's. Its power resides in its endless suggestiveness, its play of enigmatic forces that continue to seduce and inspire its subtlest critics." Shaw believes that the Duke represents "aristocratic vice," which has a subtle appeal because of its dramatic style: "This is because Browning has cast the Duke as the outrageous producer of a social play that must bring into harmony with the prejudices of the speaker's own taste every spontaneous action of the Duchess."

———, *The Dialectical Temper: The Rhetorical Art of Robert Browning* (Ithaca, N.Y., 1968), pp. 92-104.

A close examination of "My Last Duchess," which finds that the Duke "is as surely imprisoned by his senses as any inhabitant of Dante's inferno" (p. 103). "What is most repulsive in the Duke's manner is the callous precision of an insane rationalist" (p. 96).

Stevens, L. Robert, "Aestheticism in Browning's Early Monologues," *Victorian Poetry*, III (1965), 19-24.

Includes interesting comments on "My Last Duchess," "Fra Lippo Lippi," and "Andrea del Sarto."

Stevenson, Lionel, " 'My Last Duchess' and Parisina," *Modern Language Notes*, LXXIV (1960), 489-92.

2

"Count Gismond. Aix in Provence"

"Count Gismond. Aix in Provence" is significant in illustrating Browning's chivalric obsession with dramatic rescues of maidens in distress. No poem in Browning is more fully romantic. There are many references in *The Ring and the Book* and elsewhere to the story of Perseus' rescue of Andromeda, to St. George, and to the general medieval tradition of knightly succor of damsels variously menaced. Browning kept before him Caravaggio's painting of Perseus rescuing Andromeda from the serpent, a theme which the poet doubtless associated in his mind with his own rescue of Elizabeth Barrett from her own special predicament.

The speaker in the poem is an orphan maiden of the court of Aix in Provence, in southeastern France. She has been chosen the Queen of the tourney, to whom the honor was granted to confer the prize upon the winner. Joyous in the splendid day and in the honor conferred upon her, she attends the tourney with her two girl cousins, who are natural queens by reason of their beauty of "brow and heart."

At the tourney, for no assignable reason, the wretched Gauthier strides out and accuses her of being a strumpet worthy only of the stake:

> "Bring torches! Wind the penance-sheet
>   About her! Let her shun the chaste,
> Or lay herself before their feet!
>   Shall she whose body I embraced
> A night long, queen it in the day?
> For honour's sake no crowns, I say!"

Obviously innocent of the foul accusation, she is stunned to silence, when out strides Count Gismond in her defense. She immediately recognizes her rescuer and intuitively knows that her innocence will be vindicated in the combat:

> Till out strode Gismond; then I knew

  That I was saved. I never met
His face before, but, at first view,
  I felt quite sure that God had set
Himself to Satan; who would spend
A minute's mistrust on the end?

In a world of blacks and whites, she is wholly sure of the issue and is not at all surprised to see Gismond cleave the caitiff to the breastbone and drag him before her to confess his lie, a feat he accomplishes in spite of his significant disability. In accordance with Browning's doctrine of elective affinities, whereby two people may fall in love in an instant, Gismond and the rescued Queen fall in love on the spot, and in approved fashion he throws his mailed arm about her protectively, "Against the world." They flee romantically many miles to the south and in time are blessed with two fine sons, the elder fashioned in the image of his father in spirit and knightly carriage—a man clearly destined to rescue damsels in distress.

"Count Gismond" represents the early romanticism of Browning, but, more importantly, it represents the concept of moral justice that Browning always associated with men of valor in defense of beauty and innocence. It should not be forgotten that when Flush, his wife's dog, was stolen and held for ransom, Browning was for a time determined to hunt down the culprits and avenge himself in a duel, an eventuality which Elizabeth and the fates happily opposed. The substance of the poem is in reality an extended cliché, it must be confessed. It serves to illustrate, if imperfectly, one side of the poet's character that never can be forgotten.

John V. Hagopian has recently challenged the traditional interpretation of this poem, finding that the speaker is lying, that Gauthier was indeed her guilty lover, and that Count Gismond was duped.[1] Hagopian cites her reluctance to continue her tale until she is certain that Gismond is out of earshot ("See! Gismond's at the gate, in talk/ With his two boys: I can proceed") and her falsehood at the end, when she tells Gismond that she has been telling Adela how many birds her tercel has struck since May, a fact she has not mentioned at all. If these circumstances seem most imperfectly to support her guilt and the sweeping falsity of her life, they support most admirably her wish to spare Gismond embarrassment in hearing the recital of a story so full of chivalric praise of his manhood and valor. If, in fact, Gismond should overhear her account of his valorous act, he would learn nothing to incriminate his wife, and hence her hasty white lie cannot be motivated by a desire to keep him in ignorance.

1. John V. Hagopian, "The Mask of Browning's Countess Gismond," *Philological Quarterly*, XL (1961), 153-55.

SUGGESTED READINGS

DeVane, William C., A *Browning Handbook* (2nd ed., 1955), p. 110.
DeVane argues that "Count Gismond" is firmly in the heroic and chivalric tradition, with overtones of the Perseus and Andromeda legend: "The incident in *Count Gismond* is imaginary, and the hero is characteristically a Browningesque hero of the chivalric tradition. He is equipped to see virtue through evil appearances, and leaps to its defence. It is an illustration of the medieval belief, in which Gismond's wife who is the speaker fully shares, that 'God will have a stroke in every battle.' It should be observed that virtue is instantaneously recognized, as it so often is in Browning's poetry."

Hagopian, John V., "The Mask of Browning's Countess Gismond," *Philological Quarterly*, XL (1961), 153-55.
A provocative article challenging the traditional interpretation that the poem, "Count Gismond," represents the triumph of justice over villainy, the rescue of innocent virginity from oppression and slander, the Perseus and Andromeda legend:
". . . Browning has structured the Countess's monologue to suggest that she is lying and that Gauthier is indeed the rejected lover, perhaps even the father of the elder son. The strongest clue to this reading is in the psychological and symbolic significance of the ending. The Countess, who continues her tale only when she is certain that Gismond was out of earshot—'See! Gismond's at the gate, in talk/ With his two boys: I can proceed' (ll. 49-50) suddenly breaks off with a lie:

. . . Gismond here?
And have you brought my tercel back?
I was just telling Adela
How many birds it struck since May.

The fact is, of course, that that is *not* what she has just been telling Adela; the Countess is obviously capable of deceiving Gismond" (p. 154). Hagopian finds support for his belief in the guilt of the Countess in "her unusual sensitivity to phallic imagery

'. . . and scarce I felt
His sword (that dripped by me and swung)
A little shifted in its belt. . . .'
(ll. 110-12)

These lines are merely gratuitous where they occur unless they indicate the Countess's conscious or unconscious response to male sexuality" (p. 155).

Shaw, W. David, *The Dialectical Temper: The Rhetorical Art of Robert Browning* (Ithaca, N.Y., 1968), pp. 73-75.

Mr. Shaw finds that in "Count Gismond," Gauthier's staging the speaker as queen is "a form of obsessional neurosis, in which he parades her forth as the spectacular beauty he would like to possess. He represents as actuality what is merely a sexual fantasy. The only way he can gratify this fantasy is by making this outrageous charge against her: 'Shall she whose body I embraced/ A night long, queen it in the day?' "

Tilton, John W., and R. Dale Tuttle, "A New Reading of 'Count Gismond,' " *Studies in Philology*, LIX (1962), 83-95.

An essay questioning Browning's purpose in yoking together under the heading 'Italy and France' in *Dramatic Lyrics* (1842) the two poems which he later separated and renamed "My Last Duchess. Ferrara" and "Count Gismond. Aix in Provence." The authors cite the critical disapproval of the second, in contrast to the praise lavished on the first; and they come up with a novel explanation: "Count Gismond" has been wholly misinterpreted. Properly understood "Count Gismond" emerges as a highly complex and subtle psychological study, worthy to be paired with "My Last Duchess." "The discovery, stated simply, is that Browning has subtly individualized the speech of the Countess and therein has provided a means by which we are able to interpret her character and situation . . ." (p. 84). The Countess, far from being the innocent victim of a lie, is in reality the liar and whore Gauthier pronounced her to be, evidence of which fact is discovered in her interest in falconry and in the many words in the poem which may be used in the ancient sport: "The Countess has been telling Adela about her Tercel [see the last three lines of the poem]. Throughout the narration she has expressed herself in terms of falconry, and because of a perversion of values peculiar to her character, she has conceived of both Gauthier and Gismond as falcons engaged in a bloody sport immensely joyous to her . . ." (p. 85). She was not the helpless prey fought over by two hawks, but was herself a hawk "observing the fight and awaiting the outcome when she could 'make her own kill,' that is, grasp the opportunity which would best satisfy her needs. . . . Indeed, it becomes evident that this orphaned 'innocent' had gone so far as to lie with Gauthier. Far from being maligned by Gauthier, she was justly accused" (pp. 87-88).

3

"In a Gondola"

"In a Gondola" has always been considered to be among Browning's lyrical and imaginative successes. The poem is a study in illicit love, reminiscent of "The Statue and the Bust" and "Respectability." Its libretto might well have been out of Italian opera, for the sense of doom reminds one of the increasingly somber mood of *Tosca*, but the interest is not so much in young love as it is in the character of the lovers and their behavior in the face of the death that stalks them. Several of Browning's favorite dramatic devices are employed in this poem: one is the attempt to hold the infinite moment, to protract an instant in time by a projection of the imagination. The male lover, like Pippa, plays at living other lives through imagination, projecting himself and his paramour into exotic and fabulous scenes. Unlike *Pippa Passes*, however, the interest in this poem is not to escape reality and to live in fancy other and happier lives, but rather to experience a heightened awareness that the reality of the moment is greater and more magical than fabulous romance. It should be noted that the nameless man is far more "romantic" and imaginative than the woman, whose interest is more on the passing moment, the reality of their love, and their imminent danger. The difference between the romanticism of the two is reminiscent of *Romeo and Juliet*, in which romantic Romeo, who is in love with love, addresses the moon, almost to the neglect of his mistress, whereas she counsels him to swear not by the moon, the inconstant moon, but to address his attentions and plans to their immediate circumstances, their love, and to the dangers that lie in wait for them.

At the beginning of the poem, we are given a brief exposition. It becomes clear that the woman is married to an unnamed man, referred to only as "Himself." He, aided by two other men, possibly including a father, brother, or henchman, is in hot pursuit of them. Unlike the principals in "The Statue and the Bust," these lovers have the courage of their convictions and, for good or ill, fulfill themselves in their love. In the former poem, the husband is unmistakably an inconscionable cad, a tyrant who locks his bride in her room, allowing her to see the world only through the window looking out upon the square. We are not given such details about the husband of the woman in the gondola, but we assume from her manner that he is equally intolerable, although his character here is in fact irrelevant, for the emphasis is not on the morality or immorality of the wife's adulterous union, but solely on the souls of the lovers under stress.

It is important to understand the scene, for the import of the words depends upon it. They are making love in the gondola, not merely talking of love. They know that they have no time to plan or to dream of fulfillment, which must be seized in the passing moments they have before they are caught; and to protract the moment of bliss, they seek an ultimate communion of the body and spirit which will be proof against time and death. Like Pippa, the woman in the gondola wants this moment to have no end and no limits:

> Do, break down the partition-wall
> 'Twixt us, the daylight world beholds
> Curtained in dusk and splendid folds!
> What's left but—all of me to take?
> I am the Three's: prevent them, slake
> Your thirst! 'T is said, the Arab sage,
> In practising with gems, can loose
> Their subtle spirit in his cruce
> And leave but ashes: so, sweet mage,
> Leave them my ashes when thy use
> Sucks out my soul, thy heritage!
>
> (ll. 26-36)

The image of the Arab sage who can take the spirit from the gem, leaving but ashes, helps to explain the lover's indifference to the stab wounds at the end of the poem, for his spirit has escaped and only ashes remain for the Three to wreak their vengeance on. It should be noted that nowhere else, except in the scene in the shrub house in *Pippa Passes*, is there such bold sexual imagery in Browning.

Her lover sings of the scenes behind the shuttered windows and doors facing onto the canal, and he knows that unhappiness lies behind them, in contrast to their complete fulfillment. Poor Agnese, he notes, closes the shutters to conceal from the world the shame of her prostitution. Gray Zanobi has purchased a bride, and one is reminded forcibly of the terror and misery of Pompilia in a similar circumstance. The Pucci Palace—like the Institute in "Respectability"—is aglare with the lights of a great ball, and not one of the smiling hypocrites cares whether the host is hanged.

She breaks into this aside with a discourse on kissing that in its frank sexuality is unique in Browning:

> The moth's kiss, first!
> Kiss me as if you made believe
> You were not sure, this eve,
> How my face, your flower, had pursed
> Its petals up; so, here and there
> You brush it, till I grow aware
> Who wants me, and wide ope I burst.
>
> The bee's kiss, now!
> Kiss me as if you entered gay
> My heart at some noonday,
> A bud that dares not disallow
> The claim, so all is rendered up,
> And passively its shattered cup
> Over your head to sleep I bow.
>
> (ll. 49-62)

Like Pippa, the lover projects himself in imagination into other lives, romantic and fabulous, but, unlike Pippa, he does so only to return to his delightful communion, to heighten by contrast his greater joy:

> What are we two?
> I am a Jew
> And carry thee, farther than friends can pursue,
> To a feast of our tribe;
> Where they need thee to bribe
> The devil that blasts them unless he imbibe
> Thy . . . Scatter the vision forever! And now,
> As of old, I am I, thou art thou!
>
> (ll. 63-70)

Here may be seen a dramatic expression of Browning's belief that one should embrace the passing moment as a good in itself, not escape into fantasy or into myth, unless, perhaps, one should do so only to prove the passing moment's greater bliss, an entirely unusual and anti-romantic procedure.

After exploring the exotic charms of imaginative fable, the lover turns to his love to see whether he might imagine a scene or employment which might bring them greater delight than the present one:

> Oh, which were best, to roam or rest?
> The land's lap or the water's breast?
> To sleep on yellow millet-sheaves,

Or swim in lucid shallows just
Eluding water-lily leaves,
An inch from Death's black fingers, thrust
To lock you, whom release he must;
Which life were best on Summer eves?
(ll. 79-86)

Next he asks whether "thought of mine" might improve her, and he fancies her winged like an angel in unutterable radiance, only to break off the fantasy to return to the greater joy of the reality he is embracing:

Rescue me thou, the only real!
And scare away this mad ideal
That came, nor motions to depart!
Thanks! Now, stay ever as thou art!
(ll. 100-04)

This sentiment is a direct expression of one of Browning's most cherished ideals: the superiority of the real over the ideal, the Christian existentialist credo that being transcends essence, that the actual for man properly is superior to the vague ideal, that the sum of life is to embrace it in joy and gusto.

In spite of his resolution to have done with "the mad ideal," it is the woman, not the man, who is able to face reality. She flings her jewel from her hair, knowing that such a gesture is consonant with their imminent death; but, faced with certain extinction, she still makes practical plans: if she ties back the jasmine by her window, his servant, Zorzi, should contrive to communicate with hers, Zanze, for there is urgent news, but if she displays a black ribbon, keep away!

As they debark, he is stabbed, predictably, but his death is a triumph, not a defeat, for he dies in a moment of fulfillment which could not be heightened in joy, and so they have succeeded in protracting the infinite moment. One is reminded of the perversion of the attempt to stop time in a moment of supposed beauty in "Porphyria's Lover," but in that poem the lover is wholly mad and he himself kills Porphyria to preserve the perfect moment.

In "In a Gondola" the lover dies with a philosophical indifference which comes perilously close to destroying the dramatic climax (he has thought only for her beauteous hair that his blood will mar), until one remembers the atmosphere of doom which hangs over the poem and the perfection of their love, which they have consciously striven for in their certain knowledge that in their moment of fulfillment death will part them—only to join them a moment later for ever. He dies upon the heights of bliss and so has no regrets.

SUGGESTED READINGS

DeVane, William C., *A Browning Handbook* (2nd ed., 1955), pp. 114-16.
DeVane discovers "In a Gondola" to be one of Browning's greatest metrical triumphs, but the drama sinks into melodrama in the death scene at the end, possibly reflecting the influence of Bulwer-Lytton's plays: "The device of sending the illicit but happy lovers past scenes of unhappiness for the sake of contrast is a device used a number of times by Browning, notably in the poem *Respectability* (1855); in *Pippa Passes* he uses the device with a difference. The artifice of sending the imagination upon far quests in order to accentuate the supreme excellence of actuality is also a favored one with Browning. *In a Gondola* has always been reckoned one of his greatest metrical triumphs, but the melodramatic situation and action remind the reader too much of the early Victorian theater" (p. 116).

Kenmare, Dallas, *An End to Darkness* (London, 1962), pp. 139-40, 186-87.
"*Porphyria's Lover* has throughout an affinity with the closing thought of *In a Gondola;* death is greeted as a friend at the moment of supreme fulfillment; to continue to live would be too difficult. After a transcendent experience, life is always dangerous, since day by day there is fear of assault on the once-realised, and since jealously guarded, ideal . . ." (p. 140).

4

"Johannes Agricola in Meditation"

"Johannes Agricola in Meditation," a powerful study of religious mania, appeared together with "Porphyria's Lover" under the title "Madhouse Cells" in *Dramatic Lyrics* (1842). It first appeared in *The Monthly Repository*, edited by Browning's friend W. J. Fox, a Unitarian minister. Johannes Agricola (1492-1566), Luther's secretary for a time, became the originator of a doctrine called by Luther "Antinomian," for it rejected the Mosaic law of the Old Testament, maintaining that it was revoked by the dispensation of the New Testament. Browning, in a note accompanying the first appearance of the poem, quotes from the *Dictionary of All Religions* (1704):

> . . . they say that good works do not further, nor evil works hinder salvation; that the child of God cannot sin, that God never chastiseth him, that murder, drunkenness, etc. are sins in the wicked but not in him, that the child of grace being once assured of salvation, afterwards never doubteth . . . that God doth not love any man for his holiness, that sanctification is no evidence of justification, etc.[1]

The historical Agricola believed that the Christian did have moral obligations but that the New Testament served as a sufficient guide for him, but Browning chose to place him among the sizable group of antinomians who absolved the child of grace—the elect—from compliance with the moral code. Agricola, in Browning's poem, considers himself to be among the elect, predestined to salvation regardless of the "sins" he may commit, because his evil deeds, as a result of his state of election, are transformed to good in the perpetration.

Of special interest is Browning's detestation of Johannes and of all others of his persuasion. Every line of the poem establishes his loathing of such mania, which strikes at the heart of Browning's whole moral and

1. William C. DeVane, *A Browning Handbook*, 2nd ed. (New York, 1955), p. 123.

philosophical system. He wrote only one other poem on a religious subject with comparable ferocity: "Caliban upon Setebos." Both poems represent points of view that make God's plan a mockery. In the first, God is made to appear callously fraudulent in his cynical favoritism; in the second, he is viewed as a brutal sadist. But in both poems God shares the stigma of irrational whim and caprice. In passing, it should be noted that Browning has been accused of having much in common with the character of both Johannes and Caliban, and of most of his other repellent personae.

To Browning the main function of life is to test each man, not just certain men. To consider some men as immune from God's judgment of their sins is to destroy at a stroke the moral incorruptibility of God and the moral foundation of the world as well.

Johannes, in one of the shortest of Browning's dramatic monologues, is musing on his happy condition of election and its miraculous effect in converting to virtue all the sins he may commit. Nothing can alter this wonderful predestination, not the moon or stars themselves or any conjunction of planets, for his dispensation antedated the very creation of the cosmos, and he has the power to keep "the brood of stars aloof." He represents the ultimate in egotism and madness. However heinous his sins, he is sure

> . . . that thought and word and deed
> All go to swell his love for me
> Me, made because that love had need
> Of something irreversibly
> Pledged solely its content to be.

More repellent even than his egocentric mania is his ancillary belief that while experiencing all the delights an ingenious practitioner of sin may find, he may experience the ultimate ecstasy:

> . . . as I lie, smiled on, full-fed
> By unexhausted power to bless,
> I gaze below on hell's fierce bed,
> And those its waves of flame oppress,
> Swarming in ghastly wretchedness;
> Whose life on earth aspired to be
> One altar-smoke, so pure!—to win
> If not love like God's love for me,
> At least to keep his anger in;
> And all their striving turned to sin.

It must be noted that to Johannes' sick mind, greater delight is attained by his assumption that these poor suffering creatures were in fact devoted to virtue and to the fear of God, who damned them nevertheless because they happened not to be among the elect, and Johannes jibbers in drooling delight. He gained everything at no cost, whereas they gained unending torment at great cost. The naked injustice of their punishment is a source of boundless delight.

Although "Johannes Agricola in Meditation" is a satire primarily upon the antinomians, it is safe to say that it is a satire on all religions and all men who have shared Johannes' belief. It is difficult not to assume that Browning had in mind also St. Thomas Aquinas' well-known statement in the *Summa*, "Of the Relations of the Saints toward the Damned":

> *I answer that,* Nothing should be denied the blessed that belongs to the perfection of their happiness. Now everything is known the more for being compared with its contrary, because when contraries are placed beside one another they become more conspicuous. Therefore in order that the happiness of the saints may be more delightful to them and that they may render more copious thanks to God for it, they are allowed to see perfectly the sufferings of the damned. . . .
>
> . . . Whoever pities another shares somewhat in his unhappiness. But the blessed cannot share in any unhappiness. Therefore they do not pity the afflictions of the damned.[2]

The many misunderstandings of the poem are illustrated in Dean Inge's *Studies of English Mystics,* in which he notes an alleged similarity between Browning and Johannes, the poet's "danger of antinomianism." Of all the heresies that history affords, the last one that might have tempted Browning as a victim is antinomianism, which gave the lie in the teeth to every principle that guided Browning's thinking all his life. A fundamental in all of Browning's religious thought is that God must be a God of love and justice, and another is that life is a test for all men equally. Inge, however, finds that "The Flight of the Duchess" and "The Statue and the Bust" prove his contention, an alarming misreading of both poems. Joseph E. Baker shares Inge's view:

> Browning did not believe in Hell, and was certain that he would get to Heaven sooner or later. Thus he would disagree with what Agricola says at the end, but would agree with what he says at the beginning. It is interesting to try to determine how far in the poem Agricola may be taken as the spokesman of some of Browning's beliefs . . . notice this statement in the Westminster Confession (XVII, 1): "They whom God hath accepted in His Beloved, effectually called and sanctified by His Spirit, can neither totally nor finally fall away from the state of grace; but shall certainly persevere therein to the end, and

2. Supplement to the Third Part, Arts. 1 and 2, *Great Books of the Western World* XX (Chicago, 1952), 1041.

be eternally saved." In his "Epilogue" to *Asolando* Browning expresses his "assurance" that he will be eternally saved in the end.[3]

Let us examine this interesting interpretation. The statement that Browning did not believe in hell is correct, but it must be observed that to reject hell is to reject a very large part of Calvinism, a part so large that one wonders what, if anything, remained of Calvinism in his thinking. The whole concept of election and damnation is destroyed. The statement in the Westminster Confession that "They whom God hath accepted"—i.e., the elect—shall in the end be saved is materially at variance with Browning's humane belief that all people are destined for salvation, there being no hell in God's plan. Thus, when Browning in the "Epilogue" to *Asolando* speaks with assurance of his salvation, he by no means implies that he has been singled out for special reward. All men are in a like condition—a sweeping repudiation of Calvinism. Byron also was brought up in a Calvinistic household, but no one, I think, would interpret *Cain* or *Don Juan* as embracing the tenets of John Calvin.

In rejecting the concept of hell, Browning carefully avoided the destruction of his central concept of life as a test of each man, with ultimate judgment and reward for each. There is no flaming pit of molten brimstone, it is true, but Browning's heaven is a place where each man will pursue the goals he elected to follow in this life, and his heaven is a place then of infinite degrees of attainment, growth, and satisfaction. Andrea speaks in bitterness of the certainty that his great rivals in painting will in the next world continue to outstrip him in mastery and attainment—precisely because in this life he set his sights low for easily attained goals and will be doomed to similar standards of excellence throughout eternity. If his life has been ruined by guilt and failure, largely because of the demands of Lucrezia, he will be in a like state in heaven, for there too he will have Lucrezia—"as I choose." Thus, there is a kind of equivalent of hell which each man creates for himself by his example in this life. The fact that Browning was certain that he would get to heaven in no way suggests that he shared the vicious view of Johannes that, while the innocent burned, he would be saved because of his election. It should be recalled that history teems with accounts of men of faith, piety, and elevation of spirit—not Calvinists at all—who have expressed the same serene confidence in the love and justice of God, and they have not incurred the charge that they die in the sure and blessed confidence that those not counted as they are among the elect will forever shriek from the pit of hell.

Johannes is among the rare malignant spirits whom Browning found

3. Joseph E. Baker, *"Pippa Passes" and Shorter Poems* (New York, 1947), p. 87, note.

wholly repellent. Even Guido had a case to make for himself, not a very good one, it is true, but Johannes is a vicious, heartless psychopath without redeeming qualities and with no defense except insanity. His fiendish delight in sin and in contemplating the sufferings of the innocent in hell, Browning knew, is the supreme sadism of which the human spirit is capable.

SUGGESTED READINGS

Burrows, Leonard, *Browning the Poet: An Introductory Study* (Nedlands, Western Australia, 1969), pp. 48-50 and passim.

"Antinomianism is Calvinism pushed to an extravagant extreme, and where Calvinism was, there also would be the lunatic fringe of justified sinners (like Burns's Holy Willie). Nothing more likely than that Browning himself had come across an extremist or two of this type at the Independent Chapel his parents attended, latterday Agricolas who would argue, as one so-called Methodist argued, that:

> My sins may displease God, my person is acceptable to him. Though I should outsin Manasses, I should none the less be a child of goodwill, because God always sees me in Christ. Hence in the midst of murders, adulteries and incests, he can address me with the words, 'Thou art all fair, my love, my undefiled; there is no spot in thee' (pp. 49-50)."

Willoughby, John W., "Browning's *Johannes Agricola in Meditation, Explicator*, XXI (1962), Item 5.

Finds that the central portion of the poem seems to justify the conclusion of C. R. Tracy (*Studies in Philology*, XXXIII [1936], 618) "that in it Browning intended to satirize the Calvinist doctrines of election and reprobation," but Willoughby believes that to stop there is "to falsify the overall tone of Browning's poem": "It is not simply a satire of one extreme Protestant position, but a satire of the position coupled with an appreciation of its appeal. And since Browning presents the position only through the voice of Johannes Agricola, the complexity in tone involves not so much Browning's attitude toward the underlying philosophy as his ethical judgment of the protagonist . . . it would be a mistake to consider this poem an unqualified condemnation of Johannes Agricola."

5

"Porphyria's Lover"

"Porphyria's Lover," together with "Johannes Agricola in Meditation," appeared under the title "Madhouse Cells" in *Dramatic Lyrics* (1842), No. III of *Bells and Pomegranates*. Originally both poems appeared in *The Monthly Repository* in January 1836, in which the former appeared under the title "Porphyria," the latter under the title "Johannes Agricola," both signed "Z." Each poem is a study in madness: "Porphyria's Lover" being an account of sexual dementia, the other, of religious mania. In Griffin and Minchin's *Life of Robert Browning* we discover that the former was written in April and May 1834, when Browning was in St. Petersburg, Russia.

Although "Porphyria's Lover" frequently appears in anthologies, it has rarely received the close attention it deserves. It is often merely noted that it is the earliest of Browning's dramatic monologues and the first of his studies of the criminal psychopath. Thomas Blackburn dismisses the poem with some astonishment at its frequent appearance in anthologies:

> It is interesting that such an odd little study of psychopathology should have found its way into so many anthologies. The emotions behind it seem unleavened by insight and have the same text-book quality that we find in the first series of Swinburne's *Poems and Ballads*.[1]

According to Blackburn, the poem may be summarized in a sentence:

> A girl comes to her lover at night, who very briskly strangles her because he realizes that "the good minute goes" and finds intolerable the unease which her humanity—a ghostly and unpredictable energy—causes him.[2]

1. Thomas Blackburn, *Robert Browning: A Study of His Poetry* (London, 1967), p. 59.
2. Ibid.

One might as well summarize *Macbeth* as the murder of a king by a middle-aged woman.

To my knowledge, Professor W. D. Jacobs first showed the poem to be frankly a sexual murder, a study in sexual psychopathology. He establishes the fact that the term "lover" in the title means sexual lover, and the poem thus becomes a study of a sex crime.[3]

It is, however, more than this. Far from being "unleavened by insight," as Blackburn affirms, it is a profoundly incisive study of a demented sexual weakling, living in the realm of fantasy and delusion, who kills his beloved (1) to possess her absolutely and (2) to stop time and hold her like a fly in amber—in total masculine potency that is his only in his Walter Mitty fantasies of sexual possession. It is to be numbered among Browning's poems of twisted souls who deny life and seek to find a substitute in schizoid dreams of dominance and power. It is strikingly similar, in its escape from reality, to Faulkner's "A Rose for Emily" and to Dickens's *Great Expectations,* in which Miss Havisham, when she is jilted on her wedding day, tries to preserve the dream, together with the reminder of her great malice, by stopping the clocks and staying in her bridal dress, contemplating the mouldering wedding cake in an effort to deny life and time. The dominance of Porphyria is immediately seen in the opening lines. She is the emissary of life, as her lover is of death. She moves and he sits as if dead. The initial storm scene is clearly a Freudian symbol of the violence of the madness and sexual turmoil which both share. The whole episode, pictured from the standpoint of a madman, is dreamlike, surrealistic, timeless. Porphyria does not enter. He says she glides in—soundlessly, eerily amid the crashing of the storm. He does not say he watched her enter, or looked at her. Rather, "I listened with heart fit to break," as if he is puzzled by her silent entrance, but we learn that this is not the reason for his heartbreak. He is a man who cannot possess his beloved in any sense of the word, and her arrival is a humiliating challenge and the herald of certain failure. He has lost whatever masculinity he may have had, and he is unconsciously motivated as much by desire to have vengeance on her for her dominance and weakness as he is to attain sexual dominance. Immediately upon entering the room she takes charge with bustling efficiency, with every evidence that she has been here many times before and has found the room in disarray as always, and she sets about her expected tasks. It seems apparent that their meetings have been sexual assignations, as Professor Jacobs points out, but it becomes clear that she comes to her lover's lonely hut because he has psychic impotence and she can give herself to him without in reality giving herself at all. The poem, then, becomes a study in perverse sex, a study in fetishistic pseudosex.

3. W. D. Jacobs, "Browning's *Porphyria's Lover,*" *Rocky Mountain Modern Language Association Bulletin,* V, No. 2 (May 1952), 8.

Upon entering she kneels and makes a fire in the cheerless grate—for he has been sitting motionless all day in the dreary chill of his hut. Why, one asks, has he not made a fire on this cold and stormy day, to drive away the gloom and chill? The answer becomes clear: he is in a catatonic state. He cannot move. This is why he listens to her as she enters. He cannot turn his head to look. He does not speak or greet her, for he can utter no sound. He is as still and silent as Saul in his tent when David begins to play the harp for him. It must be noted that she is not at all surprised by the state of the cabin or by his immobility and silence as she comes in. She recognizes his state and apparently expects it. This is seen in the odd fact that she herself does not greet him or say one word until she makes the fire, removes her dripping cloak and shawl, gloves, and hat, and finally comes over to sit by his side. She expects nothing else from him, for he is mad. She obviously enjoys her sense of dominance and power over him and her sense of perverse security in coming to his hut to make a strange kind of love, which is not love but madness.

When no voice replied,
She put my arm about her waist,
And made her smooth white shoulder bare
And all her yellow hair displaced,
And, stooping, made my cheek lie there,
And spread, o'er all, her yellow hair
Murmuring how she loved me—she
Too weak, for all her heart's endeavor,
To set its struggling passion free
From pride, and vainer ties dissever,
And give herself to me forever.

He is incapable of putting his arm about her. She adopts the male role and places his arm about her waist. It becomes a symbol of their total relationship and his impotence. He is a kind of mechanical man whom Porphyria may manipulate and with whom she may pretend to her heart's content that she is making love. The scene is rich in suggestions of psychopathology. She brushes back her long gold hair, pulls his cheek down upon her bare shoulder (which she has exposed with deliberate calculation), and finally spreads her hair over his head and face. He is encased in her flesh and hair; the world is shut out, and he is a little child retreating to the security of the womb. She came for but one reason, to find her type of sexual satisfaction: "But passion sometimes would prevail,/ Nor could to-night's gay feast restrain/ A sudden thought of one so pale/ For love of her, and all in vain." Indeed, it is all in vain, and she finds it perversely titilating, while he is mad with desire and frustration. He needs to prove his manhood and cannot.

She does not speak her love as to an adult. She "murmurs" how she loves him, as a mother talks to a sick child. There is not a sign that she is unhappy with his catatonia. She clearly enjoys baring her shoulder provocatively and forcing his pale face to lie upon it and shielding him from reality with her long gold hair. This is what she needs and wants, and she can no more help her psychic sickness than he can. She can "give" herself to her lover only symbolically, and one doubts not that fear and inhibition have much to do with her state. It is clear that she is from a wealthy class—she has left a great party to go slumming—and she gets a perverse pleasure out of leaving the fine party, finding her way to his hut and symbolically making love, and then returning to the party with her secret—all the more exciting because of its sordid perversity. Her lover's poverty, social isolation, and psychic sickness give him a strange charm for a time.

On this tragic evening Porphyria plays her role too well, and not wisely at all. He does not content himself with being mothered and falling silently asleep upon her bare shoulder. Perhaps she had never gone quite so far or had been so sexually bold, but her lover is stirred from his catatonia at the moment when he fancies that he has found the perfect moment of possession—or the perfect substitute for possession, and he knows that he must preserve this moment forever—the moment when his sick mind fancies that he has commanded her love as only a man can:

> Be sure I looked up at her eyes
>   Happy and proud; at last I knew
> Porphyria worshipped me; surprise
>   Made my heart swell, and still it grew
>   While I debated what to do.
> That moment she was mine, mine, fair,
>   Perfectly pure and good: I found
> A thing to do, and all her hair
>   In one long yellow string I wound
>   Three times her little throat around,
> And strangled her.

In killing her, he believes that he preserves her "virtue" by giving her the strength she needs to stay with him, he preserves a perfect moment of beauty and sexual fulfillment—it is reminiscent of John Donne's "little death"—and he demonstrates and makes eternal his masculinity. He opens her lids and the blue eyes laugh, so he fancies, without a stain—a rare medical phenomenon. He fancies that she shares his maniacal joy in stopping the passage of time at the exact instant of perfect possession and beauty. In his triumph over his impuissance and the vicissitudes of time, he sees joy everywhere. There must not be one spot or stain on the white radiance of his joy—hence the clear, happy smiling eyes of the murdered girl. Since his moment of success is imperishable, he has confidence to assert without fear for his masculinity:

> . . . her cheek once more
> Blushed bright beneath my burning kiss:
> I propped her head up as before,
> Only, this time my shoulder bore
> Her head, which droops upon it still. . . .

Here is the reversal of roles he has sought for and never found, and he is fulfilled beyond his dreams. He is like the madman in Tennyson's "Maud," who deludes himself into thinking for one mad hour that he has won Maud's love and sees the world in a light of perfect beauty.

Porphyria's lover has committed two of the worst of sins: murder and a total denial of life and its limitations. He plays God and makes his own rules of conduct. He asserts his right to stop time and hold through eternity a moment he wants to be eternal—the ultimate expression of hubris. His drunken delight, in the end, is only slightly marred by his momentary perplexity: "And yet God has not said a word!" He believes that his Godlike act, his supreme denial of life, must win God's approval. From the heavens he expects a great light and a voice of thunder proclaiming, "Well done, my good and faithful servant."

SUGGESTED READINGS

Burrows, Leonard, *Browning the Poet: In Introductory Study* (Nedlands, Western Australia, 1969), pp. 51-61.

"In his drastic solution [in "Porphyria's Lover"] she can give herself to him for ever, he can possess her entirely, only through her death. Clear-sightedly the pale lover perceives that murder is more satisfactory than fornication; it is not enough for her to die the metaphorical death of the sexual climax (that favourite trope of earlier poets), she must be gathered into the artifice of true eternity. Only thus can he take and possess her and at the same time preserve her perfect purity and goodness. Only thus can he eat his cake and have it" (p. 59).

Chandler, Alice, " 'The Eve of St. Agnes' and 'Porphyria's Lover,' " *Victorian Poetry*, III (1965), 273-74.

An essay linking the two poems in a Freudian manner, reminiscent of Betty Miller's method: "We know that Browning read Keats at the same time that he read Shelley, in 1862, and that he always admired his poetry. What more likely than that he accidentally imitated 'The Eve of St. Agnes' when he wrote 'Porphyria's Lover' almost a decade later? And what more enticing way in which he reversed male and female roles and then took revenge on the dominant woman (mother?) by strangling her?" (p. 274).

Honan, Park, *Browning's Characters: A Study in Poetic Technique* (New Haven, 1961), passim.

"But a closer inspection reveals the fact that human character is, at best, only of secondary interest and importance in these poems ["Porphyria's Lover" and "Johannes Agricola in Meditation"] and that they hardly comprise 'advances' over either *Paracelsus* or *Pauline* in Browning's treatment of character" (p. 30). Honan largely agrees with J. M. Cohen that "Porphyria's Lover" is a "juvenile and unrepresentative horror poem" of small value: ". . . while this may have irritated some readers, there is truth in such a judgment. Character is no more revealed in *Porphyria* than in the average tale of Poe; the horror story itself is the thing . . ." (p. 30).

Jacobs, Willis D., "Browning's *Porphyria's Lover*," *Rocky Mountain Modern Language Association Bulletin*, V (1952), 8.

Professor Jacobs astutely points out that the poem is a sex murder. The mad lover kills Porphyria because this time she says she will not give herself to him "forever." He reacts in violence to make her his forever in the only way he knows how, in the belief that since she is too weak to make the decision she presumably wants, he will make the decision for her and thus do her the great service she really desires.

Kenmare, Dallas, *An End to Darkness* (London, 1962), pp. 139-40 and passim.

"This last extraordinary poem ["Porphyria's Lover"] is significantly ignored by many Browning commentators. . . . Two things only are quite certain: one that it is indeed a study in abnormal psychology, and the other that the kind of poet who in early youth could write a poem of such a strange passion was clearly no 'Victorian,' but rather the herald of a new era in poetry. . . . Mr. James Fotheringham in his *Studies of the Mind and Art of Robert Browning* suggests that the whole episode was only an intense dream. . . . Mr. Fotheringham adds: 'It is a romance of overpowering passion. It took place only among the wild motions of a lover's brain.' I have not, however, come across this theory elsewhere, nor can I discover what grounds Mr. Fotheringham had for the assumption."

Tracy, C. R., "Porphyria's Lover," *Modern Language Notes*, LII (1937), 579-80.

Argues that the personae in "Johannes Agricola in Meditation" and "Porphyria's Lover" are no more mad than some others among Browning's characters and that his labeling them under the general title "Madhouse Cells" reflects a certain timorous circumspection in the poet.

6

"The Bishop Orders His Tomb at St. Praxed's Church"

"The Bishop Orders His Tomb at St. Praxed's Church" is one of the most subtle of all of Browning's dramatic monologues. In its splendid blank verse Browning catches the spirit of Renaissance Italy, with its curious mixture of beauty and ugliness, grossness and sensitivity, art and luxury. Ruskin said of the poem in his *Modern Painters* (IV, 380):

> I know of no other piece of modern English, prose or poetry, in which there is so much told, as in these lines, of the Renaissance spirit,—its worldliness, inconsistency, pride, hypocrisy, ignorance of itself, love of art, of luxury, and of good Latin. It is nearly all that I have said of the central Renaissance in thirty pages of the *Stones of Venice*, put into as many lines, Browning's also being the antecedent work.

Significant as this accomplishment is—and inseparable from it—even more so is the insight into the dying Bishop's soul. Few dramatic monologues are so flawless in their sustained probing of personality and spirit. Of special importance is Browning's use of irony and incongruous juxtaposition throughout the poem. The irony is achieved by the incongruity between the dying bishop's utterances when his mind is clear and he can focus his attention on the business at hand: the ordering of a grandiose and ornate tomb; and when his mind is unclear, as the fogs of death surround him, and he lapses into the platitudinous sermonizing of the pulpit. His rational mind and his irrational ramblings have little in common, and in their memorable collision the character of the Bishop is seen against the backdrop of his age, of which he is spokesman.

In the beginning the Bishop is talking to his "nephews"—his illegitimate sons—about his plan for a splendid tomb. When his mind is sharp, he proceeds briskly to the business at hand: to bribe, wheedle, threaten, or cajole his sons into compliance with his wishes for a vulgarly expensive tomb. But when his mind cannot sustain the effort of consecutive thought, he speaks like another man from another world. In short, what Browning has done is to give us the two sides of a man, one the conscious man known to his acquaintances, and second the unconscious man, mouthing the catchphrases and stereotyped utterances of his profession without once realizing the spirit or the meaning behind the clichés he voices.

The sustained irony in the poem reflects Browning's detestation of churchly ornamentation and luxuriance. In "Christmas Eve" he expressed disillusionment with the ostentatious luxury of St. Peter's Basilica. And his disgust with the Oxford Movement in its increasing momentum toward Rome may be seen in his comment about the poem to F. A. Ward: ". . . I pick it out as being a pet of mine, and just the thing for the time—what with the Oxford business."[1] The date of the letter was February 18, 1845, the year when John Henry Newman went over to Rome.

During the Bishop's discourse, his sons are gathered about like vultures, for they are true sons of their father and suspect that the Bishop's words will bear pointedly on their own well-being, and they are right. It must be assumed that whatever filial grief they experience, if any, is not readily seen in their words or faces as they react in alternate consternation and greed to the old man's words. The demands he makes upon their purses and energy, we may assume from the Bishop's methods of persuasion, do not unduly trouble the boys, for it is clear that they will ignore his wishes while they "revel down his villas," a suggestion that squares perfectly with their desires.

The opening words indicate that the Bishop is just concluding one of his periods of fuzzy-minded sermonizing: "Vanity, saith the preacher, vanity!" The poem begins on the note of irony and concludes in the same vein, for irony is the dominant device used throughout. The contrast between his maundering quotation from Ecclesiastes and the substance of his request for the final vanity of all, a luxurious and showy tomb, sets the tone for the whole poem. At no time does the bishop note the shocking contrast between the two halves of his discourse. Immediately after mouthing words warning of the vanity of the things of the world, he launches, somewhat indirectly, into his request for the vanity of vanities. His professional utterances and his life have had but little relation. One is tempted to brand the bishop simply as a hypocrite because of this wonderful polarity, but, if the word *hypocrite* implies conscious, calculating violation of his professed beliefs, it is doubtful that he is a hypocrite. He has been so steeped in the Renaissance tradition of worldly and sensuous desire that he has given no thought to the gulf between his word and deed. The words he has just spoken, for example, have for him no real meaning, but they have a talismanic effect, a familiar sound, a comfortable feel in the mouth—but in the

1. William C. DeVane, *A Browning Handbook*, 2nd ed. (New York, 1955), 166.

most literal sense they have no meaning, not as they might apply to his life, at least. It is wholly important to be aware that there is not one sign of guilt in any word the Bishop speaks. The final rites of the Church have shriven him of any venial sins that attach to human flesh in this imperfect world, but he has no consciousness of sin or guilt, and not one suggestion of fear of damnation. He is as far removed from the terror of Dr. Faustus when he had but a bare hour to live as one may imagine. Implicit throughout is Browning's satire on both the man who should approach his death and judgment so oblivious of his mortal sins and on the Church who supplied the machinery for and the blessing upon his complacency.

As soon as the Bishop has uttered his final line from Ecclesiastes, and his mind sharpens sufficiently to get down to the business of ordering his tomb, he commands the boys to approach closer to his bed:

> Draw round my bed: is Anselm keeping back?
> Nephews—sons mine . . . ah God, I know not!
> Well—
> She, men would have to be your mother once,
> Old Gandolf envied me, so fair she was!

His command for his sons to come closer is partly explained by his need to conserve his strength in speaking, but even more by his fear that what he is about to disclose may be overheard, for one of the items he must divulge is the spot where his treasure is buried. The danger of apprising his sons is great enough without tempting his brethren in the Church with the unholy desire to dig, and one suspects that they are listening at the door.

Browning's skill in revealing the Bishop's mental state is shown by the ease with which the bishop is diverted from his theme. The mention of his sons and the slight emotional shock he experiences in realizing that for the first time he has actually acknowledged them as sons, not "nephews"—a sobering sign of his approaching death—brings the thought of his mistress, and that brings the thought of the detested Gandolf, who also lusted after this fair creature, and for a moment he forgets the ordering of the tomb. One is tempted to conclude that the Bishop found equal joy in the possession of his mistress and in the frustration that Gandolf felt in losing her to *his* detested rival. There is not a shred of Christian humility or loving kindness in the portrait of either churchman.

The thought of his triumph over Gandolf is too much for him, and his mind wanders back into the droning sounds he has uttered so often from the pulpit with no awareness of the sense of the words:

> And thence ye may perceive the world's a dream.
> Life, how and what is it? As here I lie
> In this state-chamber, dying by degrees,

> Hours and long hours in the dead night, I ask
> "Do I live, am I dead?"

The words convey much unconscious irony. At the end of this section of sustained platitude, he ends with the words, "Peace, peace seems all/ Saint Praxed's ever was the church for peace . . ."—words which in context are rich in irony, for as soon as his mind clears he forgets what he has said and confesses that in that Church there was no peace:

> And so, about this tomb of mine. I fought
> With tooth and nail to save my niche, ye know:
> —Old Gandolf cozened me, despite my care;
> Shrewd was that snatch from out the corner South
> He graced his carrion with, God curse the same!

The Church has been a festering snake pit of intrigue, hatred, and rivalry, but it has become customary to refer to the Church as affording the peace that passeth all understanding, and the Bishop violates no custom, even though he has no comprehension of its meaning. It has never occurred to him to bother one way or another about peace, when life is so full of things of consuming interest, all of which demand energetic self-interest and enterprise: getting, gaining, defeating, possessing.

He initially describes his tomb as including a slab of basalt, an inferior, dull gray stone, with nine columns of "Peach-blossom marble all":

> . . . the rare, the ripe
> As fresh-poured red wine of a mighty pulse.

Pulse means a fruit mash from which wine is made, but surely the reference is also to a strong, sensuous heartbeat—a symbol of all fleshliness that charmed the Renaissance mind, of which this poem is a study.

With reluctance, the Bishop confides to his sons that under cover of the smoke rising from a fire that gutted a part of his Church he took the opportunity of looting it of a lump of lapis lazuli,

> Big as a Jew's head cut off at the nape,
> Blue as a vein o'er the Madonna's breast. . . .

His reluctance reflects not guilt but fear that his sons will in turn demonstrate their spirit of enterprise by simply appropriating the precious stone for their own use, with a cynical disregard for his wishes—the course of action he would elect if he were standing about his father's deathbed under similar circumstances. His callous unawareness of the sanctity of anything whatever—except his own fleshly delights—may be seen in the imagery he employs to describe the stone he stole. Such outrageously anatomical images, singularly out of place in the mouth of a dying bishop, abundantly establish both his love of the flesh and his brutality. The Madonna's bosom and a Jew's decapitated head afford no discord in juxtaposition. To him there is no incongruity, for he is speaking in the manner normal among cultivated gentlemen of the Renaissance. When he asks his sons to "let the blue lump poise between my knees,/ Like God the Father's globe on both his hands/ Ye worship in the Jesu Church so gay/ . . . ," there is some ambiguity in his intent. Does he ask that the stone be put with him into the tomb, poised between his knees, or does he want it to rest between the knees of his recumbent marble figure?

Barbara Melchiori, in her *Browning's Poetry of Reticence*, affirms that he wants the stone to be placed in the latter position, and there is one good reason for supposing that this is his intent. Surely the delight of possession (clasped between the knees) would be much lessened if no one could see the stone buried in the tomb, but Mrs. Melchiori forgets that it is not the admiration of the passerby that he wants. Rather he wants to inflame old Gandolf to new excesses of envy: "For Gandolf shall not choose but see and burst!" To excite the envy of one in the tomb, what more normal place could there be than the tomb in which to place the lapis lazuli, hugged between the actual bones of his knees throughout the centuries? Gandolf could be counted upon to note the poverty of his own state in the tomb. An additional reason to suppose that the Bishop hoped to have the stone inside the tomb rather than on top is his certain knowledge that if the Church could be looted once, it could be looted twice, and about his bed stand those with the imagination and hardihood to bring it off. Moreover, identifiable loot could hardly be openly displayed.

The effort of his discourse has been too much for him, at this point, and he again, paraphrasing Job 7:6, lapses into the sermonizing that he utters so well and understands so little:

> Swift as a weaver's shuttle fleet our years:
> Man goeth to the grave, and where is he?

His mind sharpens quickly, and he again, forgetting the pious sentiment, launches into an account of the details he wishes to grace his tomb:

> Black—
> 'T was ever antique-black I meant! How else
> Shall ye contrast my frieze to come beneath?
> Those Pans and Nymphs ye wot of, and perchance
> Some tripod, thyrsus, with a vase or so,
> The Saviour at his sermon on the mount,
> Saint Praxed in a glory, and one Pan
> Ready to twitch the Nymph's last garment off,
> And Moses with the tables. . . .

The strange mixture of pagan and Christian reflects the Renaissance love of art as much as the Bishop's insensitivity to the incongruity of the frieze. There is no sign here of impiety or blasphemy, and the Bishop would have expressed dismay and incredulity if someone had remonstrated with him about the mixture of pagan and Christian. The spiritual has become lost in the sensual.

He notes with sudden alarm that his sons are not heeding his words, but are whispering among themselves. His alarm prompts him again to refer to them as his sons, but at this point he shows no over-nicety of conscience about the matter, calling Anselm "child of my bowels." He is perfectly aware of what they are whispering about, for he knows his boys and their total devotion to self-interest. They have just been told where the treasure lies, he reflects, and they are busily engaged in threatening dire punishment to any of the brothers who may sneak off to explore, shovel in hand. In shrewd understanding of their muttered conversation he says:

> Ah, ye hope
> To revel down my villas while I gasp
> Bricked o'er with beggar's mouldy travertine
> Which Gandolf from his tomb-top chuckles at!

As death approaches, the Bishop increases the demand for vulgar ostentation of the tomb. The travertine becomes one great block of jasper, to secure which he plays his trump card:

> There's plenty jasper somewhere in the world—
> And have I not Saint Praxed's ear to pray
> Horses for ye, and brown Greek manuscripts,
> And mistresses with great smooth marbly limbs?

No irony could be greater than the promise that he would intercede with St. Praxed, the virgin daughter of a Roman senator of the first century A.D., to reward his bastard sons with voluptuous mistresses.

As his mind wearies from his efforts, he mutters about the mass and the sensuous details which he recalls so well:

> And then how I shall lie through centuries,
> And hear the blessed mutter of the mass,
> And see God made and eaten all day long,
> And feel the steady candle-flame, and taste
> Good strong thick stupefying incense-smoke!

The concluding lines, beginning with line 91, are among the first of stream-of-consciousness lines extant. They are incoherent, jumbled, scattered, and ironic. He attributes the Sermon on the Mount to St. Praxed and promptly turns his thoughts to his mistress once again and to good Latin—for he shares the Renaissance love of good Latin, even though the classic discipline and wisdom are not apparent to him. Barbara Melchiori believes that Browning took the name of St. Praxed to be masculine because of the line ". . . Saint Praxed at his sermon on the mount . . . ," but surely the confusion here is in the Bishop's head, not in Browning's. If one is to assume that Browning was confused about the sex of the saint, should one also assume that he forgot who gave the Sermon on the Mount? The line, together with the lines before and after, is filled with confusion, indicative of the Bishop's dying state.

Before death, the Bishop demands that the tomb be made "all of lapiz." He threatens to give the Pope his villas if they do not comply, an idle threat, he knows, for his sons are lads of spirit; and, if they fancied that he meant what he said, they would promptly put a pillow over his face as an incentive to right action. He gaspingly demands more and gaudier pagan symbols, and, dying, reveals his fears—or his certainties—that his sons will bury him in the cheapest sandstone, which will act as a filter for his decaying body. But strong as is his fear, stronger yet is his recollection of his mistress and the envy which inflamed old Gandolf's heart.

SUGGESTED READINGS

Bonner, Francis W., "Browning's 'The Bishop Orders His Tomb at Saint Praxed's Church,' " *Explicator*, XXII (1964), Item 57.
Makes the point that the quotation from Ecclesiastes "Vanity saith the preacher, vanity!" sets the tone for the entire poem: "It is the spirit of cynicism and disillusionment which the Bishop feels as his death draws near. This tone runs in the background of the Bishop's mind throughout the poem, breaking in at intervals upon the old churchman's anxiety about the splendor of his tomb. Like the preacher, he is convinced of the emptiness of life, the certainty of death, and the uncertainty of the hereafter."

Chiarenza, Frank J., "Browning's 'The Bishop Orders His Tomb at St. Praxed's Church,' " *Explicator*, XIX (1961), Item 22.

Melchiori, Barbara, "Where the Bishop Ordered His Tomb," *A Review of English Literature*, V (1964), 7-26.
Traces Browning's indebtedness to Gerard de Lairesse's *The Art of Painting in All Its Branches*, in a highly Freudian commentary.

Milosevich, Vincent M., "Browning's 'The Bishop Orders His Tomb at Saint Praxed's Church,' " *Explicator*, XXVII (1969), Item 67.
Suggests that "it is altogether fitting that the Bishop should dwell with such anxious love on these images [i.e., of fair women, peach-blossom marble, good Latin, agate urns, grapes] because he has a terrifying vision of his world coming apart."

7

"*The Laboratory: Ancien Régime*"

"The Laboratory: Ancien Régime" is a dramatically conceived study in the psychopathology of vengeance, or more properly, a study of the soul of a woman driven mad with jealousy and desire for vengeance. The interest, as always, is not in the vengeance itself but in its poisonous effects upon the soul of the speaker. The subtitle makes the time of the action clear: the time of the old order of France, in the reign of Louis XIV. W. C. DeVane suggested that the woman who has been driven mad with hate and jealousy is modeled upon Madame de Brinvilliers, a notorious adept at poisoning, but internal evidence casts doubt on this identification. Certainly if she is to be accepted as the "minion" of the poem, she is in the earliest stage of her apprenticeship as a poisoner, for she is not adept. Rather she is the merest novice, displaying the fullest ignorance of poisons and their effects. The apothecary's shop is filled with "strange things," of which she is ignorant. Clearly she has never before purchased a poison for felonious purposes, for her questions are uniformly uninstructed. Moreover, she is entirely ready to be apprehended and punished for her crime, and she experiences a drunken elation at the thought of her bold sacrifice. It is important not to assume that she is a poisoner of experience and fame, for the whole tone of the poem is destroyed if one assumes that she is hardened in the technique of murder, especially in poisoning without detection and discovery.

So little does she care for concealment and escape that she offers the apothecary all that she has, and her body as well, for the tiny vial of poison. She has no thought for the morrow and no desire to live if she may first see her poison do its work. Her masochistic proposals to the apothecary are made in sheer spite—to get back at her faithless lover, who has found a voluptuous mistress to engage his attentions.

Enraged with jealousy, the rejected woman finds a perverse joy in the contrast she discovers between fact (her purchase of poison) and fancies of her supposed debilitating grief that she believes her lover and his new mistress are laughing about: they brazenly flaunt their love in her face, expecting her to cower and flee weeping to the sanctuary of the Church. Instead, she is buying poison:

> He is with her, and they know that I know
> Where they are, what they do: they believe
> my tears flow
> While they laugh, laugh at me, at me fled to
> the drear
> Empty church, to pray God in, for them!—I
> am here.

Her character is shown in her determination to bring art and finesse to the compounding and the administration of the poison, for she is in the tradition of the *ancien régime*, when poisoning was a fine art. It is not enough to kill. One must kill with a flair, with subtlety, with art. She wants the experience to become the whole of life, for which she is prepared to lose everything: her lover, her wealth, her virtue, and her life. For such a sacrifice, she demands an ultimate esthetic experience, for which she must pay everything. Hence her obscene proposals to the old pharmacist who is compounding the poison. While he pounds and grinds the deadly drugs—presumably a compound of arsenic, a favorite at the court of Louis XIV—she savors the passing moment, finding sweetness in her moment of strength.

The reader finds that she is small and wizened, a "minion," and she lusts for power to kill, for her rival is large, voluptuous, and exuberantly healthy. What a joy it will be, she reflects, to see the subtle workings of an esthetic poison slowly destroying the hated woman with her animal charms! Nothing blundering or crude or hasty will do, however effective it may be. It must entice the victim by its color, the enchantment of its bouquet:

> Quick—is it finished? The color's too grim!
> Why not soft like the phial's, enticing and dim?
> Let it brighten her drink, let her turn it and stir,
> And try it and taste, ere she fix and prefer!

She doubts that the insignificant drop of poison will stop the breath and the magnificent pulse of her voluptuous rival, whose charms she hates with maniacal dedication:

> What a drop! She's not little, no minion like me!
> That's why she ensnared him: this never will free
> The soul from those masculine eyes,—say, "no!"
> To that pulse's magnificent come-and-go.

Under the stimulus of her proposed vengeance, she indulges in fantasies of wholesale poisoning of all possible rivals who, like her rival, are voluptuous and thus deserving of death:

> Soon, at the King's, a mere lozenge to give,
> And Pauline should have just thirty minutes to live!
> But to light a pastile, and Elise, with her head
> And her breast and her arms and her hands, should drop dead!

She ends in a frenzy of hate and triumph, wholly demented, fancying that she will for one supreme moment attain the heights of life.

SUGGESTED READING

Shaw, W. David, *The Dialectical Temper: The Rhetorical Art of Robert Browning* (Ithaca, N.Y., 1968), pp. 68-70.
The speaker in "The Laboratory" is seen as incredibly superficial "in the literalness of her imagination, but her consistent specifications show she is a true artist. . . . The chemist functions as the lover's surrogate . . ." (p. 69).

8

"The Confessional"

"The Confessional" is a vehicle for one of Browning's most savage dramatic denunciations of organized religion. Browning, the spokesman for individuality and freedom of conscience, was always suspicious of the power of social institutions, especially the Catholic Church and the law. In *The Ring and the Book*, it must not be forgotten, if the old Pope is of admirable character and judgment, the Church itself does not come off so well. Pompilia, in pleading with the Church for redress of grievances, meets only cynical brutality and heartlessness, and Caponsacchi, in his great and moving speech, finds the Church rotten with hypocrisy.

The speaker in "The Confessional" is a young woman who has given herself passionately to her lover, Beltran. In a sudden access of guilt for her transgressions, she goes to confession to "tell the old mild father there." The old priest, far from being a mild and gentle man, is a cunning, deceitful betrayer of confidences, who promises pardon for her, provided she betray to him her lover's secrets, for Beltran is known to favor changing "the laws of church and state." The evil old priest counsels her to make love once again with Beltran and so, in the manner of Samson and Delilah, to worm from him evidence of his damnable heresy, so that he and his fellow priests may save Beltran's soul by fasting and scourging of their bodies in this worthy cause. She naïvely obeys the old father and when Beltran is making love to her she asks of him, as a special earnest of his love, that he reveal to her the secrets of their plan to alter the laws. His judgment clouded by ecstasy, he tells her all his secrets, which she purveys to the priest, sure of her virtuous motives.

Instead of praying and scourging their flesh, the priests send him straightway to the scaffold, leaving the insanely disillusioned girl screaming, "Lies—lies, again—and still, they lie!"

The setting of the poem is Spain during the Inquisition. W. C. DeVane believes the period to be "a contemporary utterance," on the score that Browning often indicates the approximate period of historical poems. The tone of the poem, the furious inquisitorial rooting out of heresy and, indeed, all forms of individualism, stamp the poem as dating from the time of the Inquisition, but nothing could be more certain than Browning's denunciation of all ecclesiastical cruelty regardless of the period when it was perpetrated. Browning detested the Oxford Movement and all it stood for, as well as all conscienceless fundamentalists.

SUGGESTED READING

Burrows, Leonard, *Browning the Poet: An Introductory Study* (Nedlands, Western Australia, 1969), pp. 139-43.

"The title ['The Confessional'] itself may be seen as ironical. The girl has initiated her own tragedy by entering the little cell of the confessional and betraying the love which she and Beltran have sealed and which the Church calls sin. Knowing now, too late, that the Church cynically used her to crush her politically deviant lover, she has been shut into a grimmer cell from which she hurls her 'confession' of infamy ('Ecrasez l'infame!) and disenchantment at the world. Yet who will be auditor and confessor here? This is a shocking and bitter 'memoir from the house of the dead.' She has unwittingly betrayed her lover to save his soul; the Church has wittingly betrayed its sacred office to remove a political enemy" (p. 143).

9

"Saul"

"Saul" long occupied a favored position in public esteem. Browning, himself, when asked to name four poems best representing his verse, selected "Saul" and "Abt Vogler" to represent the lyric.[1] W. C. DeVane remarked that the poem "possibly is more esteemed than any other among Browning's poems." During the last century especially, this poem was not infrequently called the best short religious poem in the language. "This is perhaps the grandest and most beautiful of all Mr. Browning's religious poems," said Edward Berdoe, speaking for a broad spectrum of nineteenth-century opinions. "It is a Messianic oratorio in words." Today the poem is much less admired and, indeed, is often deplored as an undramatic, somewhat static sermon in verse; and it is apparent that as the poem proceeds, the tone of the pulpit predominates over that of the stage.

"Saul" has its origin in I Samuel 16: 14-23. Samuel, after a conference with the Lord, told Saul: "Thus says the Lord of hosts: 'I will punish Amalek for what he did to Israel, in that he opposed him on the way, when he came out of Egypt. Now go and attack Amalek and utterly destroy him and all that he has, and spare not, but slaughter both man and woman, child and infant, ox and sheep, camel and ass." Saul proved himself a dutiful servant, slaughtering all the men, women, children, and suckling infants with an attention to detail which could not fail to please the Lord; but his heart forsook him when he came to putting the cattle to the sword. His strong right arm, which flinched not in the righteous carnage of infants, was stricken with disobedience when facing marketable livestock: "But Saul and the people spared Agag and the best of the sheep, the oxen, the fatlings, the lambs, and all that was good, and were not willing utterly to destroy them; but everything that was vile and despised, that they completely destroyed." The Lord, whose wrath could not be sated with less than absolute desolation, sent an evil spirit to visit the erring Saul, who had

1. William C. DeVane, *A Browning Handbook*, 2nd ed. (New York, 1955), p. 257.

failed in his duty. The young harp player David was summoned to exorcise the evil spirit from the smitten King: "So whenever the evil spirit came upon Saul, David would take the lyre and play with his hand, and Saul would be relieved and feel restored and the evil spirit would depart from him." There is no scriptural record of the vengeance wreaked on the erring spirit for its dereliction of duty.

This is the slight basis upon which the poem rests. It has been convincingly established that Christopher Smart's "A Song of David" and "On the Goodness of the Supreme Being" suggested much of the tone and manner of the poem (see DeVane, *A Browning Handbook*), and Betty Miller has discovered some interesting parallels between the imagery and tone of Elizabeth Barrett Browning's "A Rhapsody of Life's Progress" and Browning's "Saul."

The first nine sections of "Saul" (102 lines) appeared in *Dramatic Romances and Lyrics*, 1845, the seventh of the *Bells and Pomegranates*, a 24-page pamphlet selling for two shillings. The poem, enlarged to its present length of nineteen stanzas (335 lines), appeared in *Men and Women* in 1855. In 1863, when Browning redistributed his poems, "Saul" was included in *Dramatic Lyrics*, where it remains.

"Saul" shows somewhat more than a hairline scar at the juncture where the last ten stanzas were added to the first nine, in spite of considerable alteration of lines to make the addition fit smoothly. The first nine sections are very frankly a hymn to the physical delights of living, whereas the last ten are, by implication, a discourse on the inadequacy of life's physical delights, good as they are, unless they are accompanied by "soul wine," the life of the spirit. The remarkable thing is that the seam is as smooth as it is.

As the poem opens, Saul stands in his tent, as he has stood for three days, a catatonic wreck, silent and immovable. David, the young harpist, has been called to play for the stricken King and so to bring him back to health. The details Browning supplies of the nomadic life are immediately striking: the lilies entwined about the strings of the lyre as a protection against the fierce desert heat; "the sand burnt to powder"; the tent and the spear serving as an obstruction to its entrance; the gigantic figure of the King, each arm widespread along the cross-supports of the tent.

The poem immediately becomes the drama of David, not of Saul. The argument, reminiscent of *Samson Agonistes*, concerns the internal development of the young harp player, to whom Saul is a supporting character. The poem is a lesson in values and finally a great epiphany of light, a revelation and a vision of the coming of Christ—but it all happens to David. The growth is all his.

Among the charges leveled at "Saul" today is a lack of unity or direction. Altogether too much attention, it is said, is paid to David and very little about the cure of Saul, who should be the center of interest, since he is the patient, not David.[2] We are never allowed to enter the soul of the King to see the workings of David's treatment. It is true that only through his motions are we allowed to glimpse into the therapeutic process, but the truly dramatic and marvelous effects of the cure are wreaked on David, not on Saul, who, presumably, is merely cured, at least temporarily. But David will never be the same after this event. He has utterly changed, for he has seen the great light and the coming of Christ with all its meaning of love. It is doubtful that these things are visited on Saul, and his cure is only of incidental interest, a mere by-product of David's "cure." Saul is of only the slightest dramatic importance. He might be considered the patient on the operating table who merely breathes stertorously from time to time, but David is the sensitive, alive surgeon through whose eyes and heart the drama is revealed, for the changes are all within his mind and soul.

The true weakness of "Saul" lies, not in its division of attention between David and Saul, or in its failure to show the workings of David's musical psychiatry upon Saul's spirit, but in the fact that David is not dramatically believable or even very interesting. He is merely a character to whom something dramatic happens, but we can never understand precisely what happens, although we are told that it does. He is wholly unlike Fra Lippo Lippi, who lives and breathes in his tense and vibrant night upon the town, and whose every nuance and shade of joy and fear come to life before us. Browning succumbed to his besetting danger of placing message before drama and character, and as David becomes less and less, the theme becomes more and more. The great revelation takes place within the spirit of David, but when it does we remain unmoved because we have not really seen his spirit. We have merely been told about it.

The misunderstandings of "Saul" are legion. It has been declared that David's words "How good is man's life, the mere living" establishes his naïve simplicity, which has been compared with Pippa's alleged naïveté in singing "God's in his heaven—/ All's right with the world!" The two utterances are not particularly comparable. Pippa is a vitally conceived and dramatically successful character who is almost as unlikely to believe that "all's right with the world" as Guido is. She might very well agree that the *plan* of life is right, for evil is a part of that plan whereby man is tested; but to suppose that she denies the very existence of evil, as is commonly alleged, is not supported by the evidence. She has lived with evil as her familiar since her natal hour and her life has been so full of sorrow and toil and disappointment that she cannot bear to spend her one holiday of the year as Pippa, who has suffered so, and thus she plays at being, successively, "the four happiest ones in Asolo." It is altogether too often forgotten that

2. Cf. Roma A. King, Jr., *The Bow and the Lyre* (Ann Arbor, Mich., 1957), pp. 100-23.

people in literature as in life do not sing songs under oath or in any way affirm that the lyric embraces in whole or in part their philosophy of life. More often than not people simply sing and would be grievously confounded to be charged with intending the words as binding commitments, philosophical or religious.

It seems obvious that to select two lines from the scores that Pippa sings and to find in them her philosophy of life (and Browning's as well) is an affront to scholarship as well as to common sense, especially when the other lines she sings in large measure concern precisely the evil, the sin, and the crimes which her two famous lines are supposed to disavow and to deny. Not even *The Inn Album* or *Red Cotton Night-Cap Country* is so concerned with bloody deeds as is *Pippa Passes,* so full of bloody plots and violent death, and yet *Pippa* is almost universally construed to be Browning's denial of the very existence of evil.

David's case is only partially illuminated by Pippa's. There is no evidence that David has led a life of wretchedness, which prompts him to play for one mad day that life is paradise. He merely has been called upon to sing and play the lyre as a means of exorcising the evil spirit from the afflicted King, whom David loves. There is certainly far greater reason to suppose that David believes more of what he sings than Pippa does, but it must be remembered that he is doing all in his power to lift Saul out of the paralyzing depression into which he has sunk. In consequence, he sings of the simple, happy, joyous moments of physical well-being in life. What would be more natural under the circumstances? Unless one bears a resemblance to Job's comforters, he does not come to a house of sorrow equipped with the obituary column and forebodings of disaster as homeopathic prescriptions, in spite of his own mood or his private despair. We know nothing of David's frame of mind, of course, and he may or may not believe what he sings, but it is singularly unimportant. He is trying to cheer his King, not reveal his durable good spirits. Roma King, Jr., comments:

> Once before Browning had chosen a child, Pippa, as central character; and in some respects Pippa and David are alike. David's "How good is man's life, the mere living . . ." duplicates the naïve simplicity of Pippa's "God's in his heaven–/ All's right with the world!" as statements of primitive and unsophisticated innocence.[3]

King is correct in finding Pippa a far more successfully drawn character than David, who remains undeveloped. It seems doubtful, however, that Pippa could ever experience a blinding revelation of truth as David does; but for all that she is alive, and David is thinly sketched. It does not help us to understand the poem or David to affirm that he necessarily embraces

3. Ibid., p. 106.

all the words of his songs, although he probably is not an active dissenter. To find him naïvely simplistic because he sings as he does may hinder our understanding of Browning's purpose. King's implication is that David, like Pippa, sees the world through such optimistic innocence that in effect he too denies the evil that is all about him as he sings. It must not be forgotten that Saul is standing before him a massive, towering wreck, a conspicuous example of the horror that life can visit in a moment upon any man, an example of evil not likely to be lost on David.

The Bible makes clear that David was summoned to minister to the King "whenever the evil spirit came upon Saul," a detail which may suggest that David was not without experience in the camp as a musical psychiatrist, although one cannot be sure of this. Intuitively he knows that the way to help the King is to sing of life's blessings—"How good is man's life, the mere living . . ."—a choice that establishes his common sense rather than his naïveté, for Saul, it is clear, has retreated from life and would welcome death. David's first duty is to convince Saul that he must choose life, not death. As he sings, David's heart is heavy with foreboding, for he is uncertain of his method of cure, or of its success, and responsibility lies upon his spirit.

David is simple in the sense of being unsophisticated, for he is a working shepherd, not an artificial shepherd from the pastoral elegies. He is no Corydon or Adonais. He has been pronounced psychologically unrealistic because a shepherd boy simply could not speak with such symptoms of theological cultivation and intellectual maturity, and especially because his account of the Incarnation is beyond the capacity of a shepherd boy. It is indeed, but literature teems with instances of shepherds who speak with uncommon sapience and information on a variety of topics. To have David speak about the Incarnation hundreds of years before the event is remarkable, and to have him speak with insight and skill is even more so, but it must be recalled that he has been subjected to revelation, an epiphany which sets him apart from the run-of-the-mill shepherd lad as much as Lazarus is set apart from other men who have not returned from the land which lies beyond death.

If shepherds are never to speak philosophically, then a vast area of literature is dramatically invalid from Moschus, Bion, and Theocritus through Edmund Spenser, Shelley, and Matthew Arnold, to name a few. David is made to see in a flash—which has little to do with rationalistic processes—the coming of Christ, the atonement, and the love of God. King objects to the characterization of David because he "sees too much (and that through the eyes of a nineteenth-century rationalist) to be considered seriously historical. Further, not only his thought, but his diction and imagery are wholly unlike that of the Biblical David whom we know through the Psalms." On these grounds, Shakespeare's Caesar is a substantial failure, if one cares to consider him "seriously historical," and the same applies to Hamlet, whose speech rhythms are remarkably more Shakespearean than those that echoed through the drafty corridors at Elsinore. Lady Macbeth speaks of the murdered Duncan with an attention to philosophical subtlety altogether remarkable for a woman at such a time and place. It simply will not do to judge either Shakespeare's works or Browning's as history, or as anything other than what they are: works of art.

David sings to Saul of the simple things of the earth, which he has lived with and found joy in: "the tune all our sheep know," "the tune, for which quails on the cornland will each leave his mate/ To fly after the player," "the help-tune of our reapers, their wine-song," "the funeral song, praising the full life of the departed," the marriage song, the march—all songs praising the wine "of this world's life."

These enlivening songs cause Saul to shudder—and when one is in a catatonic state any sign of motion is encouraging—and the tent shakes and the jewels in his turban sparkle, but he remains in the same position, frozen in immobility. The wine of this life is good; in itself it is insufficient to effect a cure, but it makes a start.

In stanza IX, David sings in lush and ornate imagery of "manhood's prime vigor" and "the wild joys of living," supplying concrete images of a pungency that mark a new dimension in his song. His fault lies in his own imperception of the inadequacy of the mere physical, good as it is. He has yet to learn the error in his song: ". . . the mere living! how fit to employ/ All the heart and the soul and the senses forever in joy!" It must not be supposed, however, that David learns to despise the wine of this life. He learns only that it is a part of the whole of life. It is sufficient to arouse Saul but not sustain the cure: "Death was past, life not come. . . ." Still the catatonic state departs from Saul, and he begins to move his arms and his eyes and to become "Saul as before."

> . . . what next should I urge
> To sustain him where song had restored him?
> (ll. 128-29)

He has sung of life's joys and

> He saith, "It is good;" still he drinks not: he lets me praise life,
> Gives assent, yet would die for his own part.
> (ll. 134-35)

David recalls his dreams while he lay in the pasture watching an eagle circling overhead, musing upon the bird's wide vision of the world, so circumscribed to one lying on the ground, and the eagle's vision prompts him to an awareness that there must be a wider view of life than he has been singing of—the first step in the revelation to come. He commends the King for rejecting mere comforts as the whole of life, for "the branch of this life" bears fruit in the soul. But David still does not understand the significance of the illumination he dimly perceives. He still fancies that the function of the spirit is to sustain the weary flesh when age robs one of the joy of youth.

The first significant revelation to burst upon David is the lesson of growth and progress. Enjoyment of nature, romantic delight in the contemplation of sensuous beauty are imperfect, unless one grows beyond the delights of eye and ear. To David, as to Browning, nature, unless it is considered a backdrop to the human drama, is essentially without interest or significance. The soul of man, under the stress of living, with all its vicissitudes and trials, is of supreme worth.

David's analogy of the slow growth of the palm tree—successively to the height of the kid's lip, to the height of the stag's antler, to the great height of its date-laden maturity—becomes a symbol of life and its growth. The sweet and nutritious dates yield yet a further blessing: palm wine, which shall "staunch/ Every wound of man's spirit in winter." With the death of the tree, the wine yet lives, bringing comfort and gladness to the cheek and the eye. Similarly, the deeds of Saul live on, even though he is ill, and the land is blessed with his deeds and the "radiance thy deed was the germ of." Man's influence and force survive the body, as the wine the tree:

> So with man—so his power and his beauty forever take flight.
> No! Again a long draught of my soul-wine! Look forth o'er the years!
> Thou hast done now with eyes for the actual; begin with the seer's!
> (ll. 174-76)

The soul wine works its magic and Saul awakens. He regains his regal demeanor, adjusts his turban and kingly accoutrements, wipes the sweat from his face, and looks into the face of the young singer who has wrought the cure. But the change in Saul is as nothing compared with the change in David, who suddenly sees that as his love for Saul yearns to be absolute, both in this life and the next, so God's love is absolute and boundless.

At this point it is helpful to recall once again the Biblical account of Saul's plight. Jehovah, in great wrath because Saul had failed to put to the sword all the cattle, goats, and asses that remained alive after the massacre, sent an evil spirit into Saul. One cannot be wholly sure that David, a mere shepherd lad, was entirely aware of the martial background and the insufficiency of slaughter that prompted such heavy retribution to be visited by God upon Saul, but it is certain that Browning was. It is against this background of divinely conceived and divinely ordered genocide that David's revelation must be seen. It is small wonder that before the revelation David necessarily saw God as a God of wrath and jealousy, a God who could be counted upon to be divinely distressed at the sight of a man who could love far more deeply then he himself, especially when God was provoked by disobedience in those he had commanded to perform an atrocity, a commonplace in the Old Testament. In short, David's gasp as he sees that God is a God of love, not of hate and jealously and blood—a veritable Moloch—is a revelation almost beyond the comprehension of the modern reader. It becomes clear that Browning's implied intent here is to repudiate the Old Testament concept of God and to replace hate with love. Browning was later to pursue the same theme, though by different means, in "Caliban upon Setebos," which is based on Psalm 50, in which God is threatening the children of Israel with instant dismemberment for their sins, which are faithfully listed, ending with the charge that they thought ". . . that I was altogether such an one as thyself." Caliban, unlike David, has no revelation which alters his vicious primitive view of God, but rather one which confirms his brutal views—for he sees God only in his own image.

The impact of "Saul" is seen in the shocking contrast between the Old Testament God and the vision of the new God of love. In one of the earliest examples of stream-of-consciousness, David sees what Browning spent his life looking for: evidence that God is not only a God of absolute power, but of absolute love as well: "Then the truth came upon me. No harp more—no song more! outbroke—."

His incoherence is the result of his vision of the Incarnation, the one example Browning found in history that God's love is infinite, or, as David discovers: ". . . all's love, yet all's law." Power is matched by love, an electrifying discovery when one recalls that Saul, whom David loves, was reduced to a pathetic, corpse-like wreck by the Old Testament God, who, David now sees in joy, is to give way to the God of love and compassion, incarnate in Christ.

When David says

> I but open my eyes,—and perfection, no more and no less,
> In the kind I imagined, full-fronts me, and God is seen God
> In the star, in the stone, in the flesh, in the soul and the clod,
> (ll. 248-50)

he is in no sense implying that he sees a world free of evil. Rather he simply implies that power and love are perfectly mated in the creation and that the plan of life is therefore perfect, and it is perfect because it is a challenge to man to grow through struggle against evil, doubt, and frustration.

Saul recovers and wins his struggle, but David wins far more, for he sees into the infinite wisdom and purpose of the creation. David sees the dreadful error in man's fear of God, his worship of a deity wholly immoderate in his paranoid wrath, his fear that God should see man's love and happiness and be moved to anger. Rather, "Man's nothing-perfect" is in contrast to "God's all-complete" as a grain of sand is to the earth. Browning knew that everywhere the prevailing sickness in religion lies in fear, the fear of Caliban in contemplating the monstrous Setebos, the Calvinistic fear of being born to damnation, indeed the belief in hell itself, which Browning knew was incompatible with the concept of a loving God. "Saul" is a repudiation not only of the Old Testament God as seen in Saul's day but, more importantly, as seen in Browning's day, when the fundamentalists, both in and out of the Browning Societies, admired "Saul" as among the greatest of literary treasures without for a moment being aware that they themselves were the subject—or the object—of the poem.

Once having discovered that God's love is absolute, David immediately makes the giant leap: absolute love must not end with this life, for if it were to do so it would not be absolute. The "nothing-perfect" of life and man's struggle toward God's all-perfect, wherein man is tested and judged, demand a reward following the probation of life, if life is to have meaning. To suffer and to die without judgment and without compensation is cruel and meaningless. David sees that after the trials of life, man must "find himself set/ Clear and safe in new light and new life":

—a new harmony yet
To be run, and continued, and ended—who knows?—or endure!
The man taught enough, by life's dream, of the rest to make sure;
By the pain-throb, triumphantly winning intensified bliss,
And the next world's reward and repose, by the struggles in this.
(ll. 282-86)

David, speaking Browning's lifelong view of the life to come, sees eternity not as a time of rest and static fulfillment, but of striving and illimitable growth, for only in development did Browning see meaning and joy. The "reward and repose" David sees in the next life are not by any means stagnation—of all concepts the most alien to Browning—but are the growth and fulfillment which bring peace of soul and which come only through striving and progress toward a goal, not in ultimate attainment:

—'tis not what man Does which exalts him, but what man Would do!
(l. 295)

Only in eternal growth toward God and his infinite love can "love fill infinitude wholly"—a process by which the divine plan attains perfection. In the most anthropomorphic lines in all of Browning, David sees God in the very likeness of man; indeed, in the moment of rapturous love for Saul he sees God in the image of his own love:

> "O Saul, it shall be
> A Face like my face that receives thee; a Man like to me,
> Thou shalt love and be loved by, forever: a Hand like this hand
> Shall throw open the gates of new life to thee!
> See the Christ stand!"
>
> (ll. 309-13)

Stanza XIX is dramatically the most significant part of the poem, although it stands in relationship to the rest as an epilogue. It seems apparent that Browning included it for one particular reason: to oppose the notion, widespread in the century, that Christianity, whatever its virtues, robbed life of magic and myth and dreams. Throughout the century there runs a keening lament for the early simpler world in which man could find in brake and bush nymphs, dryads, and oreads, and the rainbow was a magic arch in eyes yet wide with wonder. The theme, running from Coleridge and Keats through Tennyson, Swinburne, and Arnold, appears only once in Browning's verse—in *Pauline*, his earliest published poem in which the retreat to myth and bucolic forests attracts the young romantic poet from the bustling world of reality. Tennyson's "Timbuctoo' and "The Hesperides" and "The Kraken" are fitting expressions of Tennyson's warning to the world that at all costs the color and the texture of man's dreams must not die, and the golden apple of the Hesperides must be guarded vigilantly lest it be stolen away—by science, by religion, or by the blandishments of the world. Swinburne's later shrill denunciations of Christianity in the "Hymn to Proserpine" best express the weary defeatist theme that Browning deplored.

David finds the night peopled by a new and clamorous mythology, far more powerfully conceived and vital than the pagan crew of old. It is significant that David's vision of the new world includes a multiplicity of witnesses, cohorts, angels, and demons—not a pallid company—surrendering no plume to the creatures of Greek myth.

He feels no fear, for through the tumultuous night he is concious of a hand guiding him, the same hand which Browning later felt upon his shoulder that memorable day when he discovered in San Lorenzo Square an Old Yellow Book, which he felt impelled to buy.

The dawn brings to David and the world a new peace, seen and felt in all things, for all things "felt the new law." The poem concludes in a vein of apparent pantheism in which flower, animal, snake, tree, and brook in a great harmony speak for all creation in affirmation of the truth of the revelation:

"E'en so, it is so!"

SUGGESTED READINGS

Bevington, Merle M., "Browning and Wordsworth: The Argument for Immortality in 'Saul,'" *Victorian Newsletter*, No. 20 (1961), 19-21.

Charlton, H. B., "Browning as Poet of Religion," *Bulletin of the John Rylands Library*, XXVII (1942-43), 291-98.
See the discussion of "Saul," included in this valuable essay.

Hellstrom, Ward, "Time and Type in Browning's *Saul*," *English Literary History*, XXXIII (1966), 370-89.
"Readers of Browning have long recognized that the 'doctrine of the imperfect' is a central concern in much of Browning's poetry. As applied to the individual, the doctrine asserts that the failure in this imperfect life promises success in the perfect life to come. . . . Commentators on Browning have not associated this doctrine with a similar doctrine which pervades traditional Christianity. It is there applied to historic man, rather than to the individual man, and constitutes a theory of history. This Christian theory of history and its attendant tradition of typology, I believe, provided Browning with the context in which the images of *Saul* become unified" (p. 370). Hellstrom attempts to show that in the poem Browning "sees both David and Saul as types of Christ. . . . It is Browning's recognition of vertical time—a conception of time fundamental to typology and perhaps best expressed through typology—which structures the poem and welds the imagery into an organic whole" (pp. 375-88).

McPeek, James A. S., "The Shaping of 'Saul,'" *Journal of English and Germanic Philology*, XLIV (1945), 360-66.
Indicates the influence on "Saul" of Thomas Wyatt's "Seven Penitential Psalms."

Shaw, W. David, "The Analogical Argument of Browning's 'Saul,'" *Victorian Poetry*, II (1964), 277-82.
Disagrees with Roma King, Jr.,'s essay in *The Bow and the Lyre*. Shaw maintains that if the poet's theology were as vague and amorphous as King says it is, the readers during the past hundred years would not have been so much moved by the poem: "To defend the Word of God against reason of man is not the sentimental vagary of an 'emotional agnosticism' peculiar to Tennyson or Browning, but a defense of imaginative interpretation which goes back through Blake to the Cambridge Platonists" (p. 280). Shaw believes that in "Saul," more than in any other of Browning's poems, we experience the thrill of seeing the "poet, like his speaker, soar magnificently to the 'pure white light'" (p. 281).

———, *The Dialetical Temper: The Rhetorical Art of Robert Browning* (Ithaca, N.Y., 1968), 221-33.
A stimulating examination of "Saul." Disagrees in part with Roma King, Jr.,'s conclusion in *The Bow and the Lyre*.

10

"Fra Lippo Lippi"

"Fra Lippo Lippi" is Browning's most Chaucerian dramatic monologue. It is a mightly pulse, redolent of life and laughter and sorrow, a treasure house of vitality. Fra Lippo would have fittingly made the thirtieth pilgrim on the journey to Canterbury, and great would have been the merriment.

I do not see Fra Lippo as the neurotic, twisted soul that today he is discovered to be. He is a normally complex character, but he is not unduly introspective and complicated, certainly not guilt ridden, sickly, or neurotic. The mark of the man is an extraordinary extroversion and vitality and impetuosity, characteristics not readily consonant with the picture we see of him in Roma King, Jr.'s *The Bow and the Lyre*. King interprets the whole speech of Lippo as a more or less frightened and desperate monologue designed to persuade the watch to let him go:

> Lippo is obliged to defend himself in an argument which is both an honest attempt toward a spiritual and artistic synthesis and a rationalization for his shortcomings.[1]

If this is so then the whole speech is a defense, a contrived, utilitarian, somewhat fearful attempt to win exculpation at any price, along with self-justification, and the implications are disastrous to the whole spirit of the poem. If one thing is essential in understanding the man, it is precisely that Lippo is not "forced" to make this speech at all, and certainly he is not forced to make it out of fear or self-doubt. Rather—after the initial flurry of the capture—it is the watch, the police, who are on the defensive and who experience fear of their captive, which diminishes as Lippo's humanity and kindliness become increasingly apparent. Lippo's monologue is given for the simple reason that he does not want his night of frolic and human camaraderie to end, forcing him back to austerity and endless painting of saints. He wants to talk with human beings who have

1. Roma A. King, Jr., *The Bow and the Lyre* (Ann Arbor, Mich., 1957), p. 33.

seen the world and known its delights and sufferings. The prior and his anemic followers live by the book, not by life, and Lippo, who is moderately drunk, is in the talkative, autobiographical mood of a man who has sought refuge from a termagant wife in the consolation of the bottle in the nearest pub. Every bartender knows his story and his need to tell it, for it is a hunger and a release.

As usual, Browning begins his dramatic monologue *in medias res*. Lippo is caught by the police as he leaves the red-light district, after an evening of lustful and bibulous carouse. The police—it being after midnight—are more than usually zealous in capturing victims who arouse their suspicions, and a monk, at such an hour and in such a place, arouses their suspicions very much indeed. They seize him with the callous roughness that not infrequently is the compensation for inadequate pay, especially if they are men of brutal inclination. They do not take him by the arm, but rather seize him by the throat and clap their torches to his face in a manner truly offensive to the monk, who, for a moment, *is* frightened, more by their immediate violence than by their threat of arrest. He has been out on the town many times before and he has studied men with a fidelity to detail that has often stood him in good stead. He is no monastic innocent who in desperation breaks bonds and when caught whimpers in terror. He is a man of the world, although a monk, and his *savoir faire* is that of a student of human nature, especially among such rough and bawdy types as have him in tow. He knows exactly what to say and what to do—if only they will remove their fingers from his windpipe and let him speak.

He knows enough not to deny his guilt. He has been fairly caught, and these brutal men look only for an excuse to brutalize. He openly confesses his amorous adventures, and in response to their query announces that the Carmine is his cloister, and he moreover invites them to check up on his story. The watch are suitably impressed, and Lippo, sensing his advantage, says, "Aha, you know your betters!"

> Then, you'll take
> Your hand away that's fiddling on my throat,
> And please to know me likewise.
>
> (ll. 12-14)

The watch, somewhat hesitantly, ask who he is, and Lippo toys with them, good humoredly punishing them for their violence and insolence:

> Who am I?
> Why, one, sir, who is lodging with a friend
> Three streets off—he's a certain . . . how d'ye call?
> Master—a . . . Cosimo of the Medici,
> I' the house that caps the corner. Boh! you were best!

> Remember and tell me, the day you're hanged,
> How you affected such a gullet's-gripe!
>
> (ll. 14-20)

His affected inability to recall the name of the great man who is his patron and protector is to heighten the effect of its sudden revelation. If one were apprehended in Washington, D.C., late at night under suspicious circumstances, he, like Lippo, would enjoy the event if in truth he could inform the arresting police that he was the special guest of a certain man . . . living in a large White House on Pennsylvania Avenue. The triumphal exclamation "Boh! you were best!"—meaning that you are well advised to take your hand from my throat and stand at attention respectfully—sets the tone for the remainder of the poem. From this point on, Lippo is in charge, and it is he who has the watch in tow.

Lippo, from this moment on, is in high spirits and is in absolute command. The night air, the wine, and the excitement have heightened his zest, sharpened his appetite for life, and inflamed his desire for human relationships outside the cloister. The faces of the watch, brutal and earthy, fascinate him. He wants to talk with these men and to remark their ruined faces and every line and mark of sin and weakness and nobility—if any—that he finds thereon. For good reasons Lippo was the first painter to use secular portraits in religious paintings. The watch are life on a small scale, and Lippo, the lover of life, is delighted. In the weary weeks to come, when he is painting "saints and saints and saints again" for the great man he can recall this pulsating moment in life and paint from memory the faces, so unlike the pale masks that silently glide down the dim halls of the monastery, shut off from life by grim walls.

His first duty, after suitably apprising the watch of his power and position, is to chide them, with the gentle indulgence reserved for the powerful, for their unnecessary brutality:

> But you, sir, it concerns you that your knaves
> Pick up a manner nor discredit you. . . .
>
> (ll. 21-22)

There is no fear, certainly, seen in these lines, and no anger. Lippo is having too much fun for either, and he is in no more mood for passing severe moral judgments than was Chaucer at the Tabard Inn:

> He's Judas to a tittle, that man is!
> Just such a face! Why, sir, you make amends.
> Lord, I'm not angry! Bid your hangdogs go
> Drink out this quarter-florin to the health
> Of the munificent House that harbors me
> (And many more beside, lads! more beside!)

And all's come square again. I'd like his face—
His, elbowing on his comrade in the door
With the pike and lantern,—for the slave that holds
John Baptist's head a-dangle by the hair
With one hand ("Look you, now," as who should say)
And his weapon in the other, yet unwiped!

(ll. 25-36)

If Lippo is alleged to be motivated by fear of arrest, how is one to explain his opprobrious treatment of the watch? Does a man who is wholly devoted to currying favor with the police pause in his defense to note aloud that one of the arresting officials looks like Judas and that his companion might pose for a murderer of classical brutality? If the watch are genuinely menacing, why do they accept his insults without reaction of any kind? Nothing in the poem supports the interpretation that Lippo is fearful. He has nothing to fear; but the watch do—or fancy that they do. Lippo is not interested in pressing his advantage, for he wants not fear from them but talk. He wants to "sit and set things straight now, hip to haunch," and it is clear that his wish is a command. They sit, and Lippo in high spirits tells of his escapade.

Throughout Lippo's recital, Browning manipulates the rhythm and pace of the lines to fit the mood. When Lippo tells how he leaned out of the window, heard the song and the titter of women, and fashioned his rope ladder of "Curtain and counterpane and coverlet," as a means of escape to life, the lines are rapid and breathless with excitement:

Round they went.
Scarce had they turned the corner when a titter
Like the skipping of rabbits by moonlight,—three slim shapes,
And a face that looked up . . . zooks, sir, flesh and blood,
That's all I'm made of! Into shreds it went,
Curtain and counterpane and coverlet,
All the bed-furniture—a dozen knots,
There was a ladder!

(ll. 57-64)

When he tells of his return from the night of love and wine—just before the watch seize him—his language slows to the pace of a funeral procession:

And so as I was stealing back again
To get to bed and have a bit of sleep
Ere I rise up to-morrow and go work
On Jerome knocking at his poor old breast

With his great round stone to subdue the flesh,
You snap me of the sudden.

(ll. 70-75)

One of the finest uses of irony in Browning is the picture of Lippo throwing down his brush in the middle of painting old Jerome, the ascetic saint, and fleeing with breakneck speed after women of the streets—and, later, of Lippo's return with leaden steps to pick up the brush and depict the upraised stone, the bruised breast, the saintly uplifted eyes. The irony is not unconscious: Lippo has a keen sense of humor, and the key to his humor is irony and incongruous juxtaposition. It is entirely unbelievable that a man so gifted with the ironic sense—which in essence is a gift of perspective—could be the divided, tormented, guilt-ridden character that he is often pictured as being. The best defense against such a state is precisely the kind of humor and irony that Lippo possesses beyond all other characters in Browning. The shocking juxtaposition of old Jerome, an absurd figure with his great round stone upraised to subdue lust, with Lippo risking his neck to satisfy his own lust is not lost on the erring painter, whose manner is a composite of mock repentance and bubbling humor, not guilt or fear. Tomorrow he may go to confession, but tonight is still tonight. Lippo knows that his conduct would appear irredeemably scandalous to the prior, but at the same time he knows that the prior has renounced half of life and its delights in pursuit of his crippling self-denial. The essential difference between the two men, Lippo knows, is that he is alive and joyous amid the treasures of earth's beauty, but the prior is sick with renunciation and gray with unfulfillment. Lippo is by no means an abandoned profligate. He is not one to scorn the spirit and religious life of his fellow monks. What he scorns is their denial of life and their state of neurotic imbalance which are the bitter fruits of their vows.

It is certain that a man as sensitive to the nuances of life as Lippo has some pangs of conscience, some doubt, at times, about his conduct. He is alive, wonderfully alive, and to be alive is to have wonder and doubt and unceasing groping toward truth. This is at the heart of all of Browning's thinking, it should be remembered, and of Lippo's as well. He objects to the closed mind of the prior. Men like the prior have no doubts; they are placidly content, untempted by life, and in consequence they are half men, dead to the lights and colors and shades of life. To be alive is to be tempted, and it must be confessed that Lippo all too often routs temptation by the ready expedient of giving in to it, but there is little doubt that Lippo would defend his human frailty on the ground that he does not always fail and even failure is an earnest that he is alive to life and its test.

Roma King, Jr.'s statement that Lippo's speech is, at least in part, a rationalization of his failure is surprising:

> Though always coherent, the sentences in the earlier part are less consciously formulated than those in which he later tries to express his theory of art, or, still later, those in which he rationalizes his failure.[2]

It seems to me that Lippo is no more rationalizing his failure than is the Wife of Bath, with whom he bears some comparison. Browning's concept of success may be seen in Caponsacchi's speech to the court and in "How It Strikes a Contemporary." The emphasis is always on wholeness, not on self-denial. Inevitably the successful man is enraptured by the wonder of life in all its parts:

> He walked and tapped the pavement with his cane,
> Scenting the world, looking it full in face.

No better description of Lippo might be found than this description of what Browning thought a vitally alive poet must be. Lippo is earthy, sensually alive, but yet sensitive, artistic, and in the truest sense spiritual, without being dogmatic or negative. The prior would certainly condemn in the strongest terms Lippo's night of carouse and his rationale for it, his monkish lips severely pursed and his shaven head wagging in judgment. Lippo most probably would judge the prior with greater charity, for he knows life and its bewildering diversity.

If one assumes that Lippo's monologue is a cover for or conveyance of guilt and failure, an entirely different picture emerges, one which strips the poem of its Chaucerian tone, its zest for life, and much of its humor. The poem loses its whole character as Lippo loses his.

When the monk flips a quarter-florin to the watch to drink the health of the munificent house that harbors him (he is careful to remind the watch from time to time of the power he can call upon in time of need), he is not bribing them. He is in no need of bribing anyone. He has the upper hand and feels obliged, in human sympathy, to allay their fears of the retribution they have imagined may be their lot, and he says, to make his gesture unmistakably clear, "Lord, I'm not angry!" The coin is given in simple good spirits to human beings no longer menacing to him and, quite frankly, frightened of him.

After asking the watch whether they might have a piece of chalk or wood coal with which he might sketch their brutal but human faces—an extravagantly unwise thing to say if one is fearful of arrest—Lippo confesses to them that he is indeed the painter of whom they say they have heard many a story. And once the introductions, as it were, are over he

2. Ibid., p. 39.

commands them to sit down and have a good talk, "hip to haunch." They are not reluctant, for the command is given in warmth of spirit and their fears subside:

> What, brother Lippo's doings, up and down
> You know them and they take you? like enough!
> (ll. 40-41)

What they have heard is that Lippo not infrequently breaks his sacred vows and behaves in a manner distressingly contrary to churchly ideals; but their faces reveal delight and approval. They are now currying favor with Lippo, and Lippo is delighted. He has seen "the proper twinkle" in their eyes, and he practically commands them to sit for the talk he wants to round the evening out. What he thirsts for is not clemency but simply warm human relationships and perhaps understanding—something he has not found in the monastery, and his spirit yearns for the human touch. This is why he tells his story of human frailty, for these men are gifted beyond all others with the frailty, natural and acquired, which should command understanding and sympathy as well.

Lippo's account of his flight from the Medici Palace is both a confession and an examination of life and its demands. It is carnival time, and spring and love and romance are in the air, and he was three weeks shut within his mew, painting saints and saints and saints again until he could stand it no longer. The implication here is not that he objects either to saints or to the painting of saints—but that life offers more than this. When he says that he could not paint all night—a tongue-in-cheek detail, for one rarely paints by the light of flickering lamps—he merely means that he was girl watching from his window. It is not fresh air that prompts him to put his head out of the window, as he affirms, but rather the song of girls in carnival time.

Lippo's prologue to his short autobiography is a simple but confusing question, which has led to much critical misfortune: "Come, what am I a beast for?" Lippo is not in the throes of penitential confession, far from it. He is not admitting to depravity or viciousness, but rather to his kinship with the animal world. Lippo knows that life itself is the great gift of God, a gift that man must accept in joy, not guilt. Only through the flesh can the soul grow large. To deny one's body is to deny God's plan and to set in motion the medieval dualism so jealously perpetuated by the Church in its denial of the worth and dignity of man. All men are beasts, being formed of flesh and blood, and they are men because a spark disturbs their clay, not because they deny their kinship with the rest of life. The brief autobiography which Lippo's words introduce is as far removed from any taint of guilt as anything in literature. It is the fresh new world of Renaissance lust for life in its joyous denial of the Middle Ages. It is as redolent of life and joy and suffering as anything in the language, and it is wholly alive.

Lippo's racy account of his childhood is marked by a sinewy directness and economy. Anglo-Saxon monosyllables predominate and fall like hammer blows as the monk tells his story. I think it highly unlikely that the autobiography is a document which Lippo could swear to under oath. Just how much is fact and how much invention one cannot determine, but the recital is essentially true, if not to fact, to Lippo's recollection of fact:

> I was a baby when my mother died
> And father died and left me in the street.
> I starved there, God knows how, a year or two
> On fig-skins, melon-parings, rinds and shucks,
> Refuse and rubbish.
>
> (ll. 81-85)

Twenty lines later his period of starvation has substantially lengthened:

> But, mind you, when a boy starves in the streets
> Eight years together, as my fortune was,
> Watching folk's faces to know who will fling
> The bit of half-stripped grape-bunch he desires,
> And who will curse or kick him for his pains. . . .
>
> (ll. 112-16)

When Aunt Lapaccia, to whom he was entrusted after the death of his parents, found him doubled up in the street from hunger, she took him to the Convent of the Carmelites. Lippo's first encounter with the monks is rich with irony:

> "So, boy, you're minded," quoth the good fat father
> Wiping his own mouth, 't was refection-time,—
> "To quit this very miserable world?
> Will you renounce" . . . "the mouthful of bread?" thought I;
> By no means! Brief, they made a monk of me;
> I did renounce the world, its pride and greed,
> Palace, farm, villa, shop and banking-house,
> Trash, such as these poor devils of Medici
> Have given their hearts to—all at eight years old.
>
> (ll. 93-101)

The fat father, wiping his fat mouth while asking the starving boy to renounce the world—at the age of eight—is a blood brother to Chaucer's monk. The great belly, the vast wrinkles on the holy neck, the red cheeks shiny from the fat of the leg of chicken or pheasant clutched in the pudgy hand did not escape Lippo's notice, nor did the irony. But if there was irony, there was also chicken, and Lippo was starving. The oath he took was not for nothing. The good bellyful, the warm serge, the encircling rope were the visible signs of security and physical well-being, and Lippo places a high premium on both.

The monks' attempt to teach Lippo Latin was doomed from the start. Lippo, like Browning, was not formally educated, and both placed great store on experience and life. The sixty lines in which Lippo extols the virtues of starving in the streets as a means of refining the soul's and senses' acuteness to the nuances of life are unique. It must not be forgotten that Lippo's tough and sinewy speech is given to men peculiarly qualified to understand the hunger, the hardships, and the despair he talks of, if not the whole of his account of the benefits that must accrue, but it is safe to assume that they nod in agreement:

> Why, soul and sense of him grow sharp alike,
> He learns the look of things, and none the less
> For admonition from the hunger-pinch.
> (ll. 124-26)

His speech grows more rapid and excited as he waxes to the theme of his painful schooling in the streets, which honed his powers of observation. He learned to look at faces and read the soul therein—the first and the last lesson in survival in the streets. It is true that Browning never starved in the streets, but he, like Lippo, never wearied of studying the faces and the souls of all whom he met. This part of the monk's harangue is as much a part of Browning's credo as Lippo's more formal strictures on art later on.

The memories those days of hunger and privation crammed into his head are almost uniformly of sordid, vicious, petty, mean, murderous, pitiable events and people. These he treasured up and later painted with faithful fidelity, passionately in love with life the while. The monks, when shown his murals on the cloister wall, "praised loud/ Till checked, taught what to see and what not to see. . . ." Unconsciously these "simple bodies," until checked by their "betters," judged the murals by the touchstone of art: fidelity to life:

> "That's the very man!
> Look at the boy who stoops to pat the dog!
> That woman's like the Prior's niece who comes
> To care about his asthma: it's the life!"
> (ll. 168-71)

The prior "stopped all that in no time." The monks, being trained only in obedience, surrendered their private judgment in this as in all other matters and promptly saw that to say of a work of art "it's the life!" is not to praise but to detect its sin and corruption, life being a pretty dirty business, to be suitably deplored, not painted. The prior wants "no more body than shows soul," for he hates life and wants to keep it at bay. Why, he asks, should Lippo "put all thoughts of praise out of our head/ With wonder at lines, colors, and what not?" And Lippo replies:

> Now, is that sense, I ask?
> A fine way to paint soul, by painting body
> So ill, the eye can't stop there, must go further
> And can't fare worse!
>
> (ll. 199-201)

The prior wants stereotypes: "never mind the legs and arms!" The function of painting, in his opinion, is to remind people to pray, to make them forget life, to "Make them forget there's such a thing as flesh."

Lippo's comment

> You should not take a fellow eight years old
> And make him swear to never kiss the girls

is not so much rebellion against monastic vows as it is a sad, philosophical objection to the denial of life that marks the Church and to the unfair means employed to seduce a small starving boy to renounce life for a piece of bread. Lippo's whole evening is one protracted rebellion. His words are a calm, measured protest against the folly and the dishonesty and the poverty of men like the prior, who are more to be pitied than scorned, for they have never lived. Lippo knows that life is greater than art or religion either, for it embraces both, not the other way around, and his vows, in consequence, rest lightly upon him:

> I'm my own master, paint now as I please—
> Having a friend, you see, in the Corner-house!
> Lord, it's fast holding by the rings in front—
> Those great rings serve more purposes than just
> To plant a flag in, or tie up a horse!
>
> (ll. 226-30)

Lippo is waggishly implying that when he returns home from a bibulous night of revelry, the hitching posts serve as guide posts and supports when the wine has dominion.

The monks respond to his rebellion by never failing to point out that he will not form a third with Angelico and Lorenzo, and Lippo, with mock sadness, replies:

> . . . bless us, they must know!
> Don't you think they're the likeliest to know,
> They with their Latin?
>
> (ll. 240-42)

Lippo is about as honest as it is possible for a man to be, and he is making a plea for honesty in others. Too many people "tell too many lies" and hurt themselves thereby. They waste their lives in pursuing things they detest, and he rejects both the hypocrisy and the waste of man's life:

> For me, I think I speak as I was taught;
> I always see the garden and God there
> A-making man's wife: and, my lesson learned,
> The value and significance of flesh,
> I can't unlearn ten minutes afterwards.
>
> (ll. 265-69)

Again, immediately after these lines, Lippo in fun and sham repentance says, "You understand me: I'm a beast, I know." It should be noted that he has just enlisted God as his co-partner in his set of values, and his teacher, as well. If he is wrong in setting great store on the flesh, who was his teacher? Who but God, who made man's wife and taught all men the joy in life and the wonder and the power? And who tries to make him "unlearn ten minutes afterwards"? The prior and all men like him who deny the value of life and the significance of flesh in God's plan. It is doubtful that the police fully understand the shades of meaning Lippo intends, but it makes little difference. Living largely on the level of the flesh, as they undoubtedly do, they still are not likely to comprehend the painter's moral defense of the value of the flesh as the co-partner of soul, the organ through which soul finds selfhood and joy, but they find Lippo's values entirely agreeable and inspiriting.

If the words he speaks just before he says "I'm a beast" do not make his intent clear, the words which follow must do so. He launches into an account of Hulking Tom, the young apprentice who is a younger Lippo, dedicated to the wonder of life and the worth of the flesh: "He picks my practice up—he'll paint apace,/ I hope so—though I never live so long,/ I know what's sure to follow." Tom does not mind the monks any more than Lippo does, and furthermore he too "lets no atom drop"—the hallmark of the vital, alive artist. Lippo's account of Tom is totally approving and not without a sense of pride in the shaping of his artistic heir. He is Lippo's immortality—"though I never live so long."

The words which follow are Browning's clearest and most vigorous defense of God's plan in the creation of beauty:

> . . . you've seen the world
> —The beauty and the wonder and the power
> The shapes of things, their colors, lights and shades,
> Changes, surprises,—and God made it all!
>
> (ll. 282-85)

Lippo is in love with life, not with part of life but with all of it. In painting God's works, one should count it a crime "to let a truth slip"—and his night on the town is to be counted among the pursuits of truth.

In mock repentance Lippo pleads the excuse of the night air which has gone to his "unaccustomed head like Chianti wine":

> —That is—you'll not mistake an idle word
> Spoke in a huff by a poor monk, God wot,
> Tasting the air this spicy night which turns
> The unaccustomed head like Chianti wine!
> Oh, the church knows! don't misreport me, now!
> (ll. 336-40)

The idle word to which he refers is his denunciation of the monks for their belief that he has done a splendid thing in painting a fresco of Saint Laurence in such a manner that the people coming to prayer have in anger scratched and poked the paint off the faces of the slaves in attendance at the saint's roasting. According to one of Lippo's brother monks, "Your painting serves its purpose!" and Lippo adds, "Hang the fools!"

Immediately after this quasi-bitter denunciation of the ecclesiastical mentality which would yoke art to morality, Lippo makes a mock-serious apology for his night on the town. The irreverent tone he has just used in judgment of his peers supplies the clue to the tone of his ironic apology and, more important, to his "plot to make amends" by painting a great and comprehensive religious painting, the great *Coronation of the Virgin*, later to hang in the Belle Arti in Florence. The whole thrust of his foregoing commentary on art has been to establish his contempt for traditional religious painting and for the stunted artistic mentality which fails to revere the natural and the real in life, epitomized in Fra Angelico and Lorenzo Monaco, who followed conventional rules in painting. Lippo is not by any means condemning the paintings of such men as worthless, but rather as limited, circumscribed, and bound to a narrow view of life. Lippo, according to Browning, is the first of the great realists in painting who find their inspiration in actual life, here and now. Lippo may be considered a Renaissance Browning, and this loose identification should be kept in mind in assessing Lippo's purpose in discussing the great painting he plans—or plots—to make amends. No one who is genuinely repentant "plots" to make amends. Lippo is going to show the prior and all brothers—all his critics who look over his shoulder as he paints and shake their heads in grave disapproval—that he can equal and outdo both Brother Angelico and Brother Lorenzo, if he has a mind to. He writhes in annoyance when pronounced inferior to them:

"It's art's decline, my son!
You're not of the true painters, great and old;
Brother Angelico's the man, you'll find;
Brother Lorenzo stands his single peer:
Fag on at flesh, you'll never make the third!"
(ll. 233-37)

Lippo is going to make them eat their words by painting a picture in the established tradition which will prove that he is in fact the third with his vaunted rivals, that to "Fag on at flesh" in no way is inimical to his genius, and that he has surpassed in execution and comprehensive detail all religious pictures extant. To achieve these three objectives, he is willing to slave for six months in the style he deplores: the stylized, bloodless, representation of celestial and pious figures. He will show them a thing or two. He will pack more figures with whiter faces amid more stock ecclesiastical devices than Lorenzo ever dreamed of putting onto one canvas, and, travesty though it will be, it will also be a great painting, one that will prove to those "with their Latin" that he is the peer of the mighty pair of painters judged to be peerless:

It's natural a poor monk out of bounds
Should have his apt word to excuse himself:
And hearken how I plot to make amends.
I have bethought me: I shall paint a piece
. . . There's for you! Give me six months, then go, see
Something in Sant' Ambroglio's! Bless the nuns!
They want a cast o' my office. I shall paint
God in the midst, Madonna and her babe,
Ringed by a bowery flowery angel-brood,
Lilies and vestments and white faces, sweet
As puff on puff of grated orris-root
When ladies crowd to Church at midsummer.
And then i' the front, of course a saint or two. . . .
(ll. 341-53)

Lippo is in great good humor—and still feeling the effects of the night and the wine. The Lippo of this poem is a creation of Browning, as much as Macbeth is Shakespeare's, and the picture Lippo describes is not the same as the masterpiece that is admired today in Florence. Indeed, there are reasons to doubt that Lippo kept to his bibulous resolution to paint a religious picture to end all religious pictures, packing the work with a multitude of heterogeneous characters as a near-parody of stock religious paintings. All that is certain is that at this time, under these circumstances, he is resolved to play this hearty joke and at the same time win the fame which he does not scorn in his heart. When his hand was in, month after month, undoubtedly his love of art, religious or not, triumphed over his sense of tomfoolery. What is important is not the picture hanging in Florence, but his words about the picture he plans to paint.

Lippo plans to include (in addition to God, Madonna and babe, fifty angels, St. John, and St. Ambrose) Job, "The man of Uz (and Us without the z,/ Painters who need his patience)." Such an incongruous inclusion perfectly contradicts the notion that Lippo is contrite and repentant. As if to make absolutely clear which painter is in especial need of patience, who shall appear down in a corner but Lippo himself?

> I, in this presence, this pure company!
> Where's a hole, where's a corner for escape?
> Then steps a sweet angelic slip of a thing
> Forward, puts out a soft palm—"Not so fast!"
> —Addresses the celestial presence, "nay—
> He made you and devised you, after all,
> Though he's none of you!"
>
> (ll. 368-74)

Is this the proper mood of penance? To paint a *reductio ad absurdum*, high jinks played upon his critics who carp at him for being insufficiently reverential of saints and angels and lilies? The ultimate joke is to paint himself in his "old serge gown and rope that goes all round" in this holy presence, as if it had all been a mistake: "I, caught up with my monk's-things by mistake. . . ." The figure in the corner of the painting which Browning and others have thought to be Lippo is in reality the very Reverend Francesco Maringhi, who commissioned the picture for the altar of the church associated with the Benedictine nunnery of Sant' Ambroglio. The Latin inscription in the picture, *Iste perfecit opus* ("This one brought the work to completion") applies as well to Canon Maringhi as to Lippo, but it suited Browning's purpose to assume that the figure was that of the painter, for the most irreverent and incongruous joke of all depends on this identification. Still pretending that his presence in the painting was an inexplicable mistake, Lippo in mock seriousness supposes that he is frantically seeking escape from the angelic company, among whom his presence is an affront: "Where's a hole, where's a corner for escape?" He is saved not by a saint or an angel but by a "sweet angelic slip of a thing," who is commonly identified with his divine mistress, but who seems to have sufficient charms to suggest to the monk an earthly amour, involving a close call under embarrassing circumstances, not unlike those in the picture:

> Under the cover of a hundred wings
> Thrown like a spread of kirtles when you're gay

And play hot cockles, all the doors being shut,
Till, wholly unexpected, in there pops
The hothead husband!

(ll. 379-83)

It is an error ruinous in its consequences to see in this scene evidence of Lippo's genuine penance or his sudden reverence for pious, pure saints, or religious paintings. King finds that the picture "becomes a kind of penitential office through which Lippo is cleansed (his particular sin is that he has reduced woman to a mere animal) and made a part of the holy communion."[3] I find no evidence that he has reduced woman to the status of a mere animal. Certainly the young slip of a thing he fancies in the picture does not regard him so; rather she addresses the entire heavenly company in his stout defense and seems oblivious of his reputation with women.

The conclusion, the most Shakespearean in Browning, is deliciously subtle in its humor:

Go, six months hence!
Your hand, sir, and good-bye: no light, no lights!
The street's hushed, and I know my own way back,
Don't fear me! There's the gray beginning. Zooks!

(ll. 389-92)

His words, "Don't fear me!" perfectly contradict the belief that Lippo has been arguing his case in fear. He feels constrained to put *their* minds at rest, and it will be noted that he does not beg their leave to go or bandy words about whether the charge is dropped. There has been no charge or thought of a charge since line eighteen. He has been in perfect mastery of the night's episode. He has dominated the watch, honestly confessed his own weaknesses, astonished them with his reading of life, and, finally, he dismisses them imperiously as the gray dawn appears. They in turn, make all speed to the nearest tavern to drink out the quarter-florin to the munificent house that harbors their night's strange guest.

SUGGESTED READINGS

Irvine, William, "Four Monologues in Browning's *Men and Women*," *Victorian Poetry*, II (1964), 155-64.
Finds that the "whoring monk," who appears in an unsympathetic light at the beginning of the poem, in the end is found to be less guilty than the respectable citizens who have "exploited him." Mr. Irvine argues

3. Ibid., p. 50.

that in Lippo may be seen the Victorian writer and in the Medici and the hypocritical prior may be seen the wealthy, respectable members of society who expected men of letters to pay "lip service for their own hypocrisy" (p. 157).

"With the hypocrisy of pretending to live by too lofty a code, Lippo contrasts the sincerity of responding joyously to the world and one's own biology. The opposition is really pointed. To deny one's impulses, to do what most people expect, is to tell a lie. 'As it is,/ You tell too many lies, and hurt yourself' " (pp. 260-61).

Kendall, J. L., "Lippo's Vision," *Victorian Newsletter*, No. 18 (1960), 18-21.

Litzinger, Boyd A., "Incident as Microcosm: The Prior's Niece in 'Fra Lippo Lippi,' " *College English*, XXII (1961), 409-10.

Makes the point that the prior's "niece" is in reality his mistress, in much the same fashion as the bishop who orders his tomb at Saint Praxed's has "nephews," who are in reality his sons. The terms are transparent euphemisms used to preserve appearances. The importance of the fact is that "its acceptance prejudices us against the Prior and his theory of 'proper' art, and it goes far towards casting a more sympathetic light upon Fra Lippo, who is unable to conceal his strayings as cleverly" (p. 409).

Omans, Glen, "Browning's 'Fra Lippo Lippi,' A Transcendentalist Monk," *Victorian Poetry*, VII (1969), 129-45.

In his abstract, Omans says: "The concept is basically that of Kantian transcendentalism, which Browning acquired through his friendship with Carlyle. The transcendentalist views the material world (flesh) as a symbolic projection of a supersensuous world of immutable ideas (soul). Yet these ideas are perceivable only through their material symbols. Thus, it is only by means of an accurate portrayal of the flesh that the artist, Lippo, is able to suggest the true value of soul. By so doing, Lippo elevates himself toward soul or God, and, in turn, elevates other less gifted persons by sharpening, first, their awareness of the world of physical symbols and so leading them to a glimpse of the ideas themselves" (p. 129).

Oman's perceptive argument, then, is that Lippo seeks to discover and thus to reveal to others the world of permanent and immutable ideas, or soul, which lies behind the world of phenomena and which is revealed symbolically only through the world of phenomena to man, who lives as part of that world.

Phelps, William Lyon, *Robert Browning*, new ed. (Indianapolis, 1932), pp. 203-06.

Professor Phelps sees in the inclusion of Lippo in his old clothes down in the corner of *The Coronation of the Virgin* evidence of Lippo's impudent, good-humored practical joke. The picture "is a representation of the painter's whole nature, half genius, half mucker—the painting is a glory of form and color, and then in the corner the artist had the assurance to place himself in his monk's dress among the saints and angels, where he looks as much out of place as a Bowery Boy in a Fifth Avenue drawing-room. Not content with putting himself in the picture, he stuck a Latin tag on himself, which means, 'This fellow did the job.'

"Browning loves Fra Lippo Lippi, in spite of the man's impudence and debauchery; because the painter loved life, had a tremendous zest for it, and was not ashamed of his enthusiasm . . ." (p. 205).

Shaw, W. David, "Character and Philosophy in 'Fra Lippo Lippi,'" *Victorian Poetry*, II (1964), 127-32.

"The final picture of Fra Lippo as a blushing sensualist, hiding for very shame among the 'company' of the blest, is Browning's unobtrusive way of reminding us, especially after the monk's lofty discourse on the sacramental status of nature, that the interaction between flesh and spirit, personality and ideas, which is the very condition of his art, must not be suspended" (pp. 131-32). Shaw emphasizes the point that just as the monk cannot separate spirit and flesh, so the reader cannot separate the characters of Browning's poems from their ideas. "Fra Lippo Lippi" remains a triumphant example of the fusion in Browning's monologues of the character and the ideas which he embraces.

11

"A Toccata of Galuppi's"

"A Toccata of Galuppi's" is one of the most beautiful and moving poems in the Browning canon, and in subtlety one of his finest achievements. Browning was especially interested in the compositions of Baldassare Galuppi (1706-85), an Italian composer celebrated for his work in light opera and the toccata, a "touch-piece," a prelude or overture which touches upon moods, often of considerable gravity, in a gay or superficial manner. Galuppi, like the whole rococo school of eighteenth-century Italian musicians, had only a surface gaiety, which served to hide the sad undertone of his awareness that all in the end is vanity and dust. He knew that the gay life of frivolity was hollow and ephemeral, that the Venetian whirl of love and kisses and romance on the Grand Canal was but emptiness, the hectic flush on the cheek in the approach to death. He had no concept of immortality, and his sense of the passing of life's delights was as bitter in his mouth as it was in Cleon's. But if life is in the end a sad cheat, let life while it lasts be gay and joyous and full of song and kisses! This is the light, gay surface to the music, bearing in its deeper current a sober, sad undertone: *sic transit gloria mundi.* The sensitive listener is made to creep through every limb as he listens to Galuppi's "cold music" and hears the sad warning that all life is as ephemeral as that of the butterfly Venetians. A life devoted to truth, rationalism, and science will no more assure immunity to death than will the masques and balls of the Venetians —for all must die.

The basic theme in the poem is the search for values and meaning which are proof against time—man's most persistent search. Juxtaposed are scientific rationalism and sensuous hedonism, which are placed in a kind of counterpoint, as are the surface gaiety and the subsurface sadness in Galuppi's toccata. Galuppi reveals the hollowness of Venetian life, but the music is not a condemnation of Venetian life, or of rationalism either. Rather it is a melancholy musing on the emptiness and fleetingness and vanity of all life. Under the warmth and light and love, his toccata is indeed "cold music," for it is essentially about how all things must die.

In the poem a British scientist (whether or not he is a professional or a dilettante is not made clear and is really irrelevant) is listening to this toccata, under conditions that are left to the reader's imagination. It seems unlikely that the scientist is playing the music, for, except on the intellectual level, he has had little to do with music, love, gaiety, and the whole emotional life. He is the kind of man Matthew Arnold repeatedly warned would inherit the earth unless the ominous trend toward diminution of spirit, through unbridled rationalism, were reversed:

> But no, this heart will glow no more; thou art
> A living man no more, Empedocles!
> Nothing but a devouring flame of thought—
> But a naked, eternally restless mind!
> ("Empedocles on Etna," ll. 327-30)

The great warning of Arnold's "Empedocles on Etna" is that

> The brave impetuous heart yields everywhere
> To the subtle contriving head.
> (ll. 90-91)

The scientist is but half a man. He is a thinking machine, dead to love and romance (though not to art), who, like Empedocles, might lament:

> We had not lost our balance then nor grown
> Thought's slaves, and dead to every natural joy.
> (ll. 248-49)

This is essentially the problem of the scientist in "A Toccata of Galuppi's," with one exception: the scientist has spent his entire life in intellectual pursuits, to the exclusion of "every natural joy." He has *never* known the simple country joys, the light-hearted laughter of the whole personality. But, above all, he has not known love. He has experienced the aridity of soul which the Spirit in Tennyson's "Timbuctoo" predicts will shortly come upon the world when keen Discovery (science) robs man of his creative imagination and his capacity to dream and to live in simple-hearted joy.

At the beginning of the poem, the scientist is shocked to find through the vision Galuppi's music conveys to him that the Venetians—in the period of Italian decadence—led such butterfly lives of love-making, dancing, and frivolity. He takes the meaning of the toccata "with such a heavy mind," for he has been so steeped in science that he has been unaware that another side of life exists. He has not known the life of the Venetians, with its gaiety and romance and emptiness. He has never been out of England, but through the magic of the music, "it's as if I saw it all." He is both repelled and fascinated by a vision of the emotional life of which he has no experience. He finds it hard to believe that young people actually lived the life of sustained merrymaking, for he has improbably fancied that young people spent their time in intellectual pursuits, as he has:

Did young people take their pleasure when the sea was warm in May?
Balls and masks begun at midnight, burning ever to mid-day,
When they made up fresh adventures for the morrow, do you say?

Was a lady such a lady, cheeks so round and lips so red,—
On her neck the small face buoyant, like a bell-flower on its bed,
O'er the breast's superb abundance where a man might base his head?

The idea of basing his head on the superb abundance of a lady's breast is most disquieting to a man who has been warmed by nothing more human than a Bunsen burner, but it becomes clear that he is deeply shaken by the image, and his dead emotional life stirs within him.

In fancy he sees through the music the scene of two young lovers, masked for a ball, listening to Galuppi playing at the clavichord. They love music, but the moon is out, and on the Grand Canal a gondola and love await them:

Well, and it was graceful of them—they'd break talk off and afford
—She, to bite her mask's black velvet—he, to finger on his sword,
While you sat and played Toccatas, stately at the clavichord?

The lovers, too, hear (in the scientist's fancy) the thoughts conveyed by the music. In one of the most ingenious conceptions in Browning the several notes, chords, and dissonances speak and are heard:

What? Those lesser thirds so plaintive, sixths diminished, sigh on sigh,
Told them something? Those suspensions, those solutions—
    "Must we die?"
Those commiserating sevenths—"Life might last! we can
    but try!"

A "lesser third" (composed of a tone and a semitone) shows the key to be minor, whereas a "greater third" (composed of two whole tones) shows the key to be major. The "diminished sixths" are sixths possessing a semitone less than a minor sixth. A suspension ("Those suspensions, those solutions") is the stoppage of one or more of the parts of the music, while the others move on, producing a dissonance, which gives a melancholy effect, in the poem suggesting the possibility of death to the young lovers in Venice: "Must we die?" The "commiserating sevenths," less mournful and more pleasing, suggest more cheerful thoughts to the lovers: "Life might last! we can but try!" The kissing and love-making are renewed and then interrupted by "the dominant's persistence till it must be answered to." The note is finally one of the inevitability of death, which must come to cut off "lives that came to nothing, some with deeds as well undone. . . ."

The scientist is profoundly shaken by his vision of eighteenth-century Venetian life, with its gaiety and love. He knows that the awakened forces in his soul will neither slumber again nor leave undisturbed his monomaniacal rationalism:

> But when I sit down to reason, think to take my stand
> nor swerve,
> While I triumph o'er a secret wrung from nature's close reserve,
> In you come with your cold music till I creep thro'
> every nerve.

He has rationally assumed that "the soul, doubtless, is immortal—where a soul can be discerned"—the position of the scientific agnostic. From the music he gets the ironic assurance—voicing his own feeling of superiority over the pleasure-loving Venetians—that surely he will rise to immortality, for he is learned in the sciences and mathematics: "souls shall rise in their degree. . . ." But the Venetians, so he hears, are doomed to extinction for their butterfly lives—a sentiment that but a short time before would have fallen on sympathetic ears. Now, however, he is no longer complacent or superior and he cannot cast the first stone.

The final stanza illustrates the dramatic change which comes upon the scientist. He has moved from his stiff-necked condemnation of the Venetian frivolity, which he did not understand or even recognize. Far more moving, however, than his sudden view of a whole new way of life—a life repudiating reason and knowledge, as he has repudiated love, gaiety, and emotion—is his examination of his own one-sided life and poverty of spirit. Both he and the Venetians have elected only half of life and both have thus lived stunted, incomplete lives. He is not unlike Childe Roland in his journey into the recesses of his psyche, and he too makes a painful assessment of his condition, which gives him a far more tolerant view of the Venetians, whose one-sidedness he has shared in reverse:

> "Dust and ashes!" So you creak it, and I want
> the heart to scold.
> Dear dead women, with such hair, too—what's
> become of all the gold
> Used to hang and brush their bosoms? I feel chilly
> and grown old.

"A Toccata of Galuppi's" is one of the most brilliant of Browning's poems of contrast of two radically different ways of life. It is superbly conceived in imagery and dramatic situation which elevate the poem above the flat statement that often marred Browning's later work. In dramatic situation we see one of his most enduring themes: the need for wholeness in man, and the tragic consequences of a repudiation of life in any of its parts. The question of the ephemeral quality of life remains unanswered, as it must. Clearly, the scientist, in spite of his dedication to truth, has no greater assurance of immortality than the Venetian lovers in their fool's errand to the grave. This poem gives no easy answers and avoids a pat formula. Life and death remain the great mysteries which are beyond man's understanding, but while trying to solve the riddle of existence, man must seize life with his whole spirit, not with just part of it.

SUGGESTED READINGS

Burrows, Leonard, *Browning the Poet: An Introductory Study* (Nedlands, Western Australia, 1969), pp. 150-56.

"Like 'A Grammarian's Funeral'—but with a significant difference of stress and tone—'A Toccata' holds in tension two opposed attitudes to life and unlike the former poem does not press a solution of the problem" (pp. 155-56).

Ridenour, George M., "Browning's Music Poems," *Publications of the Modern Language Association,* LXXVIII (1963), 369-77.

Professor Ridenour makes the point that in Browning's music poems there is the premise that the culture of a country and of a time is reflected in its music and that "this culture is especially approachable through its music." The Englishman who has expected to find Galuppi's music reflecting his sentimental notions of what eighteenth-century Venice was like is surprised to find it "embodying quite a different aspect of the Rococo: clear and elegant, to be sure, but ironic, witty, destructive. Galuppi's music suggests one quality of the eighteenth century, its skeptical rationalism, commenting cynically on some of its more winning illusions" (p. 373). Ridenour discovers that the music of Galuppi represents a "split in the mind of the century." The two resulting parts do not "annihilate" each other and there is no "genuine synthesis, outside the imaginative form that lets us consider them together." The split is a permanent division, "found both in the speaker of the poem, an idealistic Englishman of the nineteenth century, interested in science (a 'Victorian'), and in the poet, who sets facts against fancies to define a new harmony, of a sort, in his poem" (p. 373). The meaning, however, Ridenour finds, is not wholly Galuppi's, for his music, in a sense, "supports the values he deprecates. The Venetians are right in enjoying it; it is 'their kind' of music" (p. 374).

Shaw, W. David, *The Dialectical Temper: The Rhetorical Art of Robert Browning* (Ithaca, N.Y., 1968), pp. 136-39.

"The speaker [in 'A Toccata of Galuppi's'] tries to formulate a hypothetical syllogism whose antecedent is that 'Butterflies' like the Venetians never owned a soul, and whose consequent is that they must die. But denying the consequent, he is able to deny the antecedent and to infer that the man who is immortal is the man who possesses, like himself, the highest kind of soul; as a moralist with scientific interests, he therefore concludes that he will 'not die': 'it cannot be!' "

Whitla, William, *The Central Truth: The Incarnation in Robert Browning's Poetry* (Toronto, 1963), pp. 76-78 and passim.

"The kind of life that is presented in the poem is the life of Venice, that is, the life of the world; it is itself fleeting and based on the senses. There seems to be love in the poem, but it is a shallow love, not the merging of the soul of the lover in the soul of the beloved that Browning demands. . . . The people of Venice who wasted their lives did not prepare for their deaths by living deeply and nobly . . . life was not lived, and all has come to dust and ashes, while the music of Galuppi points its rather bitter moral."

12

"An Epistle Containing the Strange Medical Experience of Karshish, The Arab Physician"

"An Epistle Containing the Strange Medical Experience of Karshish, the Arab Physician" is a powerfully conceived dramatic epistle, in effect indistinguishable from a pure dramatic monologue. The title is fully ironic in that the burden of the poem in reality has nothing whatever to do with a strange *medical* experience, but rather with a strange spiritual experience. Karshish, the Arab physician, is impelled to write to his mentor, Abib, because of the miracle of the resurrection of Lazarus from the dead; but, to avoid the charge of being naïvely credulous, he goes to great pains to fill his letter with the scientific observations that he knows Abib expects from a rational medical colleague. He longs to give assent to the fact of the resurrection and to the incalculable implications that it carries. The informing device in the poem is the tension between Karshish's rational scientific skepticism and the intolerable impulse he feels to accept the astonishing evidence that there is another world from which Lazarus returned. If the story of Lazarus is true, he knows that he must view life and death in a new and wonderful light—a light in the darkness of his entire scientific training.

Karshish begins his letter to Abib with a protestation of his devotion to science, an affirmation to assure Abib that he is proof against the superstitions and impostures that prevail against the credulous, those not grounded in science:

> Karshish, the picker-up of learning's crumbs,
> The not-incurious in God's handiwork
> (This man's-flesh he hath admirably made,
> Blown like a bubble, kneaded like a paste,
> To coop up and keep down on earth a space
> That puff of vapor from his mouth, man's soul)
> —To Abib, all-sagacious in our art,

Breeder in me of what poor skill I boast,
Like me inquisitive how pricks and cracks
Befall the flesh through too much stress and strain,
Whereby the wily vapor fain would slip
Back and rejoin its source before the term,—
And aptest in contrivance (under God)
To baffle it by deftly stopping such:—
The vagrant Scholar to his Sage at home
Sends greeting (health and knowledge, fame with peace)
Three samples of true snakestone—rarer still,
One of the other sort, the melon-shaped,
(But fitter, pounded fine, for charms than drugs)
And writeth now the twenty-second time.

(ll. 1-20)

Among the most subtle and effective ironies in Browning is this prideful credo of intellectualism, which contains in it the evidence that his vaunted science is pitiably primitive, hardly to be distinguished from the crudest mummeries of the credulous. Although the childish imagery of the creation of man is admittedly figurative, it nevertheless reveals imaginatively the state of medicine and science in Abib's day. The salutation to Abib as "all-sagacious in our art," immediately after this evidence of the larval state of medical knowledge that is Abib's is splendidly ironic. Karshish's flattering description of his mentor as inquisitive in all areas of medical cures is to force Abib's attention on the purely medical aspects of the case of Lazarus so that the spiritual implications may be drawn to his attention subtly, a hedge against his indignant wrath at the credence that Karshish can ill conceal in viewing the resurrection.

The irony is sustained by his sending three samples of "true snakestone," the witch doctor's remedy for snakebite. Although Karshish is, for his day, a learned man, he does not know the name of "the other sort" of snakestone and describes it, as a child might, as "melon-shaped." His long and ceremonious salutation establishes two points: (1) the pride Karshish naïvely takes in his supposedly advanced medical knowledge, and (2) his veneration for his master Abib, whose state of knowledge is much the same as that of his student.

Karshish's journeyings to Jericho and beyond have been marked by considerable hardship, but they count as nothing in view of the scientific advantages that have accrued to one "studious in our art." He has been attacked by a lynx, stripped and beaten by robbers twice, and once he was declared a spy on his journey to Jerusalem. But at last he has come in reasonable estate to Bethany, which

> . . . lies scarce the distance thence
> A man with plague-sores at the third degree
> Runs till he drops down dead. Thou laughest here!
> (ll. 36-38)

This figurative estimation of distance, although intended to amuse, is calculated to keep before Abib the fact of Karshish's total devotion to medicine and to suggest that his skill is so far advanced that he can predict with great accuracy precisely how far a man with a given disease at a particular state can run before he drops dead. More important, it reveals the arrogance and the impostures of the medical fraternity of the day and their heartless and crudely primitive minds—fittingly matching their accomplishments in science.

He professes to be glad to unburden his traveler's scrip of the medical notes of the condition of medicine in Jewry:

> A viscid choler is observable
> In tertians. . . .

And there is a happier cure for the falling sickness than is known to Abib, the all-sagacious. There is also a webless spider with mottles on an ash-gray back:

> Take five and drop them . . . but who knows his mind
> The Syrian runagate I trust this to?
> (ll. 48-49)

The spider, which may have been one of the Lycosids, or wolf spiders, or various ground spiders having mottled gray backs, was frequently mentioned in the primitive pharmacopoeia as a potent medicine—when pounded with fragrant healing oils—for diseases of the eye or ear. Sir William Lister, it is reported, recommended a distillation of boiled black spiders as a cure for wounds, a fact which permits the satire to apply to ages much later than that of Abib. Undoubtedly Karshish was about to describe a prescription he made of five spiders dropped in wine or oil or boiling water, suitable as a remedy for the gout or stone, as the medical fancy might suggest. But his attention is averted to the likelihood that the letter will never be delivered into Abib's hands, for the Syrian runagate, whose eye disease Karshish has treated by blowing a sublimate (made of a colloidal suspension of spiders?) up his nose, may choose to throw it into the nearest ditch. The attempted cure of eye disease by means of nose drops is significant in assessing Karshish's skill as a physician and the irony of his pride.

He begins an account of a cure he learned at Zoar for scalp disease, but he stops short, saying that zeal outruns discretion, for, he suggests, the runagate may steal the secret. This ploy is to impress Abib with Karshish's sagacity in refusing to entrust valuable medical secrets to strangers. But—and this is one of Browning's most subtle ironies—since the runagate blinks gratefully and promises to deliver the letter faithfully (although Karshish, being a man of the world, doubts his honesty), what would it hurt to entrust to the letter, not medical secrets that are worth stealing, but a worthless story of a novel case, hardly worth the writing?

> Suppose I write what harms not, though he steal?
> I half resolve to tell thee, yet I blush. . . .
>
> (ll. 64-65)

The story of Lazarus, he suspects, is the most momentous story the world has known, and, although he fears to be thought credulous, he is impelled to write, defensively affirming from time to time his belief in the palpable fraud and worthlessness of the event. Lazarus's "case has struck me far more than 't is worth." He apologizes for the turn his letter is taking (from worthwhile science to a worthless story), but he has explained the fear of theft that has prompted the change. It does not occur to him that Abib might ask why he should write about it at all. Karshish advances the peculiar drama of the case, writing that Lazarus has "gone from me but now," an emphasis that he hopes will be more favorable to his wishes than to say, "I have but now gone from him." He insists that the root of his interest is medical, reminding Abib that clearly Lazarus suffered from an "ailment" entirely proper to the purview of medicine. This is his spurious justification for recounting the miracle, and he disarms Abib's censure by saying:

> 'T is but a case of mania—subinduced
> By epilepsy, at the turning-point
> Of trance prolonged unduly some three days:
> When, by the exhibition of some drug
> Or spell, exorcisation, stroke of art
> Unknown to me and which 't were well to know,
> The evil thing out-breaking all at once
> Left the man whole. . . .
>
> (ll. 79-87)

The medical jargon is calculated to please and reassure Abib of the soundness of his protégé's mind and spirit, but the remaining portion of the sentence, which is eighteen breathless lines, may not be so reassuring. Karshish, in his excitement, gradually abandons his cool objectivity, and turns to the effects of the resurrection upon Lazarus. He hedges no longer. He speaks as if the fact of the strange return from the grave were an established fact, and he examines the effects of the experience upon the man. He utters one of Browning's most basic philosophical beliefs: that man in the mortal state must be preserved from absolute knowledge. Lazarus has been exposed unnaturally to the truth of eternity, and the imprint of absolute truth upon the walls of the house of life—the mind and soul of Lazarus—permits of no palimpsest or addition of the half-truths that are life's peculiar hallmark. Henceforth the "just-returned and new-established soul" will read the "fancy-scrawls" which the vision of the Absolute indelibly imprinted on his soul.

In a resurgence of guilt and fear of Abib's reaction, he adds: " 'Such cases are diurnal,' thou wilt cry." But Karshish affirms that in this case devotion to the Absolute does not give way "to time or health," but rather like saffron has tinged the man, "flesh, blood, bones and all!"

Again Karshish insists that his interest in the case is medical:

> Think, could we penetrate by any drug
> And bathe the wearied soul and worried flesh
> And bring it clear and fair, by three days' sleep!
> (ll. 113-15)

Lazarus's resurrection, miraculous as it is, is not by any means an unmitigated good. He is alive and hale, it is true, but he eyes the world like a child, is as obedient as a sheep, folds his hands and watches the flies with consuming interest, while ignoring matters accounted by man as of transcendent importance. Life's values are no longer his, for they are cheap and mean in the light of the heavenly radiance which he has experienced:

> —we call the treasure knowledge, say,
> Increased beyond the fleshly faculty—
> Heaven opened to a soul while yet on earth,
> Earth forced on a soul's use while seeing heaven:
> The man is witless of the size, the sum,
> The value in proportion of all things,
> Or whether it be little or be much.
> (ll. 139-45)

Lazarus's ways are not man's ways, nor are his values man's, and he is as bewildered by man's inability to share his new heavenly vision and values as they are by his alteration, the visible result of his "opened eyes." He follows perforcedly "some thread of life" and yet cannot enter into the life beyond until his time has run in this life:

> The spiritual life around the earthly life:
> The law of that is known to him as this,
> His heart and brain move there, his feet stay here.
> (ll. 183-85)

Lazarus is pictured as a pitiable creature, sourly distracted, bored by the tawdry goals that pass for values in life, and yearning for the release of death. Sick with bewilderment, torn by conflicting impulses, he is impatient with life but aware that "It should be" is balked by "here it cannot be." He is truly a man without a world, a stranger to earth and an alien from heaven. He plies his trade obediently to God's will,

> Professedly the faultier that he knows
> God's secret, while he holds the thread of life.
> (ll. 200-01)

He longs for the gentle touch of death again, which alone can restore him to equilibrium. His body and soul already are "Divorced even now by premature full growth," and they long to be free of each other.

Karshish plays the role of psychiatrist with Lazarus, insulting him to see whether by shock he may not find truth:

> "How, beast," said I, "this stolid carelessness
> Sufficeth thee, when Rome is on her march
> To stamp out like a little spark thy town,
> Thy tribe, thy crazy tale and thee at once?"
> (ll. 221-24)

Lazarus, who has seen God, is not to be provoked by an ignorant leech who has seen but little and knows less. A strange parallel develops between the two men. As Karshish has been impatient with the arrogant ignorance of primitive medicine men, so Lazarus is impatient "At ignorance and carelessness and sin":

> An indignation which is promptly curbed:
> As when in certain travel I have feigned
> To be an ignoramus in our art
> According to some preconceived design,
> And happed to hear the land's practitioners
> Steeped in conceit sublimed by ignorance,
> Prattle fantastically on disease,
> Its cause and cure—and I must hold my peace!
> (ll. 235-42)

This passage, illustrating as it does Browning's concept of the relativity of knowledge and the need to search forever for an unobtainable total truth, is one of the delicious ironies of *Men and Women*. All men are in varying degrees "steeped in conceit sublimed by ignorance," but only the wise and humble can know this, and Karshish is not to be numbered among this small group. Compared to Lazarus's vision of the Absolute,

Karshish's truth or Abib's is the mummery of witch doctors and the rattling of bones around primordial fires, but this they cannot know.

As he nears the end of his recital, Karshish again becomes weary of betraying his credulity to Abib, and again he reaffirms his medical interest in the case. He has not sought out the Nazarene physician who wrought the wondrous cure, for he died in a tumult, accused of wizardry. He seeks to win the good opinion of Abib by pronouncing Lazarus a madman, whose words, of course, cannot be trusted, especially since he insanely believes that the same Nazarene physician was God himself, the infallible sign of madness:

> —but why all this of what he saith?
> Why write of trivial matters, things of price
> Calling at every moment for remark?
> I noticed on the margin of a pool
> Blue-flowering borage, the Aleppo sort,
> Aboundeth, very nitrous. It is strange!
>
> (ll. 277-82)

The reference to borage is mere window dressing to distract Abib's attention from the emotional excitement in the letter and from Karshish's will to believe, which more and more abounds. He apologizes for his long and tedious recital of so unworthy a case, pleading his weariness. It matters not, he reaffirms, whether the letter miscarries, for the substance is not worth the effort expended either to write it or to read it, and on this note he bids Abib farewell.

But, gripped by an uncontrollable excitement, he adds a postscript which must betray to Abib the vast amazed belief that he has been struggling to conceal:

> The very God! think, Abib; dost thou think?
> So, the All-Great, were the All-Loving too—
> So, through the thunder comes a human voice
> Saying, "O heart I made, a heart beats here!
> Face, my hands fashioned, see it in myself!
> Thou hast no power nor mayst conceive of mine,
> But love I gave thee, with myself to love,
> And thou must love me who have died for thee!"
> The madman saith He said so: it is strange.
>
> (ll. 304-12)

There is little doubt that Karshish later regrets sending this indiscreet letter, for in spite of the final line, it is clear that he does not regard Lazarus as mad, but rather as blinded by the light of another world, and one wonders, as does Karshish, what Abib thought as he read the letter.

An interesting problem arises concerning Lazarus's retention of absolute knowledge upon his return to life. Did he gain absolute knowledge at all or only an approximation? Did he gain absolute knowledge but did his return to life rob him of a part of it, in the manner of Wordsworth's "Immortality Ode"? It is impossible to pronounce with certainty, but in view of Browning's theme that the next world is much like this in its endless aspiration, striving, and growth, it may be that even there absolute knowledge is at the end of a long—and eternally receding—path. Like Moses, perhaps, Lazarus saw God and truth, not in one full epiphany of revelation, but dimly in the burning bush.

The question is of some importance, for it is made clear that Lazarus has fear, and fear is the product of doubt, uncertainty, and ignorance, none of which is compatible with possession of absolute knowledge:

Wonder and doubt come wrongly into play,
Preposterously, at cross purposes.
Should his child sicken unto death,—why, look
For scarce abatement of his cheerfulness,
Or pretermission of the daily craft!
While a word, gesture, glance from that same child
At play or in the school or laid asleep,
Will startle him to an agony of fear,
Exasperation, just as like.

(ll. 157-65)

Whether Lazarus returns with absolute knowledge imperfect or intact, it is certain that he returned with knowledge that must be denied to man on this side of the veil between this world and the next. The poem examines dramatically the effects upon a man forced to live in this world after being exposed to the knowledge of heaven. The result is a catastrophe. It is, however, a gross error to suppose that because absolute knowledge is properly forbidden to man, all knowledge is a vain and futile and pernicious pursuit, as has been alleged. Knowledge and the intellect in Browning are never disparaged; only the abuse of intellect is, or its usurpation of the roles proper to emotion, intuition, and love. The theme—that the test of life is abrogated and rendered null by the vision of the Absolute—is entirely incidental to the revelation of motive and wonder and fear in Karshish's soul, a soul under stress. Few poems are at once so rich in psychological subtlety and in irony.

SUGGESTED READINGS

Altick, Richard D., "Browning's 'Karshish' and St. Paul," *Modern Language Notes*, LXXII (1957), 494-96.

"Like 'Caliban' and 'Cleon,' 'Karshish' can and should be read in two ways: as Browning's reconstruction of a significant, albeit imaginary, event in the history of religion, and as a satiric commentary on the intellectual and theological forces aligned against traditional Christianity in the nineteenth century. When we read it on the former—literal—level, the poem acquires extra edge if we detect the hovering presence of St. Paul" (p. 474). Professor Altick finds some parallels and some differences between the lives of Karshish and his contemporary, St. Paul. The most notable difference is that the Saint perceives truth through intuition, whereas Karshish attempts to find truth through the senses and the intellect.

Charlton, H. B., "Browning as Poet of Religion," *Bulletin of the John Rylands Library*, XXVII (1942-43), 271-306.

Includes some valuable comments on "An Epistle of Karshish."

Collins, Thomas J., *Robert Browning's Moral-Aesthetic Theory, 1833-1855* (Lincoln, Nebr., 1967), pp. 136-40.

Finds the scientific and medical observations strewn throughout the epistle Karshish is writing to be the result of weariness he has suffered from his travels. Karshish feels obliged to report dutifully to his mentor, but "he records his thoughts haphazardly, as they come to him." "But his descent to the mention of such a trivial matter as the superior quality of Judea's gum tragacanth, combined with such cursory medical opinions, reminds him of the original purpose he had in writing the letter—to describe a strange medical phenomenon that he is rather embarrassed to admit has caught his attention—'I half resolve to tell thee, yet I blush,/ What set me off a-writing first of all.' "

Irvine, William, "Four Monologues in Browning's *Men and Women*," *Victorian Poetry*, II (1964), 155-64.

" 'Karshish' dramatizes curiosity and inquiry; 'Cleon,' pride and possessions. Yet both follow the same strategy. In one, human nature measures scientific materialism against Christianity; in the other, late Hellenism. In one, the speaker seems startled and unprepared for his own highest impulses; in the other, he has found no expression of them in the thought and religion of the period" (p. 163).

13

"'Childe Roland to the Dark Tower Came'"

" 'Childe Roland to the Dark Tower Came,' " Browning informs us, was written in Paris in one day, January 2, 1852, in compliance with his resolution to write a poem every twenty-four hours. It is difficult to imagine a day bringing fruit more golden. Since its appearance readers have sought for an allegorical meaning, and the richest diversity of interpretations has arisen, many laughably imaginative. Browning two years before his death was asked by a stranger whether he agreed with an allegorical interpretation he brought to the attention of the poet. He replied:

> Oh, no, not at all. Understand, I don't repudiate it, either. I only mean I was conscious of no allegorical intention in writing it. 'T was like this: one year in Florence, I had been very lazy; I resolved that I would write something every day. Well, the first day I wrote about some roses, suggested by a magnificent basket that some one had sent my wife. The next day Childe Roland came upon me as a kind of dream. I had to write it, then and there, and I finished it the same day, I believe. But it was simply that I had to do it. I did not know then what I meant beyond that, and I'm sure I don't know now. But I am very fond of it.[1]

Browning repeatedly denied that the poem had any allegorical significance or moral purpose. He insisted that it was simply a dramatic vision inspired by Edgar's song in *Lear*, Act III, scene iv, in which Edgar, disguised as a madman, says of his nightmare journey, the original of Roland's:

> Who gives anything to poor Tom? whom the foul fiend hath led through fire and through flame, through ford and whirlpool, over bog and quagmire; that hath laid knives under his pillow and halters in his pew; set ratbane by his porridge; made him proud of heart to

1. Lilian Whiting, *The Brownings* (Boston, 1917), p. 261. Although the admirable resolution was made in Florence, the composition of " 'Childe Roland' " occurred in Paris.

ride on a bay trotting-horse over four-inched bridges, to course his own shadow for a traitor.—Bless thy five wits! Tom's a-cold.—O do de , do de, do, de.—Bless thee from whirlwinds, star-blasting, and talking! Do poor Tom some charity, whom the foul fiend vexes.

At the end of the scene Edgar sings:

Childe Roland to the dark tower came,
His word was still,—Fie, Foh, and Fum
I smell the blood of a British man.

When the Reverend John W. Chadwick asked the poet if the central purpose of the poem could be summarized in the words, "He that endureth to the end shall be saved," Browning replied, "Yes, just about that." Such protestations have done little to discourage allegorical explication. Edward Berdoe in his *Browning Cyclopedia* (pp. 101-05) summarizes a number of interpretations of bewildering diversity:

Mr. Kirkman, in the paper already referred to [*Browning Society Papers*, Part iii, p. 21], says "There are overwhelming reasons for concluding that this poem describes, after the manner of an allegory, the sensations of a sick man very near to death. . . ." Mr. Nettleship, in his well-known essay on the poem, says the central idea is this: "Take some great end which men have proposed to themselves in life, which seemed to have truth in it, and power to spread freedom and happiness on others; but as it comes in sight, it falls strangely short of preconceived ideas, and stands up in hideous prosaicness." Mrs. James L. Bagg, in the *Interpretation of Childe Roland*, read to the Syracuse (U.S.) Browning Club, gives the following lesson of the poem:—"The secrets of the universe are not to be discovered by exercise of reason, nor are they to be reached by flights of fancy, nor are duties loyally done to be recompensed by revealment. A life of *becoming, being,* and *doing,* is not loss, nor failure, nor discomfiture, though the dark tower for ever tantalize and for ever withhold."

Berdoe, after reviewing the several interpretations, apparently felt constrained to top their wild flights of fancy, and did:

For my own part, I see in the allegory—for I can consider it no other—a picture of the Age of Materialistic Science, a "science falsely so called," which aims at the destruction of all our noblest ideals of religion and faith in the unseen. The pilgrim is a truth-seeker, misdirected by the lying spirit—the hoary cripple, unable to be or do anything good or noble himself; in him I see the cynical, destructive critic, who sits at our universities and colleges, our medical schools and our firesides, to point our youth to the desolate path of Atheistic

> Science, a science which strews the ghastly landscape with wreck and ruthless ruin, with the blanching bones of animals tortured to death by its "engines and wheels, with rusty teeth of steel"—a science which has invaded the healing art, and is sending students of medicine daily down the road where surgeons become cancer-grafters (as the Paris and Berlin medical scandals have revealed), and where physicians gloat over their animal victims—
>
> "Toads in a poisoned tank,
> Or wild cats in a red-hot iron cage,"
>
> in their passion to reach the dark tower of knowledge, which to them has neither door nor window.

Berdoe's suggestion is a notable exercise in sustained nonsense, an admirable equipoise of imperception and private bias. It is true that Browning was fully opposed to vivisection and, indeed, was Vice-President of the Victoria Street Society for the Protection of Animals, but it takes an inventive imagination and a sturdy disregard for evidence to find this poem to be an anti-vivisectionist statement. David V. Erdman, in his "Browning's Industrial Nightmare,"[2] has found the poem to reveal Browning's detestation of the evils, not of vivisection but of industrialism. Berdoe's statement, written in the closing years of the last century, very largely anticipated much recent criticism of the poem:

> Most of the commentators agree that when Childe Roland "dauntless set the slug horn to his lips and blew '*Childe Roland to the Dark Tower came,*' " he did so as a warning to others that he had failed in his quest, and that the way of the Dark Tower was the way of destruction and death.

Browning's reluctance to explicate his verse is well known, and is best seen in his apparent approval of Mrs. Orr's *Browning Handbook*, which he read in MS., and which he later said was filled with the most peculiar interpretations. In view of such evidence one is cautious in supposing that Browning's agreement with the Reverend John W. Chadwick's query about the theme of the work is wholly trustworthy. But it does seem strange that if he intended to reveal the depth of error and final failure he would agree with a diametrically opposed interpretation.

None of Browning's poems has been so ingeniously studied and interpreted to find its hidden meaning. In line with an unfortunate trend in Browning scholarship in recent years, the poem has been seen as an expression of Browning's own failure. Betty Miller's *Robert Browning, A*

2. David V. Erdman, "Browning's Industrial Nightmare," *Philological Quarterly*, XXXVI (1957), 417-35.

Portrait, which is a destructive and fanciful account of the poet's supposed psychiatric inadequacies, is notable in this connection.

W. C. DeVane is correct in his finding that the source of much of the imagery in the poem is Gerard de Lairesse's *The Art of Painting in All Its Branches,* a book which Robert found in his father's library and which he read repeatedly. But I cannot wholly accept DeVane's statement, "That Browning's conscious intention was not allegorical, we know: the poem came upon him 'as a kind of dream.' "[3] It is true that Browning said the poem came upon him as a kind of dream and he furthermore denied that he had a consciously allegorical intent, but the fact that a poem "came upon" one as a kind of dream in no way means that it was written in a similar state, and that there was no conscious allegory does not rule out allegory that was implicit. Coleridge's "Kubla Khan" is the most notable instance of a poem supposedly *written*—or almost transcribed— from the recollections of an opium dream, but it seems obvious that neither Browning's poem nor Coleridge's was conceived, planned, and written in a dream, although each may have been rooted in dream. Coleridge insisted upon the dream character of the poem, and its fragmentary state, to obscure the fact that the supposed fragment was in fact a complete, imaginative vision of the glorious life he would have led if he had married his "damsel with a dulcimer," Mary Evans, his early sweetheart, instead of Sara Fricker, with whom he lived in misery. Browning insisted on the dream character of his poem because he knew that the psychiatric searching of the poem would have been misunderstood. Even today it is, when the technique is familiar. " 'Childe Roland' " is one man's journey into his heart of darkness, where at every turn he meets the unknown terrors of his soul.

Perhaps the most perceptive study of the poem appears in Thomas Blackburn's *Robert Browning: A Study of His Poetry.* He very properly says, "In *Childe Roland* we find his most startling use of landscape to create a sense of the mystery and labyrinthine complexity of the human psyche and the strange, often savage fauna which inhabit it. The poem describes man's journey into the interior darkness of himself in order to confront that nexus of destructive energy which Jungians call the Shadow."[4] He perceptively finds a striking parallel between Browning's poem and Conrad's triumphant study of man's journey into the steaming jungle of his psyche: *Heart of Darkness.*

The poem must be read on two levels, just as Conrad's study must be. On the surface level, it is an allegory of each man's journey through life to death, and as such it affords the most crushing reply to the critics who

---

3. *Handbook,* p. 231.

4. Thomas Blackburn, *Robert Browning, A Study of His Poetry* (London, 1967), p. 193.

have found Browning to be a complacent optimist, prattling about how "All's right with the world." On another and more important level, as Blackburn points out, it is a study of the individual's most lonely and terrifying journey—into himself—the dread journey that each man must make before he comes to the Dark Tower. It is the two levels, working in counterpoint, which make this Browning's most original and powerful poem, if not his most satisfying or pleasant. It is a forerunner of such powerful studies as Conrad's *Heart of Darkness*, Franz Kafka's *The Trial* and "The Metamorphosis," and T. S. Eliot's *The Waste Land*.

" 'Childe Roland,' " of all of Browning's poems, is the most deeply rooted in the primitive myths and legends of evil, commonly incarnated in the form of bulls, minotaurs, serpents, lions, dragons, and assorted monsters. It is a fearsome pilgrimage into the dark night of the soul, with horror piled on horror. Everywhere through the poem is the desperate fear of a nightmare half-recognition of unknown danger and evil, savage, irrational, implacable. It is man face to face with himself, all the comfortable exculpations and rationalizations stripped away. It is thus a study in terror and at the same time a surrealistic account of life. It should be noted that in this really terrifying experience, there is not one thing of which one should be afraid. Every fear is wholly within the soul of Roland. He never meets any direct menace or danger, but he suffers the extreme torments of terror, which come not from without but from within, for the journey into his psyche is presented in terms of his journey to the Dark Tower.

The old Pope in *The Ring and the Book* says, "All to the very end is trial in life"; and of all the poems Browning wrote, " 'Childe Roland' " best and most fearfully illustrates that theme. The trials are twofold: the "real" day-to-day evils and frustrations that face each man from birth to death, and, more fearsome, the dark forces of evil that lurk in his soul, conflicting, blind, unrecognized savage energy, alien to the conscious spirit. The evils which Roland encounters every step of the way are clearly within him, for at no time does he meet anything that is evil. Rather he (1) arrives at a spot at which some vast and hideous evil has just taken place, or (2) at a spot where some unknown and fearsome evil is about to take place.

Betty Miller in her *Robert Browning, A Portrait* purveys the theme that Browning was psychologically undeveloped and twisted, a stunted mamma's boy, Oedipally attached to his domineering mother. I resist her attempt to identify Childe Roland with Browning, especially her particular theme that the poem reveals Browning's neurotic fear of failure as a poet, for no man could have written with such insight into the dark forces of the soul without having probed his own soul with uncommon courage and maturity. To write this poem, one must have made the journey, but this is not to say that *this* journey is through Browning's soul. Rather, it is the journey of Everyman, and Browning was content to let the world in good time discover his meaning.

In the first stanza, typically, Browning begins *in medias res*. The quest has begun and Childe Roland has come to a crossroads, where a cripple, seemingly foul and twisted by double dealing and deceit, points out the path Roland must follow on his quest. We are not told what the quest is, other than that it is some quest for the sinister Dark Tower, but we do not need to be told. It is the quest into the heart of darkness which every man must make sooner or later. The cackling, hideous cripple points down an ominous tract where "all agree/ Hides the Dark Tower." No one, it seems, in the poem or out, agrees with anyone else about what the Dark Tower is. It seems unmistakable that on the surface level the Tower is death, and the imagery makes this certain, but on the deeper level it represents the end of the terrifying journey through the soul. The fact that life and the goal of this dread journey are one clearly indicates that the journey is coterminous with life itself. Browning never wearied of saying that the soul of man was the only thing really worth writing about, and he criticized Tennyson for failing to focus on the souls of his knights in the *Idylls* instead of the moonlight on the battlements.

From the first line of the poem to the last, one is increasingly impressed with the unreal nature of things, the dreamlike character of Roland's fear and suspicion. Nothing makes sense. Why does Roland ask the way to the Dark Tower if, as he says, "all agree" that the Tower lies down the path the cripple indicates? The cripple, in point of fact, does nothing fearful or menacing. He merely points out the road in answer to Roland's query, and Roland immediately fancies the cripple's glee at securing another "victim," for what purpose or in what sense we are not told. Clearly this is the land of terror, the land of the soul. Even more irrational is what Roland takes as evidence of the cripple's malice: "What else should he be set for, with his staff?" To his mind the staff is evidence enough of his foul intent, and he would be astonished to discover that others might consider the evidence inadmissible. Roland is in the grip of terror of the unknown, which he does not understand and cannot fight. In the land of the psyche the sword and the lance are of no avail.

It is important to be aware of the elaborate care that Browning takes to show that not one of the terrors is real *in earthly terms*. Roland "guessed what skull-like laugh" would follow him down the ominous path, but he hears none. He wonders what crutch will write his epitaph in the dusty thoroughfare, but the dust remains undisturbed.

It is significant that Roland begins his account of his journey with a choice. Is the cripple directing him toward his destination or to some vague horror? He cannot know beyond doubt, for the essence of choice is doubt, wherein man is tested. "Life is just the terrible choice," the old Pope in *The Ring and the Book* assures us, and " 'Childe Roland' " might be a protracted illustration of his wisdom. Roland debates the probable merits of the advice agonizingly—as the Pope judges Guido—and makes his choice, for good or ill. Roland makes it clear that his mood is one of hopelessness, sustained by enough courage to let him yearn for "some end" to the quest, even though hope of success is nearly dead. To the knight-at-arms, if success was unattainable, the code demanded that one meet failure in the quest with knightly resolution. Only the recreant caitiff abandons the quest. A point of interest is Roland's statement that in the search he has spent years and wandered the world through, while his hopes "dwindled into a ghost." The word "Childe" means a young knight who has yet to prove his courage, and clearly Roland is not young. The implication is that every true knight remains in a sense "Childe," for "all to the very end is trial in life," as the Pope reminds us. The courage of one day has no carry-over to the next, which is a new day, a clean slate, with a fresh set of trials, with illimitable choice and chance for failure or success. " 'Childe Roland' " is very close to Hemingway's "Old Man and the Sea" in point of the courage and the test of man.

It has often been noted that stanzas V and VI owe much to John Donne, whom Browning admired. It has not been noted that the two levels of sensation and thought here—that of the sad speaker bidding farewell to the dying man and that of the dying man himself—suggest the dual levels on which the poem is written. The patient is conscious of his existence on two levels of life, and he desires only that (on both levels) "He may not shame such tender love and stay," i.e., recover (on one level) and abandon the quest (on another). Life and the quest are both irreversible. To return from the quest empty-handed is the one thing unthinkable, and, similarly, he feels that to return from the squat ugly Dark Tower of death would be to be recreant. Just to fail while striving seems the maximum success possible.

His fears are wholly irrational and fantastic, as in a fever dream. The grim day at its close seems to send one last red leer to see the "plain catch its estray"—Roland. How the plain will catch him he does not bother to inquire, but his terrors are increased by the improbable nature of the plain:

> For mark! no sooner was I fairly found
> Pledged to the plain, after a pace or two,
> Than, pausing to throw backward a last view
> O'er the safe road, 't was gone; gray plain all round. . . .

Such geographical eccentricities do nothing to allay his fears. Like Conrad's Marlow, Roland has embarked on the quest into the labyrinthine recesses of his soul. There is no turning back: "I might go on; naught else remained to do." It is a nightmare, terrifying, inevitable, irreversible:

> So, on I went. I think I never saw
> Such starved ignoble nature; nothing throve:
> For flowers—as well expect a cedar grove!
> But cockle, spurge, according to their law
> Might propagate their kind, with none to awe,
> You'd think; a burr had been a treasure-trove.

The land's portion is "penury, inertness and grimace." Perhaps the most significant lines in the poem are in stanza XI:

> "See
> Or shut your eyes," said Nature peevishly,
> "It nothing skills: I cannot help my case:
> 'T is the Last Judgment's fire must cure this place,
> Calcine its clods and set my prisoners free."

It is indeed the Last Judgment which can cure this place (the soul), purify its clods by fire, and set life's prisoners free for the next life.

Nature seems to have just completed a civil war of some obscure sort, but the one thing that is denied Roland is any certainty, any glimpse of evil. He arrives always just after the commission—or apparent commision—of violence, which adds the terror of the unknown to the scene:

> What made those holes and rents
> In the dock's harsh swarth leaves, bruised as to balk
> All hope of greenness? 't is a brute must walk
> Pashing their life out, with a brute's intents.

The terrain, bruised and flattened by some brute in obscure and irrational conflict, yields to an area inconceivably hostile, in which the grass "grew as scant as hair/In leprosy." It should be noted that the menace is conjectural; almost nothing *is: it seemed, looked, might have been, may have been, sounded like, it would seem*. Nothing is real but the horror it produces in Roland's mind, which finds malignity in everything. The blades of grass "looked kneaded up with blood," and one "stiff blind horse" seems "Thrust out past service from the devil's stud!" Roland is not sure whether the horse is dead or alive, for in this land of uncertainty, the borders of life and death are ambiguous. In this land, values are reversed, it seems. The poor horse, the picture of suffering, appears to be a monster of wickedness *because* he has suffered unimaginable torments.

The dual nature of the journey is best seen in Roland's words: "I shut my eyes and turned them on my heart." He hopes to recall earlier, happier sights to inspirit him before the great fight that he knows lies before him

—although he has no idea whom he must fight or where or why. He recalls Cuthbert and Giles, brave knights who failed in the quest and ended in shame. Again there is the element of uncertainty in the memory of his shame and punishment: ". . . what hangman hands/ Pin to his breast a parchment?" Over the scene hangs a sick horror of unknown depravity and public disgrace which make Roland's present horror seem almost acceptable:

> Better this present than a past like that;
> Back therefore to my darkening path again!
> No sound, no sight as far as eye could strain.
> Will the night send a howlet or a bat?
> I asked: when something on the dismal flat
> Came to arrest my thoughts and change their train.

Throughout the journey runs the query: what terror is next to come? An owl or a bat, perhaps? His imagination conjures up the fears, for not one frightful thing really happens to him. The reason is that he is in a wholly strange and terrifying country: the journey into his soul, the voyage up the Congo River into the Heart of Darkness, the terror of the encounter with Self.

A small river "crossed my path/ As unexpected as a serpent comes. . . ." In this nightmare, things come to him, all as if by stealth. He never sees something from afar and makes his way toward it. Rather it secretly approaches him to startle and unnerve. The little river, to his overheated imagination, seems as if it "might have been a bath/ for the fiend's glowing hoof. . . ." Nothing appears innocuous, everything is an obscure menace. Everything is personified. By the river the alders "kneeled down over it," suggesting to him that it is the bath of Satan, and willows along the bank "flung them headlong in a fit/ Of mute despair, a suicidal throng. . . ." He instinctively imagines that the river must have done them some dreadful wrong, "Whate'er that was. . . ."

The path he is on apparently comes to the river, not at a crossing or at a bridge, and he is forced to wade across, unquestioning, but shuddering in terror lest he step upon a dead man's cheek or spear a baby, thinking it is a water rat. The land across the river is, if anything, even more frightful. Some vague and hideous warfare has desolated the land, but not one combatant remains in the ruins of the place. Roland is doomed to arrive just after horror and to imagine what must have been:

> Who were the strugglers, what war did they wage,
> Whose savage trample thus could pad the dank
> Soil to a plash?

No battle before could equal the insane ferocity that must have rent this land, a titanic struggle marked by the pain and dementia of wild cats in a "red-hot iron cage." Not the least of the terrors lies in the fact that there are no footprints leading to this "horrid mews" and none out of it. The contending forces did not come and did not go, for they are always there, deep within the soul of man. He discovers an engine which, in his imagination, he thinks must be designed to "reel/ Men's bodies out like silk"—an image which prompted David V. Erdman to conclude that the poem was written to show the conditions in industry that were destructive of body and spirit.[5] Certainly the image is as shocking and powerful as any Browning employed, but, again, the horror is only in the fevered imagination of Roland. In the kingdom of the psyche, the imagination is king. The nightmarish quest leads him through a destroyed wood, through a marsh ("it would seem"), and through a diseased area where the soil bursts into boils. Reality is always just out of reach. He encounters a palsied oak, "a cleft in him/ Like a distorted mouth that splits its rim/ Gaping at death, and dies while it recoils." Everything is at war, all is split, and harmony is but a memory. A vast black bird, "his wide wing dragon-penned," brushes by—a perfect symbol of the fearful fauna of the soul.

The plain gives way to mountains, but alas, there is no respite from horror. He does not come upon the mountains; in this phantasmagoria, they come upon him: "How thus they had surprised me,—solve it, you!"

Here is the most direct invitation to the reader to solve for himself the mystery of this dread quest. It is true that Browning denied that he wrote conscious allegory, but it must also be remembered that he said he would not necessarily repudiate allegory found by his readers. Perhaps the major theme of *The Ring and the Book* is the relativity of knowledge. Each man sees truth through the perspective of his own total context. Here the reader is invited to solve the riddle as best he can, and, indeed, as he must.

At times Roland seems about to break the bonds of the nightmare which grips him, but he can only approach the barriers of sleep and sink back:

> Yet half I seemed to recognize some trick
> Of mischief happened to me, God knows when—
> In a bad dream perhaps.

Intuitively he knows that he has come to the end of his quest. In the midst of the two hills, like "two bulls locked horn in horn in fight," stands the Tower: the great mystery of death and the great mystery of man's soul, which join at the Dark Tower. The images of death that surround the encounter with the Tower make the symbolism clear:

---

5. Erdman, "Browning's Industrial Nightmare," pp. 417-35.

The tempest's mocking elf
Points to the shipman thus the unseen shelf
He strikes on, only when the timbers start.

The encounter with death and with the dark forces of the soul is man's loneliest journey. Nothing helps. All is hostile, and death is the arch fear that all men must meet alone:

The hills, like giants at a hunting, lay,
Chin upon hand, to see the game at bay,—
"Now stab and end the creature—to the heft!"

His vision swims and his hearing is impaired as a noise tolls like a bell in his ears, recalling the names of his peers who came to this same ugly, squat Tower and were lost in the final encounter.

And yet
Dauntless the slug-horn to my lips I set,
And blew. "*Childe Roland to the Dark Tower came.*"

Berdoe's belief that the defiant blast is a "warning to others that he had failed in his quest, and that the way of the Dark Tower was the way of destruction and death" is quite mistaken. This is, rather, the journey that all men must take. It is the journey through life to death, but it is also the journey man must sometime take through his soul into the Heart of Darkness. It most surely is not a false quest against which others must be warned. It is an inevitable quest and it ends in death, as does all life. Success lies in man's bold perseverance, however terrifying the quest, and dauntlessly blowing the horn in a last act of courage at the Dark Tower where man's twofold journey ends in death.

SUGGESTED READINGS

Arms, George, " 'Childe Roland' and 'Sir Galahad,' " *College English*, VI (1945), 258-61.
Suggests that " 'Childe Roland to the Dark Tower Came' " is Browning's reply to Tennyson's "Sir Galahad."

Burrows, Leonard, *Browning the Poet: An Introductory Study* (Nedlands, Western Australia, 1969), pp. 161-69.
"The poem [" 'Childe Roland to the Dark Tower Came' "] has an undeniable power and intensity, but without doubt it is uncharacteristically mysterious, refusing to supply answers to questions which a reader is prompted by the poem's imaginative force to ask. What is the significance of the Dark Tower? What is the purpose of the quest for it?

In what strange and terrible country does the tower stand? Are the terrors largely inside or outside the overtaxed, overstrained, overwrought knight-errant? Why and how have the lost adventurers failed? Does Childe Roland himself fail or succeed in the end?" (pp. 166-67).

Clarke, C. C., "Humor and Wit in 'Childe Roland,' " *Modern Language Quarterly,* XXIII (1962), 323-36.

Finds that the poem is "not the unequivocally somber tale it is often taken to be." The grotesque imagery, the buoyant rhythms, and the shocking incidents suggest those of "The Pied Piper of Hamelin." "What convinces us of the resilience of Childe Roland's spirit—the toughness of his moral fiber—is not merely his exhibition of courage on reaching the Tower, but the verbal exuberance and humor he displays (along with earnestness) in telling us how he got there" (p. 323).

Clarke finds humor and wit in such lines as the following:

As for the grass, it grew as scant as hair
    In leprosy. . . .

One stiff blind horse, his every bone a-stare. . . .

Whose savage trample could thus pad the dank
Soil to a plash? Toads in a poisoned tank,
    Or wild cats in a red-hot iron cage—

"It is doubtful whether anywhere else in his work Browning so successfully harnesses both his humor and wit in the prosecution of a serious artistic intention" (p. 323).

"On the whole my argument corroborates McLuhan's. Such complexity as there is in 'Childe Roland' is achieved within a single dimension; it is only in a limited sense, if at all, that the landscape can be said to be an inner landscape. And despite the complexity of tone, what Browning offers is not subtle exploration of a complex moral theme. Had he been more conscious of his debt to *Lear,* it is possible that he would have written a better poem" (p. 336).

Duffin, Henry Charles, *Amphibian: A Reconsideration of Browning* (London, 1956), pp. 84-86.

Of " 'Childe Roland' " Duffin says: "Browning was a narrative poet, not given to allegory: is there a single other poem of his that asks for an allegorical explanation? Of vast loosely-woven fabrics like *The Faerie Queene* and *The Pilgrim's Progress* it can be said that 'the allegory won't bite'; impose an allegorical intention on the finely etched chiaroscuro of *Childe Roland* and it bites the heart out of your enjoyment" (p. 85).

"If intention other than lyrical there was, it was unconscious. It may be Browning's instinctive reply to the *Grail.* Where Tennyson's ideal was something beautiful and divine to see, to aspire to, to wonder at, to worship, Browning's search is for something to be done, evil to be sought out, attacked and conquered: the way of morality against the way of religion, sacrifice in well-doing rather than saving one's own soul. Yet Browning's 'something' is no commonplace benevolence, but as mysterious as Galahad's vision, The Tower is evil itself: I think we may go so far" (p. 86).

Erdman, David V., "Browning's Industrial Nightmare," *Philological Quarterly*, XXXVI (1957), 417-35.
Argues that the poem is Browning's indirect attack on predatory industrialism. "As Roland crossed the spiteful river he thought he stepped on a dead man, and when he speared what he took for a water rat, it gave 'a baby's shriek.' In it we hear the 'sob' or 'cry' of the child in the factory which 'curses' the 'mailed heel' treading on child-workers in its merchant adventures. Is this river the mill stream?" (p. 431).

Golder, Harold, "Browning's *Childe Roland,*" *Publications of the Modern Language Association*, XXXIX (1924), 963-78.
A seminal article on the literature of myth and legend, commonly associated with children's literature, such as "Jack and the Beanstalk," "Jack the Giant-Killer," and so forth, on which Browning may have drawn in composing " 'Childe Roland to the Dark Tower Came.' "

Hoar, Victor, "A Note on Browning's 'Childe Roland to the Dark Tower Came,' " *Victorian Newsletter*, No. 27 (1965), 26-28.
Argues that Roland is not to be identified with the Grail hero, for there is no evidence that he is peculiarly gifted with the purity or the powers to enable him to succeed where others may fail: "Indeed, there is no reason to assume that Roland will endure the trial. He must pass a series of tests; he has not yet passed them all as he clears the wasteland. He is a young, relatively untried man; he may not even, as yet, be a knight. But he is brave, and it is this virtue that Browning seems to be recommending to his own age."

Kintgen, Eugene R. "Childe Roland and the Perversity of the Mind," *Victorian Poetry*, IV (1966), 253-58.
Pursues the theme suggested by Mrs. Sutherland Orr that "Childe Roland's description of the landscape through which he is riding might not correspond to the actual landscape" (p. 253). "Roland's descriptions, then, are as much mental as they are physical: they reveal as much about Roland's mind as about external events" (p. 253). Mr. Kintgen wisely assumes that "Beyond Roland's perception is the reader's, who should realize that Roland is battling against himself, rather than against

any outside challenges, and that the ultimate victory lies in his conquest of his human frailty" (p. 257).

Melchiori, Barbara, *Browning's Poetry of Reticence* (New York, 1968), pp. 114-39, 208-13 and passim.
Mrs. Melchiori, like Betty Miller, finds more or less direct autobiography in " 'Childe Roland to the Dark Tower Came,' " and in other poems as well. Moreover, the autobiographical elements which she discovers in the poems are rather regularly given a heavily Freudian emphasis. "Not that 'Childe Roland' was a conscious allegory of an artist's progress, difficulties, and ultimate failure. Any such interpretation taken alone would leave unexplained much of the horror imagery and would fail to account for the disturbing effect of the poem as a whole. Much more is involved. Nevertheless Browning shows constant concern in his poetry with his task as poet and artist. He took this very seriously indeed, and much, if not most, of his work is indirectly concerned with it. A nightmare of failure and defeat would therefore imply for him defeat as a poet. . . . The natural human wish for acknowledgment must have been strengthened in his case by his peculiar position as being the husband of a famous poetess, and financially dependent upon her. There was material for nightmare here" (p. 125).

Miller, Betty, *Robert Browning: A Portrait* (New York, 1952), p. 180.
"A few weeks later, on January 2, 1852, *Childe Roland*, coming upon him 'as a kind of dream,' revealed to him in a landscape fully as ominous as that of Dante's *Inferno* (all of which, Browning once wrote, I have 'in my head and heart') the retribution appropriate to his own sin: the corruption and sterility that must claim one who has failed, like many another 'poor traitor' before him, to deliver to mankind the full burden of the message with which he has been entrusted."

Phelps, William Lyon, *Robert Browning*, new ed. (Indianapolis, 1932), pp. 231-37.
"Three entirely different interpretations may be made of the poem [" 'Childe Roland to the Dark Tower Came' "]. First, the Tower is the quest, and Success is found only in the moment of Failure. Second, the Tower is the quest, and when found is worth nothing: his hero has spent his life searching for something that in the end is seen to be only a round, squat, blind turret—for such things do men throw away their lives! Third, the Tower is not the quest at all—it is damnation, and when the knight turns *aside* from the true road to seek the Tower, he is a lost soul steadily slipping through increasing darkness to hell . . ." (p. 233).

Shaw, W. David, *The Dialectical Temper: The Rhetorical Art of Robert Browning* (Ithaca, N.Y., 1968), pp. 126-35.

Mr. Shaw argues that Childe Roland is "a Lear upon the heath. . . ." And as Lear kneels down like a child to pray, so Childe Roland discovers that to be saved one must "become a 'childe' again" (p. 132).

Short, Clarice, "Childe Roland, Pedestrian," *Victorian Poetry*, VI (1968), 175-77.

Emphasizes the unreal, dreamlike character of the poem, along with the nightmare improbabilities that abound, especially the singular fact that Childe Roland appears to be on foot, an unlikely condition for a knight. "The spear which he uses as a staff in crossing the river seems to have come into his hand by an act of magic. The river forded, the spear is heard of no more. The horn upon which he blows the challenge like the spear is just there, mysteriously, at the right moment though whether Roland carried it or found it is never stated" (p. 177).

Symons, Arthur, *An Introduction to the Study of Browning* (London, 1906), pp. 118-20.

"The poem [" 'Childe Roland to the Dark Tower Came' "] is very generally supposed to be an allegory, and a number of ingenious interpretations have been suggested, and the 'Dark Tower' has been defined as Love, Life, Death and Truth. But, as a matter of fact, Browning, in writing it, had no allegorical intention whatever. It was meant to be, and is, a pure romance."

Willoughby, John W., " 'Childe Roland to the Dark Tower Came,' " *Victorian Poetry*, I (1963), 291-99.

Takes issue with the critics who have read allegory into the poem. "Where has all this analysis led? And what conclusions does it justify about the worth of ' "Childe Roland" ' as a poem"? (p. 297). After discovering that nothing could be more useless than such analysis, Mr. Willoughby finds that the speaker in the poem is an "unreal wanderer in a nightmare world of surrealistic horror. . . ." The poem, he believes, is not an allegory of anything outside the work itself but rather is a "plumbing of the unconscious mind projecting itself in the action of the poem" (p. 297). The poem concerns a mind turned in on itself, committed to a quest that is wholly uncertain both as to goal and outcome.

14

"Respectability"

Browning, the greatest singer of individualism in his age, believed that the highest tribunal of individual morality lay in the human heart, not in institutions or formal codes. This is not to imply that Browning ever believed that any code of morality is as good as another, or that they were equally worthless, but that, in the end, man is judged as an individual. The fullest exploration of the pernicious belief that, since in life there can be no absolutes, it is of no consequence what ideals and goals a man elects to pursue, is seen in "Bishop Blougram's Apology." In that poem a casuistical bishop argues that individuality is unlimited, so long as he pays lip service to established dogmas, and one's ardent pursuit of worldly power and wealth is fully in accord with the teachings of Christ and the Church. He argues so well, in fact, that most scholars have concluded that he speaks the sentiments of Browning himself, and Lord Dunsany has even argued, in his essay "Browning Is Blougram," that the bishop is in reality Browning in ecclesiastical surroundings.

In "Respectability" we see another aspect of the question of individualism in conflict with hypocritical codes. Couched in a swift and dramatic monologue, the poem is one of the most pointed in Browning. Unfortunately, the poem is widely misunderstood and is held to be quite the opposite of what Browning intended.

Two lovers are walking hand in hand down a boulevard along the Seine in Paris. Hiram Corson, in his *Introduction to Browning,* made the plausible suggestion, now widely accepted, that the couple are George Sand and Jules Sandeau, who lived together after the novelist had left her husband. The identity of the lovers is, in reality, quite irrelevant, for the dramatic moment and the conflict and resolution in their souls are all that matters, whoever they may be.

The man is the speaker. He is justifying their unconventional life and scornfully illuminating the hypocrisy of the world, which says that compliance with the moral and legal codes that society imposes on men (together with payment of certain fees) turns what would be a mortal sin into transcendent virtue. For those who cannot comply, perhaps because of an inconvenient spouse who refuses to cooperate by dying, society offers no recourse more palatable than self-denial. As an example of the contemptible hollowness of society's artificial mores, which can be flouted safely only by the rich and powerful, the pair pass the Institute, a citadel of pious, hypocritical respectability. Inside François Guizot, a constitutional Royalist, is welcoming with unctuous hypocrisy his political enemy, the Catholic Liberal, Charles Montalembert, to preserve the appearance of harmony and respectability. So much, the lover concludes, for respectability.

The conclusion of the poem is widely misinterpreted. Editors of anthologies routinely note that the line "Put forward your best foot!" implies that, much as one sees through the hypocrisy of social codes, when passing a stronghold of respectability, like the Institute, one is well advised to pretend compliance with its codes. In short, the proper response to hypocrisy is hypocrisy, a theme as far removed from Browning's point as can be imagined. Perhaps the source of the misinterpretation is Berdoe's *Browning Cyclopedia*, in which he says that the conclusion means: "We are passing the lamps: put your best foot foremost!" He believes the speaker counsels her to release his hand, drop behind, and pretend they are strangers until they are hidden by the welcome shadows beyond the lamps of the Institute. This is entirely out of keeping with the spirit and mood of the poem. The lamps, it seems clear, are not connected in any way with the Institute, but rather are the lamps ("Down the court three lampions flare. . . .")—three small lamps—before a cafe, a rathskeller, or a cave, where hypocrisy and false codes have no dominion, where lovers may be themselves. "Put forward your best foot" means not to *conceal* your love behind feigned respectability—against which the poem is a bitter commentary—but to shake the dust of hypocrisy from your feet. Let us hurry to the cafe where we can be completely and unhesitatingly honest.

15

"How It Strikes a Contemporary"

"How It Strikes a Contemporary" is an extended description of a poet, as seen through the eyes of a young, modish man in Valladolid, Spain. All critics have agreed very properly that the poem is a most effective and memorable account of the poet and his role, but few have seen the real dramatic basis of the poem. It has become a truism that it

> . . . is a portrait of the Poet as the unpoetic gossiping public of the day sees him. It is humorously colored by the alien point of view of the speaker, who suspects without understanding either the greatness of the poet's spiritual personality and mission, or the nature of his life, which is withdrawn from that of the commonalty, yet spent in clear-sighted universal sympathies and kindly meditation between Humanity and its God.[1]

The narrator, thus, has regularly been seen as a fop who speaks for the insensitive, suspicious, uncultured populace, who suspect the poet's motives, misunderstand his role, and embrace eagerly the most scandalous rumors attaching to his private life. Roma King, Jr., in his study *The Focusing Artifice*, finds the speaker untutored and bumbling:

> The speaker, a young man of mode, talks about a poet whom he has only seen and whose work he does not understand. He offers a series of impromptu, fragmentary, suggestive impressions rather than a full, consistent portrait. . . . The speaker fails to establish a relation between the man and his work; indeed, to understand what his work is.[2]

These judgments fail to see that the speaker is satirizing the crude and erroneous views of the populace. He is, indeed, revealing that the poet—at least this particular poet—is quite another sort of fellow, and since it is

1. Charlotte Porter and Helen A. Clarke, eds., *The Complete Works of Robert Browning*, 12 vols. (1898), note to "How It Strikes a Contemporary," V, 282.
2. Roma King, Jr., *The Focusing Artifice* (Athens, Ohio, 1968), pp. 99-100.

clear that his description of the poet is remarkably close to Browning's own view of the poet and his function, it seems strange to insist that the speaker is dull, vulgar, and imperceptive, a man speaking the prejudices of the townspeople, when he is in fact speaking as a corrective of their views. The evidence in the poem supports very well the conclusion that he is unusually sensitive and respectful, almost uniquely perceptive, and poetic far beyond the norm. He is young and not given to writing poetry, but for all that he has the stuff of poetry in him. It is not too farfetched to see in him some of the characteristics of the *young* Browning, just as it is almost impossible not to see in the poet he describes many of the characteristics of the *old* Browning.

No insensitive dullard, speaking for the vulgar populace, could have observed a poet with such keen insight or could have probed so deep into the soul of another. The speaker has watched the old poet with consuming interest, but more important he has seen that he has the soul athirst for knowledge of men and motive and the drama within the soul of his fellows. Nothing could be clearer than the fact that the speaker knows that the scandalous rumors are both stupid and cruel, and he repeatedly says so. Indeed, this is what the poem is about—to show how far from the truth the rumors are and to show that the true poets, in Shelley's words, are indeed the "unacknowledged legislators of the world."

I think it unlikely that the speaker is fully aware of the function or the technique of poetry, and unlike Browning, he probably has read little poetry, and he almost certainly has never studied it. Although he makes it clear that the poet he is describing is the only poet he has ever known, he has the soul of a poet without knowing it, and instinctively he sees what no book could teach him: the questing, searching, enormously interested soul of the true poet. It is true that he seems to be unaware that he has by instinct found the key to poets and to poetry, and he would be astounded to be told that he had. And he would be amazed to be informed that he has the soul of both the poet and the scholar, but he does. He has not fully formulated a conclusion from his careful and sensitive observations, and Roma King, Jr., is right in saying that he "offers a series of impromptu, fragmentary, suggestive impressions rather than a full, consistent portrait." But these fragmentary impressions are sound and sensitive and right. The fact that he would devote so much time to observing the poet is significant; that he would relate it in such careful detail is even more significant. Most significant of all is the essential respect and charity he feels for the poet and the urbane hostility he shows for the crass public who fail to see anything.

After all, it seems highly unlikely that Browning would elect to put into the mouth of an unintelligent philistine his most direct dramatic account of what a poet is and what his role must be. The poet he describes is not

Browning, but he embraces the same credo. Browning goes out of his way to supply details which are not in accord with the facts in his own life: the setting in Valladolid; the rather more dowdy clothing than Browning commonly wore; the poet's poverty; the suspicions of the townspeople; his lonely habits; the beaked nose, "Curved, cut and colored like an eagle's claw"; his relationship with the governor; and others. But the similarities between the two are far more impressive than the differences, especially their lust for life and their insatiable thirst for firsthand knowledge of the human condition and the drama of life.

"How It Strikes a Contemporary" might be considered to be a portrait of one obedient to the strictures on the nature of the poet included in "Transcendentalism: A Poem in Twelve Books," where the true poet is pictured as being one who fills his poetry with the sights and sounds and smells of earth and life. The poet in Valladolid scents the world, "looking it full in face," one of the most marvelous of Browning's images—and it must not be forgotten that it is from the mouth of a man supposed by the critics to be imperceptive and unaware of what he is observing. It will be noticed that the speaker intuitively is using the same concrete images and sights that the poet himself searches for with such keen interest, striking evidence of a considerable oneness and understanding between the two.

We see through the poet's own actions his drive to discover what is going on: he turns up an alley that is a dead end (and he knows it is), for he is not interested in getting from point A to point B, but in what part of the human drama he may discover on his way. He wears a "scrutinizing hat," and he probes the mortar of a new brick building to see how well or ill it is made—and it is from the words of the supposedly imperceptive speaker of the town's gross suspicions that we learn of these things. He watches every act of gentleness or cruelty with half an eye, and the whole town fancies that he must be an informer, but the speaker knows better: he is in reality the town's "chief inquisitor," who writes of all the doings in the city, unobtrusively, and then sends them to "our Lord the King." Later Browning removed the capitals, in line with his usual practice, "to make the allegorical meaning less obvious," as W. C. DeVane wisely notes. The reference is dual. On one level—the level of the townspeople—the King is their temporal ruler, for whom they fear the poet is spying, and they infer that he has much to do with recent scandalous events:

> Had he to do with A.'s surprising fate?
> When altogether old B. disappeared
> And young C. got his mistress,—was 't our friend,
> His letter to the King, that did it all?

But on another level—the real level, as seen by the speaker—the poet reports directly to God. The speaker is both amused and shocked by the disparity between the truth and the lurid, whispered speculations of the townspeople about the wild bohemian life they fancy the poet leads, with "four Titians on the wall,/ And twenty naked girls to change his plate!" The poet leads a quiet, reserved life, doing God's work without fanfare, and on his deathbed, the sensitive might have noted that

> Here had been, mark, the general-in-chief,
> Thro' a whole campaign of the world's life and death,
> Doing the King's work all the dim day long,
> In his old coat and up to knees in mud,
> Smoked like a herring, dining on a crust,—
> And, now the day was won, relieved at once!

It is unusual to find the supposedly unpoetic spokesmen of the "gossiping public of the day" speaking with such tenderness, such understanding, and such love.

It seems likely that the speaker is aware of the implication of his final words—"Let's to the Prado and make the most of time"—and it is apparent that he knows he is uttering the poetic credo of the old poet he has been describing. He, too, is a poet at heart, doing the King's work, for the words he has just spoken form the last line of one of the exquisitely sensitive and vital poems of the age.

SUGGESTED READINGS

Fotheringham, James, *Studies of the Mind and Art of Robert Browning* (London, 1898), p. 427.

" 'How It Strikes a Contemporary' deals with *popular mistakes* about the poet. It begins—

> I only knew one poet in my life:
> And this, or something like it, was his way.

He was a man of mark, though not after the style or for the uses of the world. His dress and bearing made you aware of that. He mixed in and noted the world, quiet, withdrawn, but full of eyes. He saw every one, stared at no one. You stared at him, and though he barely looked at you, he knew you and took your gaze as a thing of course. Not knowing what these 'ways' meant, yet sure they must have some 'use,' people said he was the 'king's spy,' and they could quote cases that seemed to be explained by it. And they mistook his private life as much as they did his public function. The poet lived in the simplest way, but the public thought he lived in a voluptuous style." It should be noted that Fotheringham finds that the "popular mistakes" that people have about a poet are held in this poem by the townspeople, not by the speaker, who sees with perceptive and sympathetic eyes.

Kvapil, Charline R., " 'How It Strikes a Contemporary': A Dramatic Monologue," *Victorian Poetry*, IV (1966), 279-83.

Shaw, W. David, *The Dialectical Temper: The Rhetorical Art of Robert Browning* (Ithaca, N.Y., 1968), pp. 86-88.
Mr. Shaw sees the speaker in "How It Strikes a Contemporary" as wholly superficial, a "gossip," who in trying to enumerate the poet's qualities can only "enumerate surface impressions like the aquiline nose or formidable brow."

16

"Andrea del Sarto"

"Andrea del Sarto (Called 'The Faultless Painter')" appeared in volume two of *Men and Women*. John Kenyon, Mrs. Browning's cousin, requested that Browning supply him with a copy of the picture of Andrea and his wife Lucrezia in the Pitti Palace. Browning, apparently being unable to comply with the request, wrote the poem instead. Andrea (1487-1531) was called "del Sarto" because his father was a tailor (Sarto), and he soon became known as *il pittore senza errori*, "the faultless painter." There seems to be no evidence that the title was given to him in any sense of irony, such as that which Browning employs. To Browning, who held that in life all perfection is denied, that to be perfect is the hallmark of easy and ignoble aspirations, the very nickname suggested failure. To those who have roamed the galleries in Italy expecting to find Andrea's many paintings conspicuously lacking in soul or *élan*, demonstrating the fatal consequences of overadherence to photographic realism, the excellence of his productions comes as a surprise. Even the silver gray which Browning notes in the poem as characterizing the dullness of spirit supposed to mark his painting is missing. The excellence of Andrea's works in no way vitiates the worth of Browning's magnificent poem. The poet was painting a dramatic and imaginative portrait of a man he knew only from the galleries and from books, notably Vasari's *Le Vite Pittori*, his chief source.

Andrea was a middle-class artist, with no great aspirations to fame, but with considerable taste and great powers of execution. He loved social preeminence and finally fell in love with a socialite, Lucrezia del Fede, wife of a hatter named Carlo Recanati, who conveniently died, permitting the pair to regularize the liaison. Lucrezia, according to Vasari, was shallow, pleasure loving, greedy, and faithless—but surpassingly beautiful. In 1518, Andrea was invited to visit the French Court at the invitation of Francis I. Leaving his wife in Florence, Andrea went to Fontainebleau, where he was royally entertained and handsomely remunerated for his artistic services. Upon the request of his wife to return to Italy, he obtained leave from the

King and departed, carrying with him a substantial treasure entrusted to him by Francis for the purchase of art treasures which would adorn the royal gallery. Perhaps at the instigation of his wife—certainly to gain favor in her eyes—Andrea spent the King's money and some of his own as well in building a house in Florence. Although he lost the favor of the beneficent King and lived in fear for his life thereafter, Andrea suffered no direct reprisal at the royal hand.

Andrea spent the remaining years of his life in Florence and died at the age of forty-three of the plague, which was then rampant, on January 22, 1531. His wife, for whom he had sacrified his honor and much of his artistic career as well, failed to tend him in his illness, fearing the pestilence, and she survived her husband for forty years.

In "Andrea del Sarto" Browning presents one of his masterly portraits of a complex and tortured soul, an artist whose dramatic monologue reveals a fractured spirit that is close to schizophrenic. Both within the artist and without, there is a memorable confrontation of values and standards, for the poem is both a rationalization and a confession at the same time. The inconstancy and irresolution of Andrea are again and again revealed in contrasts: contrasts of color, time, aspiration, resolution, artistry, love, women, and life.

Andrea is the faultless painter, in Browning the surest indication of failure, for absolute attainment is stagnation and death of the soul. Only through endless growth and struggle toward unattainable goals can man achieve success. Andrea's goals have been low and readily attained for one with his extraordinary talents, and the ashes of failure are bitter in his mouth; but at the same time he exercises his ingenuity to the breaking point to excuse his failure and to establish his position among those he wishes to be his peers: Raphael, Leonardo, and Michelangelo.

One of the ironies running throughout the poem is Andrea's ambivalence to life. He fears life and its challenge, and at the same time he is attracted by its blandishments and corrupted by its values. The schizophrenic nature of his monologue is illustrated by the duality of his self-assessment. He fluctuates throughout between self-derogation and self-exculpation, but he carefully, if unconsciously, keeps the two halves of his monologue apart, reasoning on two separate levels, on different premises, and to contrasting conclusions. It is an error to suppose that Andrea is contemptible wholly or that he is a simple failure. He is far too complex and contradictory to be labeled easily.

"Andrea del Sarte" is widely held to be one of Browning's most successful dramatic monologues, and it is the complexity and the subtlety of contrasts that in large measure account for its success. Nowhere does the poet more powerfully reveal the tension within character than in the almost bewildering opposition tearing the sick soul of Andrea. The poem begins with a contrast and ends with a contrast, and the dramatically conceived stress of soul everywhere in between is seen in terms of contrast. The initial line, beginning, "But do not let us quarrel any more/ No, my Lucrezia; bear with me for once," is a contrast between his yearning for an ideal love and the sordid reality of their empty relationship. The conjunction "But" suggests the contrast between his most recent protestation against her insistence that he sell his soul for money and his immediate total surrender. "You turn your face, but does it bring your heart?" he asks. The contrast between art and commercialism is balanced by the contrast between face and heart. He contrasts tonight's great weariness with his usual weariness, a suggestion of enervation more of spirit than of body. He makes clear that he wants only to hold her hand "as married people use"—a contrast between what truly married people do and what he and Lucrezia fail to do in their facsimile of marriage.

This simile leads to another contrast, the promise of the great profitable energy and industry that he foretells for the morrow, in contrast with his great lassitude and artistic paralysis as he speaks, if she will but put her hand in his for an hour. The simple desire to hold her hand within his hand reveals his desire to assert his male dominance of her female acquiescence, a wish which his abject, groveling surrender has made wholly ironic. His soul writhes when he contemplates her bodily perfection and her spiritual desolation, and there is the bitter contrast between the ironic fact that everyone who looks upon her calls her his—provided he has the price—but she is incapable of belonging to anyone, even her husband.

The pervasive contrast is between the silver-gray of Andrea's present life with the gold of his youth and the golden year at Fontainebleau, the contrast of what he likes to think they once were with what they have indubitably become:

—You, at the point of your first pride in me
(That's gone you know),—but I, at every point;
My youth, my hope, my art, being all toned down
To yonder sober pleasant Fiesole.
(ll. 37-40)

There is the contrast between light and dark, morning and evening, youth and age, life and death:

That length of convent-wall across the way
Holds the trees safer, huddled more inside;
The last monk leaves the garden; days decrease,
And autumn grows, autumn in everything.
(ll. 42-45)

Andrea has been sorely wounded by life, and he yearns for certainty and safety. He envies the trees, safe within the convent wall (as he is not) that shuts out the trials and dangers of life—and life's opportunities of growth and fulfillment as well. He makes quite explicit that the trees symbolize his furtive life:

> Eh? the whole seems to fall into a shape
> As if I saw alike my work and self
> And all that I was born to be and do,
> A twilight-piece.
>
> (ll. 46-49)

Andrea's self-exculpation is based on the mysterious contrast between man's instinctive assertion of his freedom of choice and the determinism which in reality guides his every act. Wherein is the guilt if fate determines man's acts?

> Love, we are in God's hand.
> How strange now, looks the life he makes us lead;
> So free we seem, so fettered fast we are!
>
> (ll. 51-53)

The technical dexterity that is his pride (and shame) is implicitly contrasted with the soul which his paintings lack, but which lies at the bottom of his heart awaiting his call, "if I ever wish so deep"—an admission that he has settled for mediocrity. But he still dreams of the great work he could do if Lucrezia would inspirit his soul. This leads to a contrast between his technical perfection and the blundering efforts of his rivals. He then ruefully admits the futility of basing pride on what lacks soul and candidly contrasts their "truer light" with his twilight-piece darkness. Their works may drop downward, but in contrast they themselves rise to heaven; his works rise toward heaven—the heaven of technical perfection—but he sits in the dust. They are volatile, alive; their blood boils at a word of praise or blame, but he has abdicated from life, and is impervious to praise or blame either, knowing exactly what he can do and how it will turn out—a mark of dead perfection:

> All is silver-gray
> Placid and perfect with my art: the worse!
>
> (ll. 98-99)

He recognizes his fractured, imperfect spirit when he says it would have been profitless to know, to sigh:

> "Had I been two, another and myself,
> Our head would have o'erlooked the world!"
>
> (ll. 102-03)

This is the cry of a man yearning for the woman who might supply the missing half of his soul needed to provide his wholeness. Although he then asserts that it is profitless to lament what might have been if she had complemented him, we see that this failure is the pivotal failure of his life, and he then accuses her directly of robbing him of "the play, the insight and the stretch—/ Out of me, out of me!"

> And wherefore out?
> Had you enjoined them on me, given me soul
> We might have risen to Raphael, I and you!
> (ll. 117-19)

At these unusually direct words of recrimination, Lucrezia, it may be safely assumed, bridles in anger, for Andrea, straightway frightened and abased, utters words that form a singular contrast with his foregoing sentiment:

> Nay, Love, you did give all I asked, I think—
> More than I merit, yes, by many times.
> (ll. 120-21)

Immediately after this contradiction, he qualifies it:

> But had you—oh, with the same perfect brow,
> And perfect eyes, and more than perfect mouth,
> And the low voice my soul hears, as a bird
> The fowler's pipe, and follows to the snare—
> Had you, with these the same, but brought a mind!
> (ll. 122-26)

In the word *perfect* used thrice, we have the basic contradiction of the poem: to attain perfection is to lose it.

Andrea contrasts his marital condition with the single state of Raphael and Agnolo and in vexation asks, "Why do I need you?"

> What wife had Raphael, or has Agnolo?
> In this world, who can do a thing, will not;
> And who would do it, cannot, I perceive. . . .
> (ll. 136-38)

The glorious days at Fontainebleau, with the King's golden look and his golden chain and the gold that filled his life, are painfully contrasted with the ashen-gray desolation of his life after Lucrezia "grew restless" and prompted him to steal and cheat and destroy his talent. He contrasts the "frank French eyes" of the noble courtiers whom he betrayed with his own condition:

> And I'm the weak-eyed bat no sun should tempt
> Out of the grange whose four walls make his world.
> (ll. 169-70)

The poem is besprinkled with a series of brief contrasts, heightening the bitterness of his present life: that between Raphael's picture of the virgin and his own; the contrast between the virgin and Lucrezia, who posed as model for the painting; Michelangelo's prognostication of Andrea's capacity as an artist, and his pitiful performance; the mortar between the bricks which he sees transformed into the illicit gold he stole from Francis; the failure of his life and what heaven holds for him; and saddest of all, the shattering contrast between his hopeful dream and the sudden realization that even in heaven his fellow artists will outstrip him, "Because there's still Lucrezia,—as I choose"—the final admission that he will elect his degradation throughout eternity.

Andrea's unsettled, fractured mental state is seen in these flashes of contrast, these violent fluctuations of wish, judgment, opinion, this telling of guilt and pride, strength and weakness, dream and fact. Andrea remains one of the most powerfully conceived and complex characters in Browning. Like scores of perplexed characters in Browning, Andrea is forced to make a choice between conflicting principles: in this instance, between his artistic conscience, on the one hand, and his love for his wife, on the other. His artistic failure is in perfect parallel with his failure in love. It is widely held that Andrea does not "love" his wife, but rather is infatuated with her body. Such a simplistic view diminishes the stress of soul and the drama alike. Although he is painfully aware of her undeveloped soul and mind, he is aware likewise that she is a human personality in the most dazzling body, and he is in bondage to her. In his love for a truly worthless woman and in his tormented knowledge that she is worthless lies the root of the terrible tension in Andrea. That she is unworthy of his love in no measure lessens his love, but it immeasurably heightens his shame.

One of the supreme ironies in Andrea's life is the fact that whatever he yearns for, in spite of the disastrous price he pays to gain it, he can never attain. The baseness of the object, again, does not lessen the irony, but heightens it. He can possess neither the body of Lucrezia in soul-satisfying fulfillment, nor her love. Throughout the poem there are signs of his ennui, a creeping enervation and despair, the result of endless frustration and failure, until he is quite content to hold her hand, not her body, which he can only dream of possessing in triumph. Were he the virile young stallion that he envies, perhaps her body would be sufficient, but in being of low sexual drive and quasi-impotence, he has nothing but the wreck of his dreams and his memories.

Nothing could be clearer than Andrea's consciousness of his doglike abasement in following his humiliating surrender with his astonishing request to hold her hand. Andrea deliberately lowers himself as a means of atonement through suffering. To strip himself of all manhood and self-respect is to gain some measure of pity and purgation, albeit at a fearful price. His request to hold her hand for an hour before she goes out to give her body—she could never give herself—to a lover is a tacit acceptance of his readiness to accept the crumbs from the table of his marriage. The hand becomes a sexual substitute, a fetish with which he has signified he will remain content. He does not have the courage to risk reopening the fight by suggesting that he deserves her act of love as a reward for his surrender to her demands, but one muses over whether his fears of his manhood do not equally silence his suggestion. He could never demand, of course. One can only speculate on cause and effect in this poem. Did Andrea's inadequacy follow the coldness and insensitivity of his wife, or vice versa? It is unlikely that either Andrea or Lucrezia at this point could tell, but it is certain that the two would have almost diametrically opposed recollections and interpretations of the years during which their marriage died.

As the hand is a substitute for herself, so also is her posing as a model a substitute for full possession. Her soul—such as it is—has never been his, of course, but in a very real sense her body has been almost as unattainable. Hence his insistence that she serve as model, for in his frustration and doubts of his puissance, he has found a voyeuristic substitute in which his manhood does not have to be proved, in which it is possible to be "perfect," as his art is perfect. In his imagination he can play the Renaissance Walter Mitty both in love and in art. In art Andrea has set his sights low to accommodate her avarice and in so doing has gained the reputation of being "the faultless painter"; and in love he has done much the same thing. If he cannot succeed, he has also hedged against failure. To him Lucrezia represents perfection of body, perhaps a perfection that should remain inviolate, virginal. One is tantalized by the degree of Andrea's syndrome: how far does he carry the belief that perfection—even in things mechanical or physical—is a sufficient substitute for an imperfect but alive, searching, growing spirit? Imperfection distresses him acutely. He is affronted by her pierced ear lobs, the solitary spots on the white radiance of her beauty. Even more desolating must have been the knowledge that, far from remaining inviolate and spotless, she is a notorious strumpet. He is well aware of the sordid nature of her assignations:

Ah, but what does he,
The Cousin! what does he to please you more?
(ll. 242-43)

It is certain that on the conscious level Andrea knows the shameful answer to his query, which he puts as much to himself as to Lucrezia, for the question is part of his suffering and atonement, but Andrea is a complicated man who has more than one level in his life. Perhaps he clings to the dreamlike belief that she simply loves to gamble and to show off the perfection of her beauty—and returns unsullied. Nothing could be clearer than his capacity to seek solace in illusion, both in his love and in his art, but his tragedy is not so much the illusion but his inability to sustain the illusion in its collision with reality.

Roma A. King, Jr., is correct in identifying Lucrezia with Eve and at the same time with the serpent that corrupted Eve and brought death into our world and all Andrea's woe:

> So! keep looking so—
> My serpentining beauty, rounds on rounds!
> (ll. 25-26)

The usual footnote to these lines, explaining soberly that the serpentining beauty is a reference to her hair, done up in buns of coiled braids, is amusing, especially in the light of Browning's allusion to Eve and the serpent. Perhaps the figure does, in part, refer to her hair, but surely the figure is meant to stamp her—not just her hair—as the serpent in the garden. As Andrea talks she is pacing back and forth, impatiently awaiting her lover, but, being Lucrezia, she walks with the undulating grace of a snake. She is a woman whose overriding compulsion is to stir desire in men. She does it both consciously and unconsciously. There is no doubt that her reply to Andrea's long monologue is simply the sinuous, undulating grace of her body as she tantalizes him with her beauty—and with his inability to hold it. She is Eve, she is temptation. She has been tempted by the snake and has fallen, and in turn she has destroyed her husband, who, like Adam, has learned the delights of lust, but unlike Adam, has no fulfillment.

When he informs her that she is "everybody's moon," the sex symbol of the time, she merely smiles, for she sees only flattery in his words, not insult, and in her smile he finds the emptiness of his life, the false values and the bitterness that have taken the color from his days and left them gray. He and his ambitions are a "twilight piece," and he detects the odor of decay and death in his bondage. His constant use of the vocative "Love" is rich with irony, for he is agonizingly aware that neither she nor he is capable of giving or receiving love. Probably he could have once, before Lucrezia, but not now. To address her so is a torment and an irony which she is incapable of understanding.

Edward Berdoe insists in his *Browning Cyclopedia* that Lucrezia is "not the cause of her husband's failure": "No woman ruined his soul; he had no soul to ruin." This paradox is a half-truth at best. It is true that there doubtless were other causes that contributed to the ruin of his soul: infirm principle, love of the world and its blandishments, self-pity. But Lucrezia was and remains the great cause of his ruin. Berdoe's assertion that Andrea had no soul to begin with largely destroys the drama of the poem, for, as Aristotle said, neither a perfect man nor an absolutely bad man can be made dramatically interesting. The drama of the poem is inseparable from Andrea's ruin of soul, his sense of loss. Tragedy involves the loss of something of value. Without such loss there is no tragedy. The drama here is precisely the Faustian theme of a man who has sold his soul and sees all that he was and might have been in ashes.

Andrea, fittingly enough, sought out his own ruin in ignominy: hence, his insistence that man is not free, that the course of man's life long since was laid down by God, absolving man of all responsibility and guilt, an assumption that he really cannot believe, though the words give a small measure of comfort in the mouth. He courted another man's wife, and, after his timely death, he married her with all the bitter consequences of his act. At her instigation, he robbed King Francis and now lives in hiding and in fear; he neglected his parents in their impoverished old age; and, most contemptible of all, he sacrifices his art for gold to pay the gambling debts incurred by his wife and her paramour. Had Andrea no soul to lose, where would have been the loss, the diminution or ruin of spirit through a tragic flaw so essential to tragedy? The poignancy of his state is his dreadful awareness of his great loss, his pitiable attempt to salvage a shred of character and manhood from the wreck of his hopes and dreams, and his consciousness of the impossibility of doing so. This is the real theme of the poem: the conflict between shame and pride, abasement and arrogance.

Andrea shares the moral cowardice of Browning's Pictor Ignotus, who elects "success" on a small scale, shielded from the world and its haggling marts, safe in the painting of stereotypes of the cloister. Andrea elects similarly an easy success—which is failure—and he too is forced to rationalize his failure:

> I can do with my pencil what I know,
> What I see, what at bottom of my heart
> I wish for, if I ever wish so deep—
> Do easily, too—when I say, perfectly,
> I do not boast, perhaps. . . .
>
> (ll. 60-64)

We see in these lines the tension in his soul. They represent, not so much fact, but frustrating longing. When he says that he can do what he wishes to do "at bottom of my heart," he is lying to himself and to the world, for if there is anything he is aware of at this moment it is simply that he cannot do anything that at bottom of his heart he wishes. His technical perfection is a reproach and a stench, the badge of failure. To attempt to attain the heights in art is an eternal challenge, demanding unceasing growth and struggle to the very end, he knows, and to do it "easily" and "perfectly" is a contradiction, a self-defeating impossibility—but he asserts the opposite of what "at bottom" of his heart he is altogether too much aware of.

One of the most richly textured lines in Browning's dramatic monologues is Andrea's desperate attempt to preserve the fiction of his success and the failure of such artists as Raphael, Michelangelo, and Leonardo:

—Dream? strive to do and agonize to do,
And fail in doing.
(ll. 70-71)

There is no more perfect statement in Browning of the essence of success than this, not failure, and deep in the heart of Andrea this truth lies like a sickness. The essentials of success to Browning lie in these lines: the dream of illimitable growth in artistic vision and power, the struggle to attain the ever-receding heights, and—most important—the failure to attain the vision of the dream. This is Browning's concept of success, for "the prize is in the process." What a delicious irony that Andrea, seeking to find some way to denigrate his superiors in art, in reality establishes their glorious success-through-failure. He knows in his heart that they have scaled the heights shut to him, and they fail only as an earnest of their transcendent vision and soul, for he confesses:

Well, less is more, Lucrezia: I am judged.
There burns a truer light of God in them,
In their vexed beating stuffed and stopped-up brain,
Heart, or whate'er else, than goes on to prompt
This low-pulsed forthright craftsman's hand of mine.
Their works drop groundward, but themselves, I know,
Reach many a time a heaven that's shut to me. . . .
(ll. 78-84)

They are immortalized by their inability to become immortal, and he is bitterly aware that he can never be their peer:

All is silver-gray
Placid and perfect with my art: the worse!
(ll. 98-99)

Even in the next world the distance that separates them will forever widen. Raphael, dead these five years, was the ideal, for he dedicated his energies to

> Reaching, that heaven might so replenish him,
> Above and through his art. . . .
> (ll. 110-11)

That the arm in Raphael's painting is "wrongly put" is not a defect, properly looked at, but rather a sign of the rightness of the soul, for "He means right—that, a child may understand." Here is Browning's lifelong view that " 't is not what man Does which exalts him, but what man Would do!" The intent makes large the life, not the fulfillment, for the glorious vision is always impossible to realize.

Alternating between fantasies of his worth and bitter acknowledgment of his failure, he reflects upon how he would have marched with Raphael up to God if only Lucrezia had counseled: " 'God and the glory!' never care for gain/ The Present by the future, what is that?"

At Fontainebleau he made the irrevocable and fatal decision, from which there is no returning. He likes to fancy that he gave up all for love, like Antony, who cast the world aside for Cleopatra with a noble gesture: "You called me, and I came home to your heart." He knows that this is an ingenious fiction, for he never came home to her heart at all. If he ever fancied that he possessed her heart, time disabused him of his error. When he requests permission to "Let my hands frame your face in your hair's gold," he utters the great forlorn wish of his life: "You beautiful Lucrezia that are mine." Of all the things he aspires to or wishes for, nothing is so little his as Lucrezia. His dishonesty is shameful when he dares to assert that his painting of the Virgin is more alive and pulsating with the fire of life than is Raphael's, for his wife Lucrezia posed for it. His rival's painting is "the better when you pray," being idealized, but his has fire and passion, but all the while he knows that his painting is a grotesque impropriety, for a wanton posed for the picture of the Virgin. He throws the matter up to her, to judge which painting is the better, well knowing that he is appealing to a biased judge, one who will find for him, not because his painting is better, but because her vanity will demand that she find for herself, as model.

As he judges the two pictures, hoping that Lucrezia will find words of comfort for him in the competition, he is encouraged to find yet another reason for his failure, a reason beyond his control: he had not the patronage of popes and kings. Allegedly, Agnolo said one day to Raphael:

> "Friend, there's a certain sorry little scrub
> Goes up and down our Florence, none cares how,

> Who, were he set to plan and execute
> As you are, pricked on by your popes and kings,
> Would bring the sweat into that brow of yours!"
> (ll. 189-93)

Immediately after uttering these words of comfort, he makes it clear that he is not at all certain that there was such a possibility even with such patronage, and in any event to please her was the guiding principle in his life, and in doing so he doomed his art. At this she smiles, and he finds the boldness to suggest that if only she would sit by him every night he would "work better"—"I mean that I should earn more, give you more." He spells out his wretched surrender as if she were a child, which in a sense she is. Soon in bitterness he realizes that the smile was not for him but for her lover who waits outside. In anguish he begs, "Let us but love each other," and adds, as she arises from his attempted embrace, "Must you go?/ That Cousin here again? he waits outside?/ Must see you—you and not with me?"

Perhaps the following line, spoken from the lowest rung on the ladder of shame, may be called his recognition scene, but he cannot resolve to change his course of action:

> Well, let smiles buy me! have you more to spend?
> (l. 223)

As Lucrezia prepares to depart, he utters the last of his attempts at self-deception, the most monstrous of all:

> I am grown peaceful as old age to-night
> I regret little, I would change still less.
> (ll. 244-45)

His reference to his peace of mind, after his tormented confession of weakness, failure, dishonesty, abandonment of principle, and spiritual emptiness is wonderfully ironic. His whole monologue has been an expression of regret and defeat, interspersed with hollow affirmations of his worth, which he knows are false. After a long account of his moral poverty, a man cannot say that he has found peace. While assuring himself that he has found the tranquil mind, his mouth is telling Lucrezia

> You loved me quite enough, it seems to-night
> This must suffice me here. . . .
> (ll. 258-59)

And his heart breaks in the ruin of his life as she departs for an evening of gambling and lust, for which he himself has been the pander.

The monologue ends on a fine contradiction. After saying, "No doubt, there's something strikes a balance," he proceeds to prove that comforting sentiment an illusion, for in the next world, as well as here, the triumvirate of immortal painters will widen their lead, and he will be left with only Lucrezia for compensation, the very person who destroyed him on earth and will destroy him throughout eternity.

SUGGESTED READINGS

Collins, Thomas J., *Robert Browning's Moral-Aesthetic Theory, 1833-1855* (Lincoln, Nebr., 1967), pp. 145-47.

"'Andrea del Sarto' is, however, more than just another statement by Browning on the necessity of integrating flesh and soul to achieve meaning. Of equal interest is the poet's comment on the cause of Andrea's failure—his complete devotion to a woman who has proven herself to be a negative source of inspiration. Andrea describes his wife Lucrezia in a language which recalls the significance Browning attaches to the potentially beneficial influence of a woman in *Sordello* and 'One Word More.' Lucrezia is his moon, but she is also everyone else's."

Honan, Park, *Browning's Characters, A Study in Poetic Technique*, (New Haven, 1961), pp. 156-58 and passim.

"The tragedy of Andrea's character is that the soulless facility of his work—represented in Lucrezia—has been inextricably merged in his own being" (p. 158).

Kenmare, Dallas, *An End to Darkness* (London, 1962), pp. 108-09, 154-57.

"He [Andrea del Sarto] cannot come to terms with his problem; to abandon all thought of love, and dedicate the remainder of his life to art is more than he is capable of doing. For him, the failure of love is the failure of life. Beside his need for perfect love, art fades into insignificance. And he is artist enough to be tortured by the betrayal . . ." (p. 109).

"Browning's greatest poem of marital disaster is undoubtedly *Andrea del Sarto*, a poem which has been variously interpreted—as so many of Browning's poems have—and the character of the 'faultless painter' viewed from many different angles. But whatever other attributes may have been Andrea's, his courageous, uncomplaining acceptance of an impossible situation reveals him as, in his way, a man of great stature. . . ." (p. 154).

Mendel, Sydney, "Browning's *Andrea del Sarto*," *Explicator* XXII (1964), Item 77.

Emphasizes that the structure of the poem is organized around the two concepts of reading (or aspiring) and grasping (or keeping in confinement)."

Phelps, William Lyon, *Robert Browning*, new ed. (Indianapolis, 1932), pp. 206-08.

"Poor Andrea! History has treated him harshly. He is known throughout all time as 'the tailor's son,' and Browning has given him in this immortal poem a condemnation that much of his work does not really deserve. For there is inspiration in many of Andrea's Madonnas. Browning, with his fixed idea of the glory of the imperfect, the divine evidence of perpetual development, could not forgive Andrea for being called the 'faultless painter.' Thus Browning made of him a horrible example, has used him merely as the text for a sermon."

17

"Cleon"

"Cleon" may be considered a companion poem to "An Epistle of Karshish," for both treat of men of learning and attainment in their search for truth and the answer to the riddle of existence. Both men are briefly exposed to the word of Christ, and both men fail to break the bonds of their traditions and seize the truth. Karshish is more open-minded than Cleon, less stiff-necked in his cultural blindness; but both men are victims of a narrow tradition that placed limits on man and his vision. "An Epistle" is an account of how Christianity might appear to an Arab physician, by training in medical science, if not by inclination, a man unembittered but inclined to skepticism. Cleon is an old man, broader than Karshish in his attainments, but narrower in his views. He is stiff and brittle in spirit and unbending of mind. Moreover he is an embittered man as he approaches the end of his life, full of success and honors, but with a heart empty and cankered with discontent.

A. W. Crawford has shown that "Cleon" was occasioned by Matthew Arnold's "Empedocles on Etna," another poem of a cultivated Greek, who as he approaches death, takes stock of his life and finds it sorely wanting. Arnold's Empedocles is in a more pitiable state than Cleon, for he has lost the capacity to feel and to enjoy, his emotional life having been sacrificed to the intellectual, and, even worse, he is at once alienated from his fellow man and, at the same time, unable to live in isolation. Suicide appears to him to be the only way out of his dilemma and he leaps into the crater with the only joy he shows throughout the poem—joy in finding oneness with the atoms.

Cleon is in no mood for suicide. Indeed, quite the opposite. His depression stems from the altogether too imminent death awaiting him, and, unlike Empedocles, he yearns to experience life and love, which he has denied himself to further his art and science. He has denied life; life has not denied him. One of Browning's pervasive views is seen in Cleon's predicament: life is always greater than its arts. Life must be lived first and written of and painted later. If one must choose between life and the representation of life, choose life.

On July 23, 1867, Arnold wrote to his brother that he had reinstated "Empedocles on Etna" in his 1867 volume at the insistence of Browning:

> I shall be interested in hearing what you think of the poems; some of them, I feel sure, will interest you. There are two or three bad faults of punctuation which you will observe and correct. "Empedocles" takes up much room, but Browning's desire that I should reprint "Empedocles" was really the cause of the volume appearing at all.[1]

Browning recognized the power of the poem, which Arnold had excluded from his 1853 volume of *Poems*, severely censuring the poem in his famous Preface to the volume:

> What then are the situations, from the representation of which, though accurate, no poetical enjoyment can be derived? They are those in which the suffering finds no vent in action; in which a continuous state of mental distress is prolonged, unrelieved by incident, hope, or resistance; in which there is everything to be endured, nothing to be done. . . . When they occur in actual life, they are painful, not tragic; the representation of them in poetry is painful also.
>
> To this class of situations . . . that of Empedocles, as I have endeavored to represent him, belongs. . . .

Arnold's sturdy belief, expressed in the Preface, that a great human action of long ago was more properly the subject of great poetry than a lesser contemporary action, might predictably meet with Browning's approval, but the tone of the Preface is strongly in favor of classical antiquity for its own sake, and this bias Browning never shared. Indeed, the opposite view grew upon him with the passing of years, as one may see in "Old Pictures in Florence," "Parleying with Gerard de Lairesse," "An Epistle," and "Cleon" itself. To Browning, since life is to be lived, as man's first responsibility, the passing moment is the most important in the whole range of human history. The passing moment is the eternally moving watershed parting the two divisions of eternity, and it is eternally unique. The moment to come, which as one looks becomes the present is the next most important and vital point in time; then follow all the moments that make up the future. The past, interesting and enlightening as it is, is comparatively unimportant. Thus, Browning could not share Arnold's special delight with the past as superior to the present and future. In "Parleying with Gerard de Lairesse" he expresses his emphasis:

1. George W. E. Russell, ed., *Letters of Matthew Arnold, 1848-1888* (New York, 1900), p. 431.

Enough! Stop further fooling, De Lairesse!
My fault, not yours! Some fitter way express
Heart's satisfaction that the Past indeed
Is past, gives way before Life's best and last,
The all-including Future! What were life
Did soul stand still therein, forego her strife
Through the ambiguous Present to the goal
Of some all-reconciling Future? Soul,
Nothing has been which shall not bettered be
Hereafter,—leave the root, by law's decree
Whence springs the ultimate and perfect tree!
Busy thee with unearthing root? Nay, climb—
(ll. 363-74)

Much as Browning liked "Empedocles" he doubtless felt considerable impatience with Arnold's belief that the Greek literature and culture properly had a peculiar grip upon the imagination of modern man, a view that could not appeal to one who believed the present and the future were of overriding importance. Browning was the poet of immediacy and the life abundant, for, as Landor suggested, he was the Chaucer of the nineteenth century.

"Cleon" is a picture of incomparable richness in its dramatic exploration of failure-in-success, a theme which fascinated the poet. It concerns the disastrous results to man of the Greek inability to see life as a continuum. Throughout the poem is seen the paralysis of soul occasioned by the finite view of life, which rigidly circumscribes man's life and limits his scope both of vision and of hope. To Browning only Christianity could tear down the barricades blocking access to the greater life and illimitable fulfillment. "Cleon" is another dramatic illustration that the demands of life are to be met, not from philosophical and artistic achievement, however perfect, but from a revelation bringing hope. Cleon, the finest product of the pagan world, admits in despair that his hope is in inverse proportion to his achievement, that the perfection of his accomplishment has brought bitterness and emptiness into his life, which soon must end.

The quotation appearing under the title, "As certain also of your own poets have said," from Acts 17:28, concludes St. Paul's words to the Athenians with whom he was provoked because "he beheld the city full of idols." He admonishes them "that they should seek God, if haply they might feel after him and find him, though he is not far from each of us: for in him we live, and move, and have our being; as certain even of your own poets have said."

This is what the poem is about: the feeling after God and finding him, or—in Cleon's case—not seeking and not finding.

Cleon is a man who has attained great eminence in all the arts and in science as well, but in his salutation to Protus the King, he elects to call himself Cleon the poet. As if to supply a sample of his craft, he couches his salutation to the King in poetic terms:

> Cleon the poet (from the sprinkled isles,
> Lily on lily, that o'erlace the sea,
> And laugh their pride when the light wave lisps "Greece")—
> To Protus in his Tyranny: much health!

Protus, in recognition of Cleon's contribution to Greek culture, has sent many gifts, which as Cleon writes are being unloaded and crowd the court and portico. The reader is at once dramatically aware of Cleon's ennui, his perfunctory interest in the kingly gifts (which significantly remain largely unidentified), but it becomes clear that his attention and interest are drawn by the "white she-slave," the "One lyric woman" who commends to him the strainer and the cup Protus's lips have graced. He would give all the gifts, whether graced by the kingly lips or not, to kiss the lips of the one lyric woman, who, he knows, is wholly unobtainable. The gifts are art, but she is life, and Cleon is surfeited by art and starved for life, of which art is but a tantalizing shadow.

Cleon, then, is seen at a moment of crisis in his life. He has lived for preeminence in the arts and sciences and he has attained his goals, in Browning always an ominous sign of failure. Old and facing the prospect of death, he is sick to think that he has not really lived and time and strength are not his to make up the loss. It is at this point that Protus's gifts arrive, accompanied by a letter requesting that Cleon interpret for him the significance of death. The query touches him on the raw, for it is on this theme that he has been ruefully thinking:

> Well-counselled, king, in thy munificence!
> For so shall men remark, in such an act
> Of love for him whose song gives life its joy,
> Thy recognition of the use of life. . . .
> (ll. 19-22)

The newly discovered bitterness that besets Cleon is precisely that if song gives life its joy, life must first give joy to song. Cleon has sacrificed life to song and the taste is of ashes. He flatters the King for his patronage of the arts and for the praise which the people shall confer on him for his "recognition of the use of life." This is his response to the praise which Protus has heaped upon him, and Cleon admits that the King's information is correct:

> It is as thou hast heard: in one short life
> I, Cleon, have effected all those things

Thou wonderingly dost enumerate.
That epos on thy hundred plates of gold
Is mine,—and also mine the little chant,
So sure to rise from every fishing-bark
When, lights at prow, the seamen haul their net.
(ll. 43-50)

His admission is made at length. He does not in a blanket assent admit to all the triumphs listed by the King. Rather he savors each one singly, with no detectable modesty. Ironically, he knows the "true proportions of a man/ And woman also, not observed before," but he has not loved a woman. His art seems to mock him. While he is unaware that he is groping for the Christian concept of immortality, he has written "three books on the soul,/ Proving absurd all written hitherto,/ And putting us to ignorance again." Browning's sense of irony is seen in Cleon's admission that "all arts are mine," a fact testified to by the *universal* acclaim of mankind—"throughout our seventeen islands."

Cleon sees life as a finite and limited experience, a whole, with adamantine boundaries. He does not see life as a continuum, an illimitable, unbroken development. Men of the modern age, he says, are of greater mind and accomplishment than their forerunners, but they, as individual men, may have attained the same height in one area as men of the "heroic age,"—his own—but the difference is that modern man excels in many areas. Significantly, Cleon uses the figure of a hollow sphere to represent man's capacity for knowledge and attainment. The sphere can never be enlarged, and so man is a prisoner within it. Early man, like a little water placed inside the ball, may touch all points upon the inner surface, for the water runs as the ball is slowly turned this way and that. But modern man is like air completely filling the sphere, touching all points at once, but because the air is impalpable, the ignorant fancy that the visible water has accomplished more, by touching first one point and then another, than the air, which touches all. The image of the sphere, a veritable prison, fits Cleon's sense of the wall placed about man's mind and spirit. When man discovered that he was enclosed within a sphere

. . . our soul, misknown, cries out to Zeus
To vindicate his purpose in our life:
Why stay we on the earth unless to grow?
(ll. 112-14)

Cleon's realization that growth is the one thing man must never be denied is balanced by the thought that perhaps Zeus at one time may have come to earth and "once for all"

> . . . showed, I say,
> The worth both absolute and relative
> Of all his children from the birth of time,
> His instruments for all appointed work.
> (ll. 119-22)

This is stagnation, death. To fix anything once for all is to stop growth and development. Painful to Cleon is the apparent contrast between the visible growth of things material and the alarming suggestion that the soul may deteriorate. Through science grapes, plums, honey—yea, even the beauty of women—all have progressed toward perfection; but is there a comparable growth in man's spirit?

Cleon has not chanted verse like Homer, or swept the string like Terpander, or painted men like Phidias—all of whom touched the confining surface of the sphere which sets absolute limits on man's achievements; but he has arrived at heights nearly as great in all the arts. Protus has asked him whether such preeminence is not "The very crown and proper end of life," an assurance that banishes all fear of death:

> "Thou leavest much behind, while I leave naught.
> Thy life stays in the poems men shall sing,
> The pictures men shall study; while my life,
> Complete and whole now in its power and joy,
> Dies altogether with my brain and arm,
> Is lost indeed; since, what survives myself?"
> (ll. 169-74)

Cleon poses a problem to Protus: if in the dawn of creation it had been possible for the King, with his present knowledge, to view all created things, he would have found only one way to improve upon their state: "Ay, by making each/ Grow conscious in itself. . . ." In the physical sense, nothing is lacking. The shells suck fasts to the rocks, fish swim, the beasts and birds move in their appropriate element

> Till life's mechanics can no further go—

but the creatures are still "mere matter," however formed to cope with their environment; the fire that is within them "has them, not they it." Lacking is the quality of self-consciousness, a quality in the soul

> "Which, intro-active, made to supervise
> And feel the force it has, may view itself,
> And so be happy."
> (ll. 212-14)

But Cleon, grown weary of thought, counsels the wisdom of letting man in the evolutionary scale remain a brute, unawakened to self-consciousness, for if death ends all, man's state is bitterness and failure:

> But thou, king, hadst more reasonably said:
> "Let progress end at once,—man make no step
> Beyond the natural man, the better beast,
> Using his senses, not the sense of sense."
> (ll. 221-24)

Here is the central issue in the poem: Cleon, a cultivated Greek, faces death and oblivion in despair, for he has, by arduous study and training in the arts, become superlatively self-conscious and cultivated, a condition which makes death intolerable. Man's vision of delight is frustratingly superior to his capacity to experience delight: ". . . . a man can use but a man's joy/ While he sees God's." Man long held that his crowning glory was to progress beyond the brutes, to grow increasingly conscious of man's life and estate, to climb the "watchtower and treasure-fortress of the soul."

> But alas,
> The soul now climbs it just to perish there!
> (ll. 235-36)

Cleon is shackled by his physical vision of the soul. The soul's illimitable aspirations and dreams are denied by the body, which wearies and sickens with the years as the soul becomes more aware and alive to growth and delight:

> We struggle, fain to enlarge
> Our bounded physical recipiency,
> Increase our power, supply fresh oil to life,
> Repair the waste of age and sickness: no,
> It skills not! life's inadequate to joy,
> As the soul sees joy, tempting life to take.
> (ll. 245-50)

Since it is apparent to Cleon that man's frustration and disappointment are in precise ratio to his soul's aspiration, it follows that man should "make no step beyond the natural man":

> I ask,
> And get no answer, and agree in sum,
> O king, with thy profound discouragement,
> Who seest the wider but to sigh the more.
> Most progress is most failure: thou sayest well.
> (ll. 268-72)

Most bitter to Cleon is his awareness that the artistic distance he has kept from life, his ivory tower of philosophical contemplation, has in his old age, heightened his sense of the horror of death. In youth, with death so far away, there seemed to be endless time to master all the arts and still—with heightened, refined delight—to taste of life, a dream which the ravages of time changed to illusion. Does the King, he asks

> . . . confound the knowing how
> And showing how to live (my faculty)
> With actually living?
>
> (ll. 281-83)

He finds no immortality in his epos of "How divers men young, strong, fair, wise, can act," for "Is this as though I acted?" His very application to the arts brought him to physical decrepitude before his time and increased his loss.

Browning's acute dramatic sense of the need of immediacy and concrete illustration is seen in Cleon's comment upon the fair slave, the lyric woman, who all this while has been indifferent to the presence of the greatest artist of the day but who turns instinctively toward the young rower whose rippling muscles are an affront and reproach to Cleon:

> I can write love-odes: thy fair slave's an ode.
> I get to sing of love, when grown too gray
> For being beloved: she turns to that young man,
> The muscles all a-ripple on his back.
> I know the joy of kingship: well, thou art king!
>
> (ll. 296-300)

To Protus's animadversion that immortality lies in one's imperishable art works, Cleon scornfully replies that if Sappho and Aeschylus "live" in their works, let them come and take the fair slave, together with the King's cup, but, alas! they cannot. Cleon's fate is deadly beyond endurance, for as his powers wane, his sense of joy and his lust for the life he has missed grow more desperately intense, and he knows that his works will serve only to mock him sleeping in his urn.

The conclusion to the poem is consummately brilliant. In his wild desperation, he fancies that there must be a future state wherein to fulfill one's thin and arid life,

> Some future state revealed to us by Zeus
> Unlimited in capability
> For joy, as this is in desire for joy,
> —To seek which, the joy-hunger forces us:
> That, stung by straitness of our life, made strait

On purpose to make prized the life at large—
Freed by the throbbing impulse we call death,
We burst there as the worm into the fly,
Who, while a worm still, wants his wings. But no!
Zeus has not yet revealed it; and alas,
He must have done so, were it possible!

(ll. 325-35)

Again, his imaginative insight is blinded by his orthodox and limited vision.

Perhaps the finest piece of sustained irony in Browning is included in the farewell to the King. Fittingly Cleon waits until the end to acknowledge the gift which Protus has sent to St. Paul, with the request that Cleon instruct the messenger how to deliver it. Cleon is mildly contemptuous of the King for his gift, which reveals to Cleon a credulity hitherto unsuspected in the ruler. His reaction is much as Abib's might be, one suspects, upon receipt of Karshish's disquieting words about the resurrection of Lazarus and its total implication. Cleon reveals in his blind rejection of what is strange and beyond his limited comprehension the classic failure of the human mind—even the scholarly human mind—and herein lies the irony. He does not know where Paulus lives, or, indeed, whether Christus and Paulus are one; but it matters not, for, he admonishes the King,

Thou canst not think a mere barbarian Jew,
As Paulus proves to be, one circumcised,
Hath access to a secret shut from us?

(ll. 342-45)

Cleon's final words, almost unbearable in their irony, reveal the dangers of intellect divorced from spirit and love. Cleon, the supreme scholar, in the most momentous event of his life, at the precise instant when he needs awareness that he stands face to face with the answer to all his spiritual needs, if he will but stretch forth his hands, relies on hearsay evidence, one of the least defensible errors in scholarship:

And (as I gathered from a bystander)
Their doctrine could be held by no sane man.

"Cleon" should be read with "Rabbi Ben Ezra" in mind, not because one contains an apparent condemnation of old age and the other an extravagant praise of it, but because of the contrast between two opposing views of life and death. Matthew Arnold's "Growing Old," a poem written in response to "Rabbi Ben Ezra," presents a view of old age that is shockingly repellent in its point-by-point recital of the horrors that age brings to every function. Indeed, the picture of old age in "Growing Old" and in "Cleon" is much alike: intolerably empty and bleak. Browning's poem, properly looked at, does everything that Arnold's attempts and fails in doing. Browning's poem is dramatic and enormously alive, whereas Arnold's is undramatic and dead—a bitter sermon in verse, without life. The two poems reveal the essential difference between the two men: to Arnold all old age must be an unrelieved despoliation; to Browning it must be so if one has not the vision which Christus and Paulus brought to rob death of its terror and to give life meaning.

SUGGESTED READINGS

Collins, Thomas J., *Robert Browning's Moral-Aesthetic Theory, 1833-1855* (Lincoln, Nebr., 1967), pp. 140-42.

"However, Cleon admits that in reality the pessimistic philosophy of King Protus is closer to the truth. 'Most progress is most failure' . . . because as man advances in self-consciousness he learns that there is joy, or realization of soul, that he can never fully experience. Man can always attempt to enlarge his capacity, but, as Browning illustrated in the case of Sordello, he is doomed to failure, without hope of ever bridging the gap between what he knows he can be and what he is."

Honan, Park, *Browning's Characters, A Study in Poetic Technique* (New Haven, 1961), pp. 163-64 and passim.

Professor Honan astutely points out the artistic and psychological advantages accruing from Browning's use of the epistolary style: "But the very process of self-identification that occurs—Cleon's seeing one element of his own being in Protus the Tyrrant [sic] is made possible only by the epistolary nature of the situation. On hand, Protus would destroy the illusion" (p. 165).

Kenmare, Dallas, *An End to Darkness* (London, 1962), pp. 122-24.

"Our chief pain, Cleon reflects, arises from incomplete vision, the incapacity to see the whole. . . . Poet, mystic, philosopher, saint, are all working in the cause of ultimate unity, working to prove the necessity for the apparently conflicting pieces of the mysterious pattern, the pieces without which there could be no whole. . . . But Cleon is tormented by doubts which a knowledge of Paul's convictions would have quieted."

King, Roma, Jr., "Browning: 'Mage' and 'Maker'—A Study in Poetic Purpose and Method," *Victorian Newsletter*, No. 20 (1961), 22-25.

18

"Two in the Campagna"

"Two in the Campagna" is Browning's finest study of imperfection in love and the essential isolation of the human heart. The theme is the finite, limited, unpredictable nature of love and the impossibility of achieving oneness with any other person, even in love. No poet of the age so often saw the riddle of life in terms of man's uniqueness, his individual personality, his essential isolation. Since the function of life is to test man in the presence of evil, doubt, and frustration, he is tested as a single unit, not as a member of a group. Arnold's "The Buried Life" and "To Marguerite—Continued" investigate much the same theme, although in static rather than dramatic terms. Browning's poem may be regarded as the precursor in spirit and mood of the most dominant theme of twentieth-century belles lettres: the alienation of the isolated spirit.

Browning, the poet of love, was also the poet of life, and the hallmark of life is failure—wherein man may find success if his aspirations are noble. He never meant that in finding failure to mark his hopes and efforts man should be immune to the pain of failure, for it is precisely the pain through which he is tested. Even love, the supreme value of life, is marked by imperfection, since life denies absolutes. In this poem Browning is denying the Romantic view of love as all-embracing, all-consuming, and absolute. Perfection implies stagnation, and stagnation is death. Only through struggle does life achieve meaning, for in struggle there is growth. Man is most severely tested when failure destroys love, his finest possession.

It is apparent that the poem was written during or after the Brownings' sojourn in Rome in May 1854. W. C. DeVane quotes Elizabeth Barrett Browning's letter of May 10, 1854, which affords striking evidence of their outings on the Campagna:

> The pleasantest days in Rome we have spent with the Kembles—the two sisters—who are charming and excellent, both of them, in different ways; and certainly they have given us some exquisite hours on the

Campagna, upon picnic excursions, they and certain of their friends. . . .[1]

The poem has long been seen as Browning's confession of his alleged unhappiness in marriage and his dissatisfaction with his wife. It seems undeniable that the poem stems from his personal experience or observation and from his outing on the Campagna, but there is no justification in identifying Browning with his persona as a means of reading confession of failure in his marriage. The greatest and most protracted fallacy in Browning criticism is the complacent identification of Browning with the creatures of his poetic imagination. Since Browning wrote of highly individual types, twisted souls, men in the grip of lust, greed, and dishonesty, this unscholarly tendency has had a peculiarly unhappy effect on his reputation and has disastrously blurred the image of the man and poet. It may be recalled that Browning, in great annoyance, wrote that the grossest misconceptions of him and his work were perpetuated by "the critics reading attentively the criticisms of their brethren, and paying no attention at all to the text criticized."[2] Careful reading of the Browning critics from his day forward affords some depressing evidence of the accuracy of his charge. Thomas Blackburn finds close identification of Browning and his persona:

"In 'Two in the Campagna,' one of his finest poems, Browning writes about the inevitable duality of human existence in relationship to his love for Elizabeth Barrett."[3]

In recent years the marriage of Robert and Elizabeth has increasingly been construed as being essentially unhappy and discordant. Betty Miller's *Robert Browning, A Portrait* is perhaps the most mischievous purveyor of this view, which fits her Freudian view of Browning. Richard Altick's "The Private Life of Robert Browning" is the most ingeniously destructive account of the character of the poet and his psychological and biological failures:

> The woman he married was six years older than he, a fact which even those with the least possible tinge of Freudianism may find relevant. And when, after fifteen years, that marriage was ended by death, he found solace among women for the rest of his long life.[4]

It might reasonably be asked whether Browning's search for consolation among women after the death of his wife might not be considered the

1. *The Letters of Elizabeth Barrett Browning*, ed. F. G. Kenyon, II, 165.
2. *Letters of Robert Browning, Collected by Thomas J. Wise*, ed. Thurman L. Hood (New Haven, 1933), p. 216.
3. Thomas Blackburn, *Robert Browning: A Study of His Poetry*, 1967, p. 49.
4. Richard Altick, "The Private Life of Robert Browning," *Yale Review* XLI (December 1951), 257.

highest tribute to Elizabeth and to the success of their marriage—and at the same time an impressive testimonial to his psychiatric health, not sickness. If it is an ominous symptom of mental and sexual aberration to find women delightful company after the death of one's wife, it might seem to follow that a settled distaste for women might be telling evidence of his matrimonial felicity and sturdy emotional fiber. I think that no one is likely to so conclude. Furthermore, it may well be surmised that Browning married Elizabeth, not because she was six years older than he, but in spite of it. Indeed, nothing is more probable, I should suppose, than that he fell in love with her and married her, age, sickness, and all, since there was nothing else to do if he loved her. To imply that he was subconsciously marrying his mother may or may not be true, but probably no more true than the charge that he was attracted by sickness, of which there is no evidence.

Browning said, after several years of marriage, that he found the greatest happiness and contentment in the simple prospect of spending a whole day in the same room with his wife. Just to be near her was his idea of happiness. In no sense does this imply that there were no differences between the two. Life is an exercise in imperfection, and they had differences of opinion on several heads: Pen's rearing and dress, Napoleon III, and spiritualism. If these are the only differences that marred their happiness, their marriage takes on the character of unearthly perfection, not a bitter yoking of incompatible spirits.

In the poem, the man recalls the glorious day in the Campagna when hand in hand, he and his wife or lover sat down on the grass, "to stray/ In spirit better through the land. . . ." He recalls a thought that has tantalized and perplexed him many a time—a thought he compares to a thread of spider's web blown about the Campagna, tortuous and tangled and exceedingly difficult to hold and follow. The thought is of the riddle of life and love and mating everywhere in the whole range of life on the Campagna:

Such life here, through such lengths of hours
   Such miracles performed in play,
Such primal naked forms of flowers,
   Such letting nature have her way
While heaven looks from its towers!

How say you? Let us, O my dove,
   Let us be unashamed of soul,
As earth lies bare to heaven above!
   How is it under our control
To love or not to love?

In these lines is seen Browning's lifelong insistence on the rightness and wholesomeness of love and sex. Fecund nature is looked upon with approval by heaven, and likewise man should be unashamed of his nature.

Love is not subject to our will, but rather is subject to the obscure working of nature, which denies all absolutes. Thus, he argues, how can he be blamed for being unable to love her completely and absolutely? He yearns for infinite love, but life sets its finite limits:

> I would that you were all to me,
> You that are just so much, no more.
> Nor yours nor mine, nor slave nor free!
> Where does the fault lie? What the core
> O' the wound, since wound must be?

"Two in the Campagna" is almost universally construed to be a study in failure in love, much as "The Last Ride Together" is. This is a mistake. It is, rather, a study of the nature of love, which is imperfect, being of this earth. Since love to Browning was the most precious thing in life, man's inability to attain perfection in love remained the great mystery. In short compass, the theme is seen in "Meeting at Night" and "Parting at Morning," in which the man, after a night of love, must return to the world of men and getting and gaining, for life puts demands on men, beyond even the supreme good, love. In these two poems it is implied that among man's deepest wishes is that love might be enough—all sufficient and lasting: "that such raptures are self-sufficient and enduring," as Browning phrased it. The second poem of the pair indicated how imperfectly this belief is realized. Love alone, however rapturous, cannot fill man's life. Nor can lovers find a common identity, however great their love.

This is the true theme of the poem, and, as such, it is a study in how *great* is his love, not how small, and at the same time it examines the mystery of why such a consuming love cannot attain the absolute ideal he yearns for. Far from being a study of a signally deficient love, it is a study of why such a transcendently beautiful love cannot pass to the next step and transcend life's limitations. It is completely clear that his love is great, in spite of its being subject to mortal limitations:

> Where does the fault lie? What the core
> O' the wound, since wound must be?

Here is the mystery of life: nothing can be perfect, and since his love is the most beautiful and powerful thing in his life, he cannot comprehend the fate that prohibits him from attaining the perfection that is reserved for the next life. His love is so great that he wishes to attain absolute oneness with his beloved, to break the bonds of self and to literally be one with her:

> I would I could adopt your will,
> See with your eyes, and set my heart
> Beating by yours, and drink my fill
> At your soul's springs,—your part my part
> In life, for good and ill.

These lines, ironically enough, are commonly understood to mean that he is lamenting his inability to return her love with any real passion and that he recognizes his deficiencies. But when he says that he would love to "adopt your will/ See with your eyes, and set my heart/ Beating by yours," he does not mean that he wishes he could equal her intensity of love, but rather that his love is so great that he wants it to fill his life completely, so that they become one in body and in spirit forever. This life denies any man, and this is the mystery he is exploring. The love to which Browning is referring, it goes without saying, is sexual love in its total context: the full interfusion of flesh and spirit. Browning knew that even this ultimate experience of love's ecstasy is but fleeting:

> I pluck the rose
> And love it more than tongue can speak—
> Then the good minute goes.

It should be noted that he makes it clear that in his act of love no words can express his delight—telling evidence of his love, not his inability to love. Nor is sex all, by any means, for in kissing her cheek, he says, "I . . . Catch your soul's warmth." But in the mortal state, "the good minute goes," and he wonders why:

> Already how am I so far
> Out of that minute? Must I go
> Still like the thistle-ball, no bar,
> Onward, whenever light winds blow,
> Fixed by no friendly star?

Nothing could be more destructive to one's understanding of the poem than the conclusion that he is an inconstant lover, footloose and fancy free, drifting like the thistle-ball from love to love. He is asking directly the theme of the poem: why in just a moment after thinking he may have attained the indissoluble oneness, the full identity with his beloved, he suddenly is "Out of that minute." He feels alone and lost and tricked, "Fixed by no friendly star," blown helplessly like the thistle-ball, unable to hold the moment of infinite communion with his beloved. How can one attain and hold the heights of rapture? One cannot, because he is mortal.

The conclusion of the poem is not a statement, as most critics believe, of the disappointment and failure the lover experiences. It states his disappointment and failure only in his reiterated inability to conquer time and to hold the moment of delight forever. He cannot bear to relinquish the moment and come down to earth, as man must:

> Only I discern
> Infinite passion, and the pain
> Of finite hearts that yearn.

The infinite passion is his—not a deficient, pallid emotion as the poem often is read—and the pain also is his, but it is not the pain of disappointment in the quality of the love he experiences, but the pain of its passing, his inability to break the bonds of life and remain on the heights of rapture forever.

W. C. DeVane, although very properly saying that the poem is the "dramatic embodiment of a mood which all men have," nevertheless believes that "The perfect antidote to *Two in the Campagna* is *By the Fire-Side*, where loves achieves perfect understanding." Properly looked at, the two poems are perfectly complementary. The one is not an examination of failure in love, the other of love perfectly attained. Both are studies of love as perfect as life permits, but the first examines the mystery of man's inability to reside in the clouds of rapture forever, and the other is a quiet study of love as communion and contemplation and adoration, quite as powerful in its way as the more sexual love in the first. But in neither poem can man remain on the heights forever. He must come down to earth before he may ascend the heights again. Browning, the poet of individualism, knew that it is precisely man's individualism which prevents his blending with another perfectly and forever, for if he ever attained this ideal, he would be destroyed as an individual. It is not the attainment which man needs and (if he fully understands himself and the laws of life) wants, but the eternal yearning and striving for perfect attainment.

The theme of "Two in the Campagna" is expressed in the words of the ancient crone, now grown young and radiant, to the Duchess in "The Flight of the Duchess":

> And thou shalt know, those arms once curled
> About thee, what we knew before,
> How love is the only good in the world.
> Henceforth be loved as heart can love,
> Or brain devise, or hand approve!

. . . .
If any two creatures grew into one,
They would do more than the world has done. . . .
(ll. 613-27)

SUGGESTED READINGS

Collins, Thomas J., *Robert Browning's Moral-Aesthetic Theory, 1833-1855* (Lincoln, Nebr., 1967), p. 134.

Mr. Collins believes that the lover speaking in "Two in the Campagna" is experiencing the bitterness of failure in love in much the same manner as does the unsuccessful suitor in "The Last Ride Together": "But the speaker [in 'The Last Ride Together'] is not very realistic: he is unwilling to face the termination of the ride, which will efface the lingering grasp he still has on his 'infinite moment'; and he wishes that the ride would continue forever so that 'the instant' could be 'made eternity.' . . . We are given an indication of the isolation he will feel when he and his lover are finally separated in 'Two in the Campagna,' which describes the painful awareness of a man who has experienced the 'good minute,' but has been unable to extend it."

DeVane, William C., *A Browning Handbook* (2nd ed., 1955), pp. 222-23.

"The poem [*By the Fire-Side*], a perfect illustration of Browning's belief in the 'good minute,' should be read with *Two in the Campagna*, where the good minute goes and the lovers fail to attain the perfect understanding which is the achievement in *By the Fire-Side*."

Kenmare, Dallas, *An End to Darkness* (London, 1962), p. 61.

"In Browning's love-poetry it is almost invariably the man who comes to understand the mysterious self-fulfillment of love in spite of apparent failure, the great truth that no real love is ever lost, that in the emotion itself lies the truest fulfillment. The heights, depths and riches experienced by the lover in his own inner world cannot really be increased by any consummation in actuality, nor can they really be minimised by the tragedy of loss. This philosophy—truly optimistic, since it robs all actual circumstances of their power—is perhaps best expressed in *The Last Ride Together*. . . . How infinitely happier he is, having lost all he desired in actuality, than the lover in *Two in the Campagna*, whose consummated love yet leaves him tormented with an insatiable longing. . . ."

"The two poems, *By the Fireside* and *Two in the Campagna* should be read together to observe the penetrating and subtle portrayal of two precisely antithetical types of love-experience . . ." (p. 139).

"This poem, like *Andrea del Sarto,* reveals a very delicate and subtle tragedy of love. The lover is trapped in a situation from which there is no escape, because there is nothing tangible in the situation to grapple with, no valid reason why he should desire escape. . . . No one is to blame for these deep tragedies of incompatibility. It is not within the scope of her nature to be 'all to him.' Such tragedies of love can well lead to death, either psychic or actual. There are certain emotional disasters which have no more substance than a cloud on a high mountain, yet can, like such a cloud, envelop and blind, and drive to destruction" pp. 184-85).

Shaw, W. David, *The Dialectical Temper: The Rhetorical Art of Robert Browning* (Ithaca, N.Y., 1968), pp. 120-23.

Mr. Shaw finds the speaker in "Two in the Campagna" to be a "scholastic Don Juan who begins by celebrating the erotic life. . . ."

"The speaker is the victim of his own analogies, and in using repulsive spider and beetle imagery, he does not 'come out' where he had planned to. 'The grassy slope,' 'brick-work's cleft,' and phallic 'towers' are erotically alluring. But the five beetles groping in the honey-meal suggest a kind of sexual mounting of the small orange cup and a teeming promiscuity that is unexpectedly hideous."

Whitla, William, *The Central Truth: The Incarnation in Robert Browning's Poetry* (Toronto, 1963), pp. 94-95.

"*Two in the Campagna* provides a marked contrast with *Love among the Ruins*. It is closer in theme to *The Statue and the Bust,* but in *Two in the Campagna* the lovers do not seize the good minute at all. They suffer the 'pain of finite hearts that yearn.' The lover strives to hold fast to the love that motivates him, but the barrier of the two selves seems to interrupt the insight that should be shared. The lovers cannot merge their separate personalities in a self-giving of soul to soul. For a moment it seems that the barrier between the lovers is about to vanish. The speaker desires to will through his beloved's will, see through her eyes, and love through her heart, but the yearning for union remains only yearning."

19

"A Grammarian's Funeral"

"A Grammarian's Funeral" is a dramatic monologue spoken by the head pallbearer as the body of a famous philologist is being carried to the top of a mountain to be buried with honor. The poem has been seen traditionally as an extreme example of Browning's doctrine of apparent failure, i.e., an illustration of the belief that man's reach should exceed his grasp, that each individual must aim for impossible heights. Richard Altick has recently challenged this view in an article entitled "*A Grammarian's Funeral*: Browning's Praise of Folly?" which finds the poem to be a satire on pedantry and a misspent life, a mock-encomium on the old misguided grammarian.[1]

In my opinion, both the traditional view and Professor Altick's dissenting view make the same mistake of attempting to read the poem as a statement of Browning's upon the success or failure of the old philologist's life, instead of seeing the poem as a dramatic monologue which forces the attention on the speaker and his mind and soul. It may very well be that Browning's views may be surmised from the words of the admiring pallbearer, but it is a mistake to begin a study of the poem by trying to find the "message," and this is the usual way in which the poem is read. "A Grammarian's Funeral" is particularly embarrassing for message seekers because of the immediate conflict of themes that is apparent: the theme that the old scholar is in truth a heroic figure of singular dedication to a lofty ideal, albeit narrow and remote from life, because he puts his faith in the next life in which to do all the living for which this life is a mere preparation; and, on the other hand, the theme, which is everywhere illustrated in Browning's poetry, that life must be lived first and philosophized and written about later. This is nowhere more directly stated than in "Parleying with Christopher Smart": "Live and learn/ Not first learn

1. Richard Altick, "*A Grammarian's Funeral:* Browning's Praise of Folly?" *Studies in English Literature,* III (1963), 449-60.

and then live is our concern." The poem, then, becomes the scene of conflicting credos. Is the grammarian in fact a hero, to be not merely defended but held up as an ideal? Or is the poem satiric? And if it is a satire, against whom is the satire directed, the grammarian or the pallbearer who speaks the lines? Or is the poem a dramatic utterance with no approval or disapproval of either implied by the author?

"A Grammarian's Funeral" has few of the obvious elements of satire. Missing is the incongruity, the shocking collision of discordant elements, which is the very stuff of satire. A sensitive reader immediately senses that "Caliban upon Setebos" is a satire, for nothing could be more incongruous than the humanoid Caliban lying at length in the muck and mire of the pit as he philosophizes on the nature of the diety. Throughout "Caliban" one becomes more and more aware of the appalling gulf separating this foul and hideous creature, in whose image he creates a foul and hideous god, from any real insight into the true nature of god. In "A Grammarian's Funeral" all this is lacking. We may not share the reverential enthusiasm of the pallbearer for his shriveled old mentor, but we are not made to laugh or to feel the grotesque incongruity of the scene.

To say that the poem is not primarily a satire does not imply that Browning therefore approved or disapproved of the speaker or his mentor or philology or intellectual pursuits of whatever description. The poem is simply another of Browning's dramatic monologues in which a person speaks and reveals the state of his mind and soul on a topic close to his heart. In this instance the speaker is an apprentice scholar—in modern terminology, he might be considered a graduate student working toward his Ph.D.—who is speaking under the emotional tension of the death of his admired advisor at a particular time in history ("Shortly after the revival of learning in Europe") when, as never before or since, the rediscovery of classical learning fired the imagination and seemed to hold the key to a rediscovery of life and the living of it. To fail to sense the excitement of the Renaissance in the speaker's encomium is to misread the poem from the first line onward. Since the secret of the good life appeared to be found in the revival of classical learning, the old scholar in his total devotion is only carrying to its logical extreme a principle clearly understood by his subordinates. It should be noted that their admonitions to him to take a little rest are founded not on their disapproval of his plan of life, but on their fear that he may drop dead from overwork.

Joseph E. Baker, speaking for a broad spectrum of modern Browning scholarship, says:

> This "grammarian" however does not apply his learning to human purposes in the spirit of the Renaissance; in his devotion to facts for their own sake he is perhaps more like a type of scholar that flourished

> in the latter part of the nineteenth century. Browning himself admires the decision "not to live"—this willingness to forego everything except study. In his glorification of specialization and his "philosophy of the imperfect," Browning was hostile to the classic demand for balanced and well-rounded perfection, and preferred an attitude that he was calling Medieval in other poems that appeared in 1855 in the same work, *Men and Women* (e.g., "Old Pictures in Florence").[2]

The bold assurance that Browning admires the decision "not to live" is one that needs careful qualification. It is by no means clear that Browning's admiration of the grammarian's way of life, or rather his rejection of life's blandishments until he has learned all there is to know, may be inferred. Nothing could be clearer throughout Browning's life than his steady belief that the first business of life is to live it fully. Baker's statement that Browning was "hostile to the classic demand for balanced and well-rounded perfection" is simply mistaken. Browning's hostility to Greek classicism lay not in its demand for the well-rounded man—the ideal of Renaissance Humanism—but in its inherent limitations which effectively prevented man's growth toward this ideal. Cleon is not a pitiable failure because he has risen to the heights in all the arts and sciences of his day, far from it. He is pitiable precisely because Greek culture, being self-limiting and perfect within the limits set, obscured the vision brought by Christ of illimitable opportunity of growth and attainment throughout eternity. Cleon is a miserable failure because he has denied life, in much the same fashion as has the old grammarian, except that he has been far broader and far more unhappy. He has written perfect love odes, but he has not loved; and his heart writhes in anguish to see the beautiful slave girl, the lyric woman, turn from him, old and gray in his honors, to follow the youthful rower with the muscles all a-ripple on his back.

Baker's reference to "Old Pictures in Florence" as supplying evidence in support of Browning's supposed hostility to the classical and well-balanced perfection should be examined. Baker is right in finding Browning to be opposed to the attainment of perfection in this life, for "the prize is in the process," not in the attainment of perfection. But perfection and balance and wholeness should not be yoked. In "Old Pictures in Florence," Browning elaborately defends his pet belief (probably the least defensible of all his beliefs) that the passage of time inevitably brings progress: "The first of the new, in our race's story,/ Beats the last of the old. . . ." It is true that the poem is a defense of the superiority of late Medieval and early Renaissance art over classical, and, even more remarkable, it is a defense of the early Medieval artists, forerunners of the great

2. Joseph E. Baker, *"Pippa Passes" and Shorter Poems* (New York, 1947), p. 436 note.

masters, as being of equal stature in the history of art—because they were essential in the sequential growth of art. But the superiority of the Medieval in no wise is due to the crippling disability of the Greek ideal of balance and wholeness. The Medieval was superior not because it was narrower in vision or scope, but rather because it was far broader and far-seeing: it saw the soul and eternity:

> . . . the race of Man
> That receives life in parts to live in a whole,
>   And grow here according to God's clear plan.
>
> Growth came when, looking your last on them all,
>   You turned your eyes inwardly one fine day
> And cried with a start—What if we so small
>   Be greater and grander the while than they?
> Are they perfect of lineament, perfect of stature?
>   In both, of such lower types are we
> Precisely because of our wider nature;
>   For time, theirs—ours, for eternity.
>
> To-day's brief passion limits their range. . . .

Greek classicism was narrow and imperfect because it had attained perfection—to Browning the infallible sign that low and easily attained goals were sought. The Medieval art is "rough-hewn, nowise polished," because it has aimed to encompass the soul and man's infinite destiny throughout eternity. Surely the scope of this mighty vision is more balanced and rounded than the limited vision of the Greeks:

> On which I conclude, that the early painters,
>   To cries of "Greek Art and what more wish you?"—
> Replied, "To become now self-acquainters,
>   And paint, man man, whatever the issue!
> Make new hopes shine through the flesh they fray,
>   New fears aggrandize the rags and tatters:
> To bring the invisible full into play!
>   Let the visible go to the dogs—what matters?"

Perhaps the best poetic statement Browning left to refute the belief that he glorified specialization and thus approved of the resolution of the grammarian not to live but to study is included in "Easter Day," a poem that is as direct a statement of belief as one can find between *Sordello* and *La Saisiaz*. In the poem Browning is examining "how hard it is to be a Christian," together with ways men have tried to find the good life, including amassing of knowledge. It should be observed that Browning is not condemning knowledge or the uses of the intellect, but the abuses of the intellect and the narrowly specialized life, which denies life. A certain similarity will be noted between the man who collects *coleoptera* and the man who collects Greek roots:

"One friend of mine wears out his eyes,
Slighting the stupid joys of sense,
In patient hope that, ten years hence
'Somewhat completer,' he may say,
'My list of *coleoptera*!'
While just the other who most laughs
At him, above all epitaphs
Aspires to have his tomb describe
Himself as sole among the tribe
Of snuffbox-fanciers, who possessed
A Grignon with the Regent's crest.
So that, subduing, as you want,
Whatever stands predominant
Among my earthly appetites
For tastes and smells and sounds and sights,
I shall be doing that alone,
To gain a palm-branch and a throne,
Which fifty people undertake
To do, and gladly, for the sake
Of giving a Semitic guess,
Or playing pawns at blindfold chess."
(ll. 150-70)

The contempt for such empty, narrow lives is everywhere apparent, but nowhere more than in Browning's denunciation even of more useful knowledge, including science, when such knowledge denies life:

I cried in anguish: "Mind, the mind,
So miserably cast behind,
To gain what had been wisely lost!
Oh, let me strive to make the most
Of the poor stinted soul, I nipped
Of budding wings, else now equipped
For voyage from summer isle to isle!
And though *she needs must reconcile*
Ambition to the life on ground,
Still, I can profit by late found
But precious knowledge. Mind is best—
I will seize mind, forego the rest,

And try how far my tethered strength
May crawl in this poor breadth and length.
Let me, since I can fly no more,
At least spin dervish-like about
(Till giddy rapture almost doubt
I fly) through circling sciences,
Philosophies and histories!
Should the whirl slacken there, then verse,
Fining to music, shall asperse
Fresh and fresh fire-dew, till I strain
Intoxicate, half-break my chain!"[3]
(ll. 864-86)

It is clear that such monomaniacal pursuit of knowledge, in defiance of life's demands, is wrong:

"What matter? I have reached the goal—
'Whereto does knowledge serve!' will burn
My eyes, too sure, at every turn!"
(ll. 896-98)

The error lies not in following intellect but in denying all else. The intellectual regimen is both narrow (certainly not balanced and well-rounded) and perfected ("reached the goal"), and Browning condemns in the clearest terms any choice of obsessional interests.

In "A Toccata of Galuppi's" the scientist, who belatedly becomes aware of the life in eighteenth-century Venice of romance, joy, and love-making, is forced to see the narrowness of his own monomania, for he is but half a man, and he recants his condemnation of the Venetian butterfly lives as he realizes that he has been as guilty as they, for life demands wholeness, not narrowness. His poignant sense of irreparable loss of something precious when he thinks of the beautiful Venetian woman (". . . the small face buoyant, like a bell flower on its bed,/ O'er the breast's superb abundance where a man might base his head?") is close to Cleon's bitter sense of his emptiness in knowing that the beautiful slave girl is wholly indifferent to him—and the real pathos in Cleon's heart is not that he thinks she is wrong in turning to the lithe, muscular rower, but that he knows she is right.

There cannot be a doubt that of all poets Browning stands foremost in his insistence that life, "the mere living," as David sang, is man's first duty. All else comes second, important as it is, not because mere living is "best," but because it is indispensable to man's attainment of all the rest—the "soul wine," which is life's true aim.

3. Italics are mine.

"A Grammarian's Funeral" must be seen through the eyes of the pallbearer, a fledgling Renaissance scholar who is wholly sincere in his admiration for the old grammarian, for they both have breathed the fire and the excitement of the new learning. The speaker has unbounded respect and admiration for the old man and hopes that he may, some day, be his equal. It is irrelevant that to us the old man is shriveled, diminished, and unattractive—the ultimate type of the dry-as-dust professor, the butt of ten thousand irreverent stories. He cannot but appear spectacularly unattractive to us, with his eyes like lead, later like dross of lead, his cough, his wizened shanks, his absentmindedness and bemused mannerisms. He seems to represent the ultimate pedant, the final perversion of scholarship, for he wishes to learn all—text and commentary and footnote; and, worse, he seems to be a miser of knowledge, hoarding with a cackling chuckle each kernel of knowledge he may find in the most esoteric footnote to a footnote. It seems apparent that he is a man who wastes the most valuable thing man has—life and its rich experience—and for the wrong reasons elects the wrong choice.

But is the grammarian, in fact, quite as narrow as this? The word *grammarian* in our day, when grammar has become a dirty word, has a pejorative force; but he is a grammarian only incidentally: he is a student of languages, of philology, which is a branch of learning both fascinating and valuable. Moreover, he is said to be a scholar in the "bard and sage," a notable addition to the scope of his inquiries. Indeed, if a man embraces philology, literature, and philosophy, he is today spread rather thin.

The pallbearer has no doubt whatsoever about the rationale of the old man's devotion to learning and his concept of its relation to life; and there is no doubt that he got his information directly from the grammarian himself. In short, he is not finding suitable reasons with which to whitewash a man whom he is to emulate: he is quoting the reasoned philosophy of the man. The most significant point in the grammarian's rationale is not his tunnel vision or his rejection of life's delights, but his resolution to experience all things in due time—in the next world. It matters not that we may pronounce him mad or mistaken or the dupe of a fraudulent philosophy. What matters is that he has lived by a philosophical regimen which, if we may trust his vocal disciple, has not only given him eyes that resembled the skin which forms on molten lead, but has also yielded an inward peace that went far to render him proof against the agonies of the stone and the gout and the cough. And his inner fortitude is founded precisely on his faith that his joys in the next world will be augmented exponentially, not because he has denied himself, but because he has prepared himself for the enjoyment of all things. Indeed, he has aimed for the stars and has found it good, all ninety pounds of him.

Did Browning "admire the decision 'not to live,' " as Baker believes? I am not sure that this is a question that can be answered, nor am I at all sure it should be asked. One knows that if Browning had been asked whether a man is wise to elect to live the grammarian's life, he would have said no. If he had been asked whether a man should trust death or not to supply illimitable time and opportunity in which to attain endlessly the heights one sought in this life, he would have said yes. The proper questions are: What stress of soul yielded such a choice of life? Was it good for the *individual* who made the choice? And what were the forces working in the pallbearer's soul that forced him to find his mentor wholly admirable? These questions can be answered with any chance of accuracy only if one sees the scene against the backdrop of the Renaissance thirst hydropic for knowledge. Browning is not laying down rules of conduct for the greater life, here or in the next world. He is recounting a moment in time in which an individual, under complicated emotions and stresses, utters his convictions upon another man.

Browning loved case making. He loved to allow a person, even a consummate scoundrel, to defend himself or to expound his view by any means at his command, including the use of false analogies, non sequiturs, misrepresentation of fact, plain lies, and poor judgment. This is one of his most individual contributions to poetry, and he has paid a high price in critical imperception, which has insisted on finding a sermon behind the dramatic mask. Browning is not speaking here of pedantry or scholarship or philology, and indeed the pallbearer is not either: he is speaking of one man whom he loved and admired, who happened to be obsessed by all three, and the burden of the poem is his passionate defense of his mentor.

The question which should be uppermost in the mind in reading this poem is not "What did Browning think?" but "How successful is Browning in revealing the soul of the speaker and the character of the old grammarian?"

Richard D. Altick makes the point that the speaker is a pedant off the old block, speaking to pedants of a like persuasion. From our standpoint the judgment is probably true, but the pallbearer is not speaking from our standpoint, but rather from that of the Renaissance, when each crumb of knowledge gave a thrill which is now lost. Altick is right in believing that although the old grammarian is the students' hero, Browning did not intend for him to be ours.[4] Browning, to be sure, is not trying to persuade us to accept the grammarian as our hero, or reject him either. His interest lies rather in showing one man's rationale for accepting him as a hero.

Samuel Johnson remarked that in writing lapidary inscriptions one is not under oath. The speaker is not insincere in his high praise, but he is in the grip of an intense emotion appropriate to the sad occasion, which

4. Baker, *"Pippa Passes" and Shorter Poems*, p. 451.

may have something to do with the encomiastic tone of his praise. The funeral affords neither the time nor the place for voicing a reasoned objection to the deceased's life; however, one feels sure that the praise is heartfelt. After all, his mentor has

> . . . settled *Hoti's* business—let it be!—
> Properly based *Oun*—
> Gave us the doctrine of the enclitic *De*,
> Dead from the waist down.

Scholars have often given up much of life for less. Here is a man whose name is imperishably attached to certain important grammatical laws. He might be looked upon as a veritable early Renaissance Grimm or Verner, names revered and memorized by graduate students of philology. How many memorial volumes of essays, compiled by admiring former graduate students, have been dedicated to scholars who likewise have settled this and properly based that under disabilities not remarkably dissimilar—and not one has used the word *pedant*. The speaker in this poem is remarkable for his honesty and candor in pointing out the deformity of the man, and there is no indication that he hopes to emulate him in this regard, but he is defending both the man and a way of life that he himself hopes to follow, at least in scholarship, if not in desiccation. He does what he can to make the vision satisfying, but it is not what we would call pedantry that needs explaining away: it is the denial of life. Pedantry in this golden dawn of learning was not thought of. When the old dying Bishop tries to wheedle his sons into spending their substance on a grandiose tomb for him, he promises to intercede with St. Praxed in heaven to bestow upon them the three greatest delights his world offers:

> And have I not Saint Praxed's ear to pray
> Horses for ye, and brown Greek manuscripts,
> And mistresses with great smooth marbly limbs?

There is no irony intended here. One is inclined to accept the Bishop's ranking of these three delights, in ascending order, of course. A historic sense is required in reading these two poems on death, for today we are spared any undue concern lest our youth be driven to excesses of lust over manuscripts or recondite erudition, although women and horses have lost but little of their charm.

The speaker is speaking reverentially of his master, "famous calm and dead"—a splendid example of the incongruity which runs throughout the poem. Fame, that last infirmity of noble mind, came to the old scholar: "Long he lived nameless"—implying that at last fame came to him, the fruits of scholarship. He became a legend in his own time, and many men have traded life for far less.

The pallbearer is fully aware of the old man's plans to live life—all of it—in the next world:

> Oh, such a life as he resolved to live,
>   When he had learned it,
> When he had gathered all books had to give!
>   Sooner, he spurned it.

One of Browning's sturdy philosophical beliefs was that the function of the next world is to fulfill our aspirations in this. The most familiar statement of his faith appears in Andrea's final words of his artistic future in the next world. In "A Grammarian's Funeral" the speaker, however, is not Browning, and the grammarian is not either, and his faith that in heaven he can make up for lost time by enjoying life belatedly must be considered to be his own, just as Andrea's is his own. But whereas Andrea's faith sounds plausible, the grammarian's sounds pathetically schizophrenic. One can possibly imagine Andrea painting throughout eternity (admittedly it is more difficult to see Lucrezia there), but it is nearly impossible to imagine the grammarian, finally having learned all, embarking on a celestial career of frivolity, gaiety, and love-making. Not even eternity could accomplish that miracle. His long life of devotion to the study and the lamp, one realizes, was not preparation for learning to enjoy the delights of youth which he had passed by as unworthy of his attention while he was young. The heartening words of how the losses of this life will be made up illimitably in the next become almost a parody of the funeral oration. "Hence with life's pale lure!" he said as he bowed over his tomes, but he was not in truth scorning the delights of life, but merely postponing them, we know: " 'Wilt thou trust death or not?'/ He answered 'Yes. . . .' " The several figures of speech used to illustrate the superhuman dedication of the grammarian to a great ideal are in fact filled with images of decay, stagnation, sickness, and death:

> So, with the throttling hands of death at strife,
>   Ground he at grammar;
> Still, thro' the rattle, parts of speech were rife. . . .

There is nothing attractive here, not even to men in the first flush of the Rebirth of learning, and the pallbearer knows it. After all, they all warned him repeatedly of his folly in such maniacal pursuit of knowledge. The words of praise are not insincere. He was a hero to them, if an unwise one. Browning's judgment of the old grammarian—which probably concurred in part with the speaker's—is not a part of the poem, except by implication. The poem, properly seen, is not propaganda for or against the grammarian and his way of life, but is one of the most successful and forthright instances of case making in the Browning canon. The reader is torn between a natural aversion to the insane pedantry of the man and, on the other hand, admiration for his faith, dedication, and obvious joy in his pursuit of knowledge. After all, no one else in Browning receives quite such an encomium, E. B. B. and Pompilia excepted:

> Bury this man there?
> Here—here's his place, where meteors shoot, clouds form,
> Lightnings are loosened,
> Stars come and go! Let joy break with the storm,
> Peace let the dew send!
> Lofty designs must close in like effects:
> Loftily lying,
> Leave him—still loftier than the world suspects,
> Living and dying.

SUGGESTED READINGS

Ariail, J. M., " 'The Grammarian's Funeral'—A Note," *Publications of the Modern Language Association*, XLVIII (1933), 954-56.

Makes the interesting point that in the line "Still there's the comment," the comment is not the commentary and footnotes to the prodigious learning of the old grammarian, but rather the comment that he intends to write about his learning—an interpretation which, if it can be proved, makes the grammarian appear less passive and self-indulgent than he is commonly considered to be: "This comment was to be made upon the basis of his sound and mature scholarship—a scholarship which would know all and which prated not of most or least, even to the crumbs. He dismisses the suggestion that time was passing with a sublime contempt nobly stated and turns fiercely back to his book. . . . And then *tussis* attacked him. Not only the weakening cough, but in pursuing his method he came upon the crux involved in the *word* itself. And as *tussis* the disease attacked him, applying his methods, he flared 'fierce as a dragon,' with a counter-attack upon the word itself" (pp. 954-55).

Burrows, Leonard, *Browning the Poet: An Introductory Study* (Nedlands, Western Australia, 1969), pp. 120-30.

The poem should be read as a dramatic monologue, not as a statement of Browning's position, for we cannot assume that the speaker is the poet. The reader is not to be classed among the unlettered and crass herd living on the level of the plain nor among the enthusiastic members of the cortege. The "detached reader" may find the "degeneration from Greek god to downright scholar not entirely a matter for congratulation, even granted the heroism of the endeavour" (p. 127).

Clarke, C. C., "Humor and Wit in 'Childe Roland,' " *Modern Language Quarterly*, XXIII (1962), 323-36.
Clarke discovers a parallel between " 'Childe Roland to the Dark Tower Came' " and "A Grammarian's Funeral," in Browning's use of wit and humor. He makes the point that the theory of living embraced by the grammarian is "transparently defective" and thus is advanced by the poet as being "at once ludicrous and noble." The view that this life is significant only as it is a preparation for eternity is distorted in the mind of the old grammarian until the fact that man has Forever means that Now is only for dogs and apes. Nevertheless, he believes, the unbalanced views of the old man are not wholly to be discounted, because his devoted followers have fully accepted and endorsed them. "What is Browning up to? How seriously are we to take the 'philosophy?' " (p. 325). Clarke finds that "the earnestness and the buffoonery do not properly sort together" (p. 325).

DeVane, William C., *A Browning Handbook* (2nd ed., 1955), pp. 269-72.
"The philosophy of *A Grammarian's Funeral* is the 'philosophy of the imperfect,' an idea which appears many times elsewhere in *Men and Women*, notably in *Old Pictures in Florence*, *Fra Lippo Lippi*, and in its reverse application is used in *Andrea del Sarto*. This philosophy found its classic expression in John Ruskin's essay *On the Nature of Gothic*, in his monumental *Stones of Venice*. . . . The idea, of course, is as truly the expression of Browning's personality as it is of Ruskin's. But it is essentially a medieval philosophy, and fits a little strangely into this poem which obviously has as its inspiration the early Renaissance" (p. 271).

Duffin, Henry Charles, *Amphibian: A Reconsideration of Browning* (London, 1956), pp. 86-88.
"If we choose to leave the passionate way of the poem ['A Grammarian's Funeral'] and separate out ideas, we may find some of them false—such as that which seems to say that the purely intellectual approach to life is best; and others doubtful—such as the need to complete this life by another. But let the poem's powerful current of feeling carry you and you perceive that all the 'ideas' are taken up into the rhythmic flow, things of beauty beyond mental analysis, and all leading to the irrefutable conclusion—'Lofty designs must end in like effects' " (p. 88).

Monteiro, George, "A Proposal for Settling the Grammarian's Estate," *Victorian Poetry*, III (1965), 266-70.
Argues that the grammarian is not so much denying this life as he is living the way he thinks best in preparation for the life to come: "For the grammarian the established doctrine of the enclitic *De* is not inconsonant with his commitment to living *toward* the next world—less

by denying this world for the next, than by living *in* this world *toward* the next" (p. 268).

Schweik, Robert C., "The Structure of 'A Grammarian's Funeral,'" *College English*, XXII (1961), 411-12.

"It seems clear, then, that the disciples' progress from the plain to the city, and through it to the mountain top, is in effect a concrete symbol for the grammarian's intellectual progress from ignorance to knowledge sought as a guide for life, and beyond that to knowledge desired for its own sake. If so, it is probably misleading to describe 'A Grammarian's Funeral' as an effort to capture the spirit of Medieval or of Renaissance scholarship, though both of these, as Browning would have defined them, are certainly part of the poem. But primarily Browning seems to be concerned with the movement of the grammarian's mind, the drama of choices, which culminates in his rejection of the Renaissance ideal of scholarship in favor of the 'philosophy of the imperfect'" (p. 412).

Svaglic, Martin J., "Browning's Grammarian: Apparent Failure or Real?" *Victorian Poetry*, V (1967), 93-103.

Takes issue with Richard D. Altick's "'A Grammarian's Funeral': Browning's Praise of Folly?"

". . . I am convinced that the late Victorians were basically right and Professor Altick is wrong, though my heart is still more or less with him" (p. 97). Maintains that the poem must be read in the context of its Platonic dialectic, which is basically that of Carlyle, Ruskin, and Tennyson: "'Move upward, working out the beast/ And let the ape and tiger die.' The text of the poem, he argues, does not justify the common assumption that the grammarian was always a scholar, that he has never 'lived' at all in the ordinary sense. He has" (p. 99).

20

"*Abt Vogler*"

Georg Joseph Vogler (1749-1814), also known as Abbé or Abt Vogler, was a famous German composer and inventor of the orchestrion, a small organ having four keyboards of five octaves each, and a pedal board of thirty-six keys. His name was probably brought to Browning's attention because John Relfe, Browning's music teacher, had studied under the master. Vogler gained considerable fame as an extemporizer, one who improvises music while playing, seeking new and unique combinations of sounds, which will usually never be played again. As the subtitle suggests, Vogler is writing after an extended period of extemporizing, but even as he speaks he is extemporizing.

The poem springs from the poignancy of the death of such beautiful sounds, sounds never to be recaptured and dying as they are played. The whole mystery of the death of beauty arises, and in the poem one sees Vogler's direct answer to the questions arising in Keats's "Ode on a Grecian Urn" and "Ode to a Nightingale," an answer predictably embracing the plan of life and finding in the death of beauty an earnest of the deathless beauty in the "house not made with hands."

Stanza I is a classic example of syntactical complexity which has occasioned much dismay, for if it is considered separate from the stanza which follows, it is grammatically incomplete. Only when the two stanzas are read together are the demands of grammar satisfied. Clearly this is a serious flaw in the poem. The initial words "Would that the structure brave, the manifold music I build" remain verbless until the initial line of the second stanza, where Vogler utters the wish: "would it [the structure brave] might tarry like his [Solomon's]." Once the grammar is seen, the sense becomes apparent. He is expressing the wish that the beautiful sounds of his improvisation might last like the palace which Solomon commanded the legions of demons to fashion for the delight of his beloved princess. Solomon, according to Jewish and Moslem legends, was given the power over demons through his possession of a seal bearing on it the "ineffable name," i.e., of God.

How glorious, Vogler reflects, it would be if the beautiful building erected by the keys—his cohorts and demons to command—were to be made adamantine and imperishable! Like Solomon's obedient legions, the keys, disparting and combining, raise the lovely structure to pleasure him, their master. The keys take all space and time for their province, plunging hell-deep to place the foundation of the structure on the adamantine rock beneath all things, while others rise to heaven to erect the gold of the walls, each note "eager to do and die, yield each his place to the rest." Here is the difference between his airy structure and Solomon's temple: his is built of the least permanent and solid of all things: invisible vibrations which die in the air of which they are a part, leaving place for the notes to follow in their rush to death. He sees his structure as St. Peter's on a festal night, the colonnades and the vast dome illuminated with light. The music, in contrast to the solidity of the great edifice, becomes in its insubstantial beauty a symbol of life and beauty, which, as Keats noted with infinite sadness, is dying as one looks at it.

The fourth stanza is probably the most clarion of hymns of praise to the power of music in all of Browning. The vision of St. Peter's in its festal glory is nothing as compared with the magical beauty of the fabulous structure he makes, for music is the one power that unites heaven and earth, fills both with a heavenly light, and erases the near and far as it triumphs over space and time, even calling forth those who arose from the primal protoplast, the primordial slime of creation. The wonderful notes have the power to cause the dead to rise and breathe in a new world which never was before, and to summon the future before its time, forming a great harmony of past, present, and future in the impalpable structure of music. And it all must die.

He comforts himself by reflecting that if he had created the structure in paint on canvas, although the eye would be delighted, the very brush strokes—the sign of the dross with which actuality mars pure essence—would constitute imperfection. If he had created it in poetry, a form of art less gross than painting, even then the technique and the structure of the verse would show through, to be studied and learnedly commented on, and inevitably some of the wonder would depart. Both painting and poetry "are in obedience to laws," but music is the finger of God, "Existent behind all laws," and only in music is it given to man to frame out of three sounds "not a fourth sound, but a star." The infinite harmony, transcending sound, yields a vision of the harmonious spheres, the ultimate wonder.

But, like Keats, in spite of his comforting reflection that music avoids the fate of the grosser arts, he is still shaken by the transitoriness of music, the glorious structure that falls even as it rises:

Well, it is gone at last, the palace of music I reared;
  Gone! and the good tears start, the praises that come too slow;
For one is assured at first, one scarce can say that he feared,
  That he even gave it a thought, the gone thing was to go.
Never to be again! But many more of the kind
  As good, nay, better perchance: is this your comfort to me?
To me, who must be saved because I cling with my mind
  To the same, same self, same love, same God: ay, what was
    shall be.

The possibility of eternal growth and progress is wonderfully sustaining in a world of eternal change, and his faith in growth is one and the same with his faith in the nature of a God of love. Change must be good in a world created with such beauty by God, for "There shall never be one lost good!" Here is where Vogler parts company fully with Keats, who found comfort in the contemplation of Platonic essences, which alone are proof against time and decay. Vogler, who speaks the sentiment that Browning repeatedly embraced, finds comfort in the endless improvement in all things, the splendid certainty that goodness and beauty last, heightened illimitably. The evils in life, he discovers, are functional (1) to test man's fidelity and courage in the face of frustration, doubt, and pain, (2) to cement bonds of brotherhood and love among men, and (3) to heighten the sense of the beautiful and the good by knowledge of their obverse.

What was, shall live as before;
  The evil is null, is naught, is silence implying sound;
What was good shall be good, with, for evil, so much good more;
  On the earth the broken arcs; in the heaven, a perfect round.

These lines are frequently quoted out of context to prove that Browning denied the reality of evil, believing, as Don Juan insists in *Fifine at the Fair*, evil is "stuff for transmuting," i.e., it is changed in its perpetration into good. A whole critical mythology has arisen over the years concerning Browning's supposed denial of evil, beginning with Henry Jones' *Browning As a Philosophic and Religious Teacher* (1891). When Vogler refers to evil as "null" and "naught," he is by no means denying its reality. He is merely affirming that in the scheme of things it is a necessary part of the creation, not to be unduly brooded upon or lamented over, for it yields fruit of good. It is not "transmuted" into good, but it brings about good, although it remains the evil it is. Because of evil we have "so much good more."

The poem is perhaps the most unqualified of all of Browning's poems in its assured optimism, and some people have found the sentiment too blatantly affirmative for our time, with the neo-barbarism, ugliness, despoliation of beauty, and the threat of genocide, prime instruments of national policy, as accepted ways of life. It is clear that "Abt Vogler" has done little in our day to enhance Browning's position as a thinker. It must be remembered that it is a persona who is speaking, but it is difficult to argue successfully that he is not revealing at least partially the views of his creator. The last four stanzas become, like "Rabbi Ben Ezra," less a drama than a sermon, and one easily forgets that an eighteenth-century composer is speaking.

Perhaps the stanza most likely to bruise the sensibilities of the modern reader is this:

> And what is our failure here but a triumph's evidence
> For the fulness of the days? Have we withered or agonized?
> Why else was the pause prolonged but that singing might issue thence?
> Why rushed the discords in, but that harmony should be prized?

Our failures in the twentieth century are on a scale beyond the powers of comprehension of nineteenth-century Englishmen. It will not do in our time to find comfort in the fact that the world has always been in trouble, that the tree of life was never quiet, as Housman knew. Today we live with genocide and the threat of genocide as our familiar, and we have seen everywhere men of pious and devout lives accepting both as instruments in international relations wholly acceptable to Christ, the Prince of Peace. It is not strange that Vogler's optimistic words seem scarcely adequate to explain Belsen, Buchenwald, Hiroshima, and Vietnam. No longer can we brush aside our failures as merely "a triumph's evidence/ For the fulness of the days," for, in spite of Vogler, we *have* withered and agonized. It may all be very well to ask "Why rushed the discords in, but that harmony should be prized?" But when the "discord" is the death by violence of uncountable millions within the span of a half century, the word "discord" becomes regrettably inadequate, especially when one considers that the "discords" of the nineteenth century have yielded to many discrete problems that appear to be insoluble if not terminal—and, most ironic of all, precisely because men have found them enormously profitable.

Vogler asserts that in a world of strife and confusion, " 't is we musicians know," a view that seems to have been Browning's own. It is clear that during the playing at the organ, Vogler has indeed been close to God and the truth, or so he fancies. In life one cannot for long remain in this rarefied atmosphere, for he is man and must return to earth, "the C Major of this life." His feet once again are planted on earth as Keats returned from his escape through poesy with the nightingale and was brought back to earth by the bell-like sound "Forlorn"—a word poles apart from Vogler's sentiment.

SUGGESTED READINGS

Duffin, Henry Charles, *Amphibian: A Reconsideration of Browning* (London, 1957), pp. 201-02.

"*Abt Vogler* shows that Browning was able to use the avenue of mystic approach to reality afforded by art. The poem falls into three parts. Stanzas I to V are unimportant, and do nothing but give, through floods of alliteration, metaphor and hyperbole, an onomatopoetic impression of organ music. The final part of the poem is a statement of Browning's belief that the imperfections of this life will be put right in the next—'on earth the broken arcs; in heaven, the perfect round' " (p. 201).

Kenmare, Dallas, *An End to Darkness* (London, 1962), pp. 213-14.

"In *Abt Vogler*, Browning wrote of the undying power of those we call dead: 'The wonderful dead who have passed through the body and gone,/ But were back once more to breathe in an old world worth their new;' they are living again, firing the mind of the musician. And not only the 'wonderful' dead, but all who have loved and lived, still live, in an even fuller sense, in the lives of those who loved them, with an influence increased by the removal of their bodily presence."

Ridenour, George M., "Browning's Music Poems," *Publications of the Modern Language Association*, LXXVIII (1963), 369-77.

"The emphatic amorality of the building [in 'Abt Vogler'] is striking. It is based on hell, and built by demons equally with angels, which is a good deal more than acknowledging the existence of evil, making it 'part of the picture,' or even making use of it. From this point of view it reminds us of 'Kubla Kahn' " (p. 374).

Shaw, W. David, *The Dialectical Temper: The Rhetorical Art of Robert Browning* (Ithaca, N.Y., 1968), pp. 140-42.

" 'Abt Vogler' (1864), like 'Saul,' is one of Browning's rare experiments in a visionary, or (as the poet himself would say) 'lyric,' mode. By speaking through Abt Vogler in his own voice, as his wife had urged, Browning is able to pass from a merely subjective point of view, in the second and third stanzas, to a sympathetic identification with the living, 'the wonderful Dead,' and 'ages' still 'to come,' and to a new use of nature at the religious stage."

21

"A Death in the Desert"

"A Death in the Desert" is one of Browning's most carefully reasoned religious poems, ranking with "Cleon," "An Epistle of Karshish," "Caliban upon Setebos," "Christmas-Eve and Easter-Day," and "La Saisiaz," dramatically inferior to the first three but superior to the last two. The poem is supposedly a manuscript account of the dying testimony of St. John concerning the truth of the Christian revelation and the divinity of Christ. The aged apostle is lying in a cave in the desert, attended by five companions and guardians. The opening twelve lines, in square brackets, are supposed to be the commentary of the owner of the manuscript wherein the occurrences in the poem are recorded. The twelfth line identifies the narrator of the poem as Pamphylax.

Pamphylax wishes to have the dying apostle speak once again words memorable or oracular in their revelation. For sixty days the revered saint has been hidden in the cave, since the issuance of a certain decree in persecution of the Christians, perhaps that of Domitian. He has been reverently moved to the midmost grotto, where noon's light might enable the faithful five to read the expected revelation that will illumine his face.

Their hopes are dashed, because St. John is about to deliver himself of a discourse to explain why special revelations and miracles, which command belief, are no longer needed. Browning is clearly writing a reply to the Higher Critics, especially David Friedrich Strauss, whose new *Leben Jesu* had recently appeared in England, and Ernest Renan, whose *Vie de Jésus* had come out the year before (1863). Both books rocked the foundations of orthodoxy with their sceptical rationalism, which Browning deplored all his life as simply destructive, and many of the faithful feared that the Church might never recover from the attack. Browning's purpose is to allay such fears and to give heart to the weary.

The descriptive scenes in the poem are among the most vivid in Browning's poetry. Browning wishes to convey a true sense of the post-Biblical scene to give the message dramatic verisimilitude:

Beyond, and half way up the mouth o' the cave,
The Bactrian convert, having his desire,
Kept watch, and made pretence to graze a goat
That gave us milk, on rags of various herb,
Plantain and quitch, the rocks' shade keeps alive:
So that if any thief or soldier passed,
(Because the persecution was aware)
Yielding the goat up promptly with his life,
Such man might pass on, joyful at a prize,
Nor care to pry into the cool o' the cave
Outside was all noon and the burning blue.
(ll. 35-45)

As the apostle's lids move "presageful of the end," the faithful attendants chafe his wrist, place a drop of wine on his lips, and break a ball of nard beneath his nostrils to stir him to utterance. All is to no avail, for he smiles in his coma, but does not awaken. Even prayer is unavailing, but when the boy in a moment of inspiration speaks the words, " 'I am the Resurrection and the Life,' " the sage awakens at once and speaks. Browning is careful throughout to keep before us the dramatic scene, lest in hearing the long monologue our attention flag and we forget the drama:

Only, outside, the Bactrian cried his cry
Like the lone desert-bird that wears the ruff,
As signal we were safe, from time to time.
(ll. 68-70)

Pamphylax, before the sage speaks the anticipated words of wisdom, interjects an editorial, following the gloss of an imaginary Theotypas, included in brackets. The burden of his words concerns St. John's concept of the triple soul of man, which Browning spent a substantial part of his life illustrating dramatically. It is of unusual significance, for "A Death in the Desert," unlike such dramatic monologues as "My Last Duchess," "A Grammarian's Funeral," and "The Bishop Orders His Tomb," to mention but three of many scores, is a poem in which the speaker becomes substantially a mouthpiece for the poet's philosophical and religious beliefs, much as the old Pope in *The Ring and the Book* speaks Browning's most cherished views. One of the most difficult tasks in Browning scholarship is to know when a character does in fact speak for his creator and when he does not. In no sense are St. John and Browning to be identified, of course, but nothing could be clearer than Browning's endorsement of such beliefs as this:

[This is the doctrine he was wont to teach,
How divers persons witness in each man,

Three souls which make up one soul: first, to wit,
A soul of each and all the bodily parts,
Seated therein, which works, and is what Does,
And has the use of earth, and ends the man
Downward: but, tending upward for advice,
Grows into, and again is grown into
By the next soul, which, seated in the brain,
Useth the first with its collected use,
And feeleth, thinketh, willeth,—is what Knows:
Which, duly tending upward in its turn,
Grows into, and again is grown into
By the last soul, that uses both the first,
Subsisting whether they assist or no,
And, constituting man's self, is what Is—
And leans upon the former, makes it play,
As that played off the first: and, tending up,
Holds, is upheld by, God, and ends the man
Upward in that dread point of intercourse,
Nor needs a place for it returns to Him.
What Does, what Knows, what Is; three souls, one man.]
(ll. 82-103)

Since St. John was the last man to see Christ alive and he himself is about to die, he speaks the question in the minds of his followers: " 'How will it be when none more saith "I saw"?' " He recalls the three stages of his ministry: for many years he journeyed about and taught " 'and men believed.' "After his exile under Domitian to the Isle of Patmos, he was bidden not to teach but to write his gospel, and again " 'men believed.' " Thereafter, he heard no further messages, was given no commands to follow, and followed his instincts and heart:

"And, reasoning from my knowledge, merely taught
Men should, for love's sake, in love's strength believe. . . ."
(ll. 147-49)

And once again men believed. But time brought age and change, and Antichrist stalked the land and men fell away. The young asserted the superiority of their youth and its acumen over his age and the forgetfulness of age. He did not call down wrath upon their heads or astound them into belief by picking up scorpions or treading on serpents with impunity. Rather he relied on lovingly recounting the simple facts of Christ's life, " 'and, in the main, I think such men believed.' "

Thus, when sickness fell upon him, he was brought to the cave wherein he now lies, and he fell asleep, comforted in the certainty that

"Though the whole earth should lie in wickedness,
We had the truth, might leave the rest to God."
(ll. 186-87)

Here begins the substance of the poem, the philosophical burden, and it is typical of Browning that the focus is on what St. John learned when facing death, not on what he could speak of at firsthand about Christ. Just as the interest in "Saul" is in the revelations that come to David, the interest here is in St. John's discovery of the folly of going to sleep in serene reliance upon the adamantine impregnability of his supposed truth. Old and enfeebled, he awakens with the scales fallen from his eyes. He sees with the percipience of those about to die the veil between life and death worn thin to admit the light that truth is a living, kinetic thing, not a treasure to be hoarded in a vault. Nor can it be founded on historical evidences and demonstration. He is the last person alive to bear witness from personal acquaintance with Christ, and after his passing, hearsay will assume dominion, and he knows that people will ask

" 'Was John at all, and did he say he saw?
Assure us, ere we ask what he might see!' "
(ll. 196-97)

He knows that he must soon pass on, and how best can one tell the young what they must know—they who are so far from death, and shielded from the light of eternity by youth and strength? In his vast old age he lies "bare to the universal prick of light" and sees what youth must grope toward, unassisted, for this is the law of life. It would defeat the function of life to establish firmly and forever unchanged even the truth of God or the truth about God, for truth is relative, growing and shaped by the needs of men. Each man is tested by the resolution of his quest for truth: " 'When pain ends, gain ends too.' " He learns to be unafraid lest after his death—and the passing of firsthand evidence of Christ—the world might forget. The world will ever forget and learn again and nothing will remain constant. "New lessons" must ever be learned

"Till earth's work stop and useless time run out,
So duly, daily, needs provision be
For keeping the soul's prowess possible,
Building new barriers as the old decay,
Saving us from evasion of life's proof,
Putting the question ever, 'Does God love,
And will ye hold that truth against the world?' "
(ll. 267-73)

The apostle says that man "needs no second proof" to seize and hold the worth of physical good. We may laugh at the myth of Prometheus and his theft of fire from the gods, but the worth of fire, once learned, is never forgotten. But it is far otherwise with matters of the soul. If man could find and hold the answers to the soul's needs, once and forever, then earth must end, being without use:

> "While were it so with the soul,—this gift of truth
> Once grasped, were this our soul's gain safe, and sure
> To prosper as the soul's gain is wont,—
> Why, man's probation would conclude, his earth
> Crumble; for he both reasons and decides,
> Weighs first, then chooses: will he give up fire
> For gold or purple once he knows its worth?
> Could he give Christ up were His worth as plain?"
> (ll. 287-94)

St. John says that no man is or may be proof against fear and doubt, and the test of life is precisely that any man may fail under the stress of circumstances, for life is risk and it is suffering. How could the disciples themselves, including John himself, desert their Lord when betrayed by the mob?

> "Even a torchlight and a noise,
> The sudden Roman faces, violent hands,
> And fear of what the Jews might do! Just that,
> And it is written, 'I forsook and fled:'
> There was my trial, and it ended thus."
> (ll. 307-11)

In spite of his betrayal, he experienced the test of life, and although, in this instance, he failed the test, " 'my soul had gained its truth, could grow. . . .' " At the time he could hardly believe that soon men, women, and children who had only heard of Christ would clasp the Cross and embrace the truth. Even then, with Christianity triumphant,

> "Well, was truth safe forever, then? Not so.
> Already had begun the silent work
> Whereby truth, deadened of its absolute blaze,
> Might need love's eye to pierce the o'erstretched doubt.
> Teachers were busy, whispering 'All is true
> As the aged ones report: but youth can reach
> Where age gropes dimly, weak with stir and strain,
> And the full doctrine slumbers till to-day.' "
> (ll. 318-25)

Truth is the one thing in life, he knows, that cannot be fixed or made immune from inquiry and doubt. It is useless for men to cry out

"Quick, for time presses, tell the whole mind out,
And let us ask and answer and be saved!
My book speaks on, because it cannot pass;
One listens quietly, nor scoffs but pleads
'Here is a tale of things done ages since;
What truth was ever told the second day?
Wonders, that would prove doctrine, go for naught.
Remains the doctrine, love; well, we must love,
And what we love most, power and love in one,
Let us acknowledge on the record here,
Accepting these in Christ. . . .' "
(ll. 366-75)

Again St. John affirms the folly of wanting fixity in matters spiritual. Fixity means stagnation and the abrogation of life's test:

"I say that man was made to grow, not stop;
That help, he needed once, and needs no more,
Having grown but an inch by, is withdrawn:
For he hath new needs, and new helps to these.
This imports solely, man should mount on each
New height in view; the help whereby he mounts,
The ladder-rung his foot has left, may fall,
Since all things suffer change save God the Truth.
Man apprehends Him newly at each stage
Whereat earth's ladder drops, its service done;
And nothing shall prove twice what once was proved."
(ll. 424-34)

Man no longer needs miracles to support his faith, nor the aid of primitive myth, the stories of man's youth, to give substance fitted to the minds of children. Man has grown beyond such childish needs. The babe one must spoonfeed with accounts of miracles to command faith, but the adult must feed himself or starve. The miracle, when used in man's dawn was " 'duly wrought/ When, save for it, no faith was possible.' " Further miracles, today, would compel belief, " 'not help.' " Nor does man need scientific demonstration to command belief any more than he needs miracles. Man finds in his love an intuitive perception of God's love, which affords ample warrant for " 'the acknowledgment of God in Christ/ Accepted by thy reason. . . .' " Nowhere in Browning does he discredit the role of intellect so long as it works with body and spirit.

St. John in no way is condemning knowledge or the intellect when he says that " 'With ignorance was surety of a cure.' " He means that a plethora of demonstration, a repletion of truth, to remove *all* doubt and ignorance (man's natural state) would eliminate the struggle of man toward truth. It is " 'death and sole death' " when man attains absolute truth, for he gets darkness from light and stagnation for growth. Here, then, is man's eternal dilemma: he finds it difficult to understand that what he must spend his whole life in pursuit of must never be caught and held secure. Each man in each generation is a truth seeker, and it must ever be so, but man must likewise ever renew his discovery that he must be denied all absolutes in life, for doubt is the greatest of man's tests:

> ". . . why refuse what modicum of help
> Had stopped the after-doubt, impossible
> I' the face of truth—truth absolute, uniform?
> Why must I hit of this and miss of that,
> Distinguish just as I be weak or strong,
> And not ask of thee and have answer prompt,
> Was this once, was it not once?—then and now
> And evermore, plain truth from man to man."
> (ll. 522-29)

Even this question—the question of why there must be questions—may not be answered absolutely and for all time, for each man and each age must seek and find the answer anew. The sum of wisdom is in the discovery that man must ever " 'pass from old to new./ From vain to real, from mistake to fact . . .' ": " 'How could man have progression otherwise?' "

> "Such progress could no more attend his soul
> Were all it struggles after found at first
> And guesses changed to knowledge absolute,
> Than motion wait his body, were all else
> Than it the solid earth on every side,
> Where now through space he moves from rest to rest.
> Man, therefore, thus conditioned, must expect
> He could not, what he knows now, know at first. . . ."
> (ll. 589-96)

St. John dies and is buried by his faithful five, who then depart to their several destinies about the world, Pamphylax to fight the beasts in the arena and to die. In conclusion, Browning adds a monitory note to Cerinthus, the heretic who denied Christ's divinity, reaffirming that Christ was indeed the son of God and the embodiment of love.

"A Death in the Desert" is the most carefully reasoned and sustained dramatic poem Browning wrote about the Christian religion. It is spared the tedium that marks "Christmas-Eve and Easter-Day" and *La Saisiaz* because of its careful attention to setting and detail, which gives a degree of authenticity to the Biblical scene and character. It is useful to compare the poem with "Bishop Blougram's Apology" to see the illimitable distance separating the spirit and the vision of St. John and the worldly Bishop who argues more in the spirit of Cerinthus than of the apostle.

SUGGESTED READINGS

Honan, Park, *Browning's Characters, A Study in Poetic Technique* (New Haven, 1961), passim.

Raymond, William O., "Browning and Higher Criticism," *The Infinite Moment and Other Essays in Robert Browning*, Toronto, 1950. See pages 32-43 for a close discussion of "A Death in the Desert."

22

"Caliban upon Setebos; or, Natural Theology in the Island"

Since C. R. Tracy's essay "Caliban upon Setebos," in 1938, it has been fashionable to see "Caliban" as a study of a normal stage in man's natural religious development, in which may be seen "an expression of Browning's own opinion on certain religious questions of considerable importance." The poem today is commonly held to be innocent of satire (although W. C. DeVane in *A Browning Handbook* considers it to be a satire), whether of the Darwinians or the Calvinists. Although Tracy admits that there may be some satire in the poem, his essay is most remarkable for the thesis that Browning wrote the poem simply to show the antiquity of religious belief and the lines of development such religious belief must have taken: the poem illustrates the belief that at every stage of his evolutionary development man has evolved a theology to fit his spiritual needs and capabilities, a theology that for the time was essentially "right" for him.[1] In short, Caliban's religious beliefs were "normal" for him and his evolutionary growth, and, indeed, were inevitable to his stage of development. In both his chapter on Browning appearing in *The Victorian Poets: A Guide to Research* and in his *Handbook*, DeVane substantially accepts Tracy's theory.

John Howard emphatically denies that the poem is a satire on anything whatever, on the puzzling grounds that Browning's interest was in the creation of a character, representative of the denizens of the primordial swamp and speaking theological sentiments appropriate to his limited development. Apparently a poet is forced to make a choice between creating character or writing satire, although Dryden's *Absalom and Achitophel* achieves its magnificent satire through its clever but cruel characterization of types that might also be considered to be denizens of a moral swamp. Indeed, it is hard to recall a successful satire which does not owe its success largely to careful, if biased and unkind, characterization.

1. See C. R. Tracy, "Caliban upon Setebos," *Studies in Philology*, XXXV (1938), 487-99.

No one would discover that the careful delineation of the character of Jonathan Wild invalidates the sustained satire in Fielding's minor masterpiece. Surely there is satire on the English country gentleman to be found in the drunken insensitivity of Squire Western, a memorable characterization.

"Caliban upon Setebos" (the title means "Caliban *talking about* Setebos") is indeed a superlative satire, but it is directed not so much against a creature in the primordial swamp as against men sunk in the religious morass of mid-Victorian fundamentalism and Calvinism, men who sat in church and embraced their creed's peculiar Setebos. The belief that Browning was picturing a view of God that was natural to a particular time or state in man's religious development is simply untenable. Browning never thought that a belief in God's unbounded pettiness, villainy, and sadism was a normal state for man to be in or to pass through, regardless of his state of growth. It was, of all beliefs, the most perverted, and perversion is the opposite of what is natural. That man has held such beliefs, Browning knew, is abundantly proved in all places and in all ages—today as well as yesterday, although the passage of time, he thought, happily brings progress. It is a satire upon the cruel, abominable Caliban, who yet lives in the minds and hearts of men, and not men who are sprawled at length in the "pit's much mire," but who are on the board of deacons, sit in the Privy Council, and preside as chairmen of the boards of great corporations. A splendid picture of Victorian sabre-tooth fundamentalism may be seen conveniently in Esmé Wingfield-Stratford's *Those Earnest Victorians*, which shows how consciously a large segment of fundamentalist parents of the age modeled themselves after the Old Testament God of wrath, brutality, and terror, the better to intimidate their cringing children.

One recalls the spiritual anguish of Annie Besant in her quest for an Almighty Good that should be proof against "the nightmare of Almighty Evil"—and her memorable collision with the great Dr. Edward B. Pusey at Oxford, who brutalized her in thunderous denunciation for her respectful request for evidence of the divinity of Christ. It was an age of many Calibans and many Seteboses, and Browning deplored them all with his whole heart, for to him the word God meant love first and power second, and terror and brutality could never be linked with the concept of God, or with any true follower of God, whether he were a parent or a renowned leader of the Oxford Movement. Annie Besant, as she left the greatest divine in the kingdom, was told: "It is not your duty to ascertain the truth. It is your duty to accept and believe the truth as laid down by the Church. At your peril you reject it."[2]

2. Arthur H. Nethercot, *The First Five Lives of Annie Besant* (Chicago, 1960), p. 48.

The good doctor made exquisitely explicit that such pursuit of truth meant eternal damnation in a hell to be contemplated only by a diseased mind like Caliban's. Poor Annie, in the words of Arthur H. Nethercot, in leaving the formidable divine, the emissary of the Prince of All Mercies, reflected: "Here was the reincarnation of the Inquisitors of the Middle Ages, perfectly conscientious according to their own light, perfectly rigid—and perfectly merciless."[3] It is not easy to determine whether Dr. Pusey saw God in the light of his own mercilessness or whether he fashioned himself after the mercilessness of this God, but probably both thought processes obtained, for both are immeasurably comforting to Inquisitors. Dr. Pusey, in his own time, in his treatment of Annie, at all events, was a Victorian Caliban, representative of a whole spectrum of cruel, unloving bigots, all of whom Browning detested.

John Howard goes to wondrous lengths in his essay "Caliban's Mind"[4] to prove that the poem was written to depict a primitive subhuman mentality, and he supplies abundant evidence from the poem to establish his case, which no one would deny. But it was written to depict all such minds, today as well as yesterday and tomorrow, for it was not conceived of as a history of one stage of man, but as a psychological study of an enduring mental disease. Howard urges caution in discovering evidence of satire on Calvinism, especially upon the omnipotence of God, "one of the main tenets of Calvinism," for Browning, he reminds us, also held this belief. This belief is held by most Christians, except by those like John Stuart Mill, who, believing that it was impossible to ascribe to the deity omnipotence, omniscience, and total love, recommended sacrificing the first on the grounds that God intended well, but even His might occasionally could not prevail against "intractable materials."

Belief in the omnipotence of God is certainly not peculiar to Calvinists, or even especially associated with them more than with other sects. It is not the belief in omnipotence that is being satirized, but rather the abuse of omnipotence, a far different thing. Browning is satirizing the doctrine of election and reprobation, the irrational, whimsical God of John Calvin, but, more than this, he is satirizing the cruel, tyrannical, sadistic God pictured in certain passages of the Old Testament, and all fundamentalists, of whatever age, who embrace the belief in such a God—a God capable of murder and genocide. It is furthermore a satire on all believers in natural theology and on the Darwinians insofar as they postulated the nature of God on the evidences to be found in the rocks or in nature, for Browning knew that such evidence, though not inadmissible, is inadequate to explain God. In a letter to Mrs. Sutherland Orr, Browning wrote of the

3. Ibid., p. 48-49.
4. John Howard, "Caliban's Mind," *Victorian Poetry*, I (1963), 249-57.

necessity of the Incarnation to reveal to man the love and humanity in God:

> The evidence of divine power is everywhere about us; not so the evidence of divine love. That love could only reveal itself to the human heart by some supreme act of human tenderness and devotion; the fact, or fancy, of Christ's cross and passion could alone supply such a revelation.[5]

Although, as in "Saul," Browning occasionally pictured God as man, he rarely thought of God in anthropomorphic terms, but he believed that it was essential that God, at one time in human history, assume human form and show his love and compassion through suffering. This vision of God could not come through science, evolution, or "Natural Theology," a term suggesting that God may be known through study of nature, his handiwork. Nothing is more certain than Browning's repudiation of such attempts to combat the threat which evolution seemed to level at the authenticity of the Scriptures as the widely circulated postulate that the disturbing fossils were in truth not fossils at all, but rather were spurious imitations which God placed in the rocks when the world was founded, as a means of testing man's faith. But Browning clearly recognized the threat of trying to discover the nature of God solely from the evidence found in geology—or in any other natural science. The only way to know God is to bring the whole man with his whole capacity to the total evidence, the most important part of which was the Incarnation.

In Caliban's conception of "the Quiet," both Tracy and Howard discover evidence of man's evolutionary growth through seeking and finding a concept of a better God than the imperfect God he has. Porter and Clarke, much earlier, noted that "even at this low stage of development a reaching toward something better is evidenced in Caliban's supposition that behind Setebos is a power which he calls the Quiet, indifferent to the affairs of man, but so far superior to Setebos as not to be actively antagonistic to man."[6] The god here pictured is, of course, the Deistic god, the indifferent absentee landlord of the eighteenth century. But is the Quiet a distant, indifferent quasi-benevolent deity? Caliban does not think so. Although the Quiet is an improvement on Setebos, he is motivated in much the same way. He is preferable only because he is sluggish and inclined to doze, much as Thomas Hardy hopefully pictured God as someday becoming—man's best hope of escaping misery.

> This Quiet, all it hath a mind to, doth.
> 'Esteemeth stars the outposts of its couch,

5. "The Religious Opinions of Robert Browning," *Contemporary Review* (December 1891), p. 879.
6. *The Complete Works of Robert Browning*, ed. Charlotte Porter and Helen A. Clarke (12 vols., New York, 1898), V, 312.

> But never spends much thought nor care that way.
> It may look up, work up,—the worse for those
> It works on!
>
> (ll. 137-41)

In Caliban's sadistic view whoever was responsible for the creation, the Quiet or Setebos, carefully planned creatures he could torment:

> His dam held that the Quiet made all things
> Which Setebos vexed only: 'holds not so.
> Who made them weak, meant weakness He might vex.
> Had He meant other, while His hand was in,
> Why not make horny eyes no thorn could prick,
> Or plate my scalp with bone against the snow,
> Or overscale my flesh 'neath joint and joint,
> Like an orc's armor? Ay,—so spoil his sport!
>
> (ll. 170-77)

Caliban does not fancy that there is much improvement in an exchange of gods, except as sloth or deficient enterprise might moderate his exercise of cruelty. The character and motives remain substantially unimproved. Indeed, it would be contrary both to Caliban's character and to the theme of the poem if he did conceive of a god of kindliness and love, for the thrust of everything Caliban says is to show his total inability to conceive of a god different in any way from Caliban himself, and he is unreservedly devoted to cruelty. Godhead, by definition, means to Caliban the power to abuse power and to be above the moral code and retribution. A super-god would only be one more completely devoted to the principles of cruelty, and the Quiet is more desirable than Setebos, not because of superior ethics, but because of inferior initiative. Caliban knows that unless the Quiet more and more lapses into sloth and indifference, the outlook is bleak, for if it becomes more aware, more developed, "The worse for those/ It works on!"

C. R. Tracy discovers that, with allowances being made for differences in the evolutionary scale, Caliban's two gods represent a theological dualism similar to Browning's. The Quiet, who represents an advance in the concept of god, is postulated through intuition, not through reason. The suggestion that Browning held a dual notion of God is amusing, but that his supposed pair of gods might in any way resemble the grotesque travesty which is Setebos or the malign but more distant Quiet is shattering. Furthermore, Browning's God is always presented as a god of love and compassion, two qualities that are incompatible with a belief that God is remote from human concerns. Much of Browning's purpose throughout his life was to show that the opposite was true. His enthusiastic acceptance of the Incarnation was founded on the belief that for God to send his only son to die to save mankind would reveal his love and refusal to be remote from human concerns.

At the heart of Howard's insistence that "Caliban" must not be considered a satire lies this belief that Browning would not satirize what he himself largely accepted:

> Since one of Browning's major beliefs included the omnipotence of God, however, one must be careful not to confuse as satire a statement of belief by Caliban, which Browning may have considered quite valid. One has only to remember Karshish's excited exclamation to his friend Abib: "So, the All-Great, were the All-Loving too" . . . *to see that Browning, far from denying the complete truth of Caliban's belief, would consider it only a limited segment of knowledge.*[7]

This statement clearly says that Browning could not find it in his heart to deny the "complete truth" of Caliban's belief and took exception to it only in that it did not go far enough, revealing only a narrow segment of truth, but that what Caliban revealed was indisputably truth, however limited. The identification of Browning's views with Caliban's is superlatively unfortunate, in understanding both the poem and Browning. One of the most persistent beliefs the poet held was the denial of damnation and divine brutality. God must be all-loving or he is not God. This is what he is saying dramatically in the poem—and in scores of others as well. But it has been Browning's malign destiny to be misunderstood precisely where he spent the most pains to be entirely clear.

In a letter to Mrs. Thomas Fitzgerald, on the occasion of her son's mental illness, when it was feared that he might do himself harm and thus might suffer damnation, Browning wrote:

> —I should never dare to attribute to God what would be injustice in a human being—nay, in a *less* degree,—and think Him capable of punishing what Himself was the agent in producing. That is my opinion, and it is inexplicable to me how people with a belief in the Mercy and Rectitude of God can have any other. Trust in these, dear Friend,—and dismiss all such fancies as derogatory to the All-Good and All-Wise.[8]

His letters and his verse, as well as the reports of friends who knew him intimately, uniformly report that Browning never wavered in his central belief that God is in fact the All-Good and the All-Wise—a God as far removed from Caliban's Setebos, or his Quiet either, as may be imagined.

7. Howard, "Caliban's Mind," 249. Italics are mine.

8. *Learned Lady: Letters from Robert Browning to Mrs. Thomas Fitzgerald, 1876-1889*, ed. Edward C. McAleer (Cambridge, Mass., 1966), p. 35.

William C. DeVane calls attention to the motto from Psalms 50.21, "Thou thoughtest that I was altogether such a one as thyself," noting that in the collected edition of 1868 the motto was omitted, but that it was restored in the collected edition of 1889. Browning, in making the restoration, commented that the omission had been a mistake. DeVane observes that the motto "helps to a comprehension of the poem." It does indeed, but I think that its importance is much greater than has been recognized. Immediately it calls attention to Caliban's primitive anthropomorphism, from which he creates God in his own image, but the context of the motto is of even greater importance. The heading of Psalm 50 reads "1 The majesty of God in the church. 7 His pleasure is not in ceremonies, 14 but in sincere obedience." The substance of God's discourse in this psalm is twofold: to register his displeasure with the Israelites (1) for their sacrificial offerings, and (2) for their disobedience in keeping the Lord's laws. It becomes apparent that his annoyance is partly that the Israelites have offered sacrifices as substitutes for their compliance with the moral code. It will be noted at once that this is precisely the method that Caliban has employed to placate Setebos. When he is caught by his cruel god, Caliban acts to win reprieve by offering to maim himself or to undergo rigorous austerities. But the most significant part of the psalm concerns God's severe condemnation of them for their sins:

> 16 But unto the wicked God saith,
> What hast thou to do to declare
> My statutes or *that* thou shouldest
> take my covenant in thy mouth?
> 17 Seeing thou hatest instruction,
> and castest my words behind thee.
> 18 When thou sawest a thief, then
> thou consentedst with him, and
> hast been partaker with adulterers.
> 19 Thou givest thy mouth to evil,
> and thy tongue frameth deceit.
> 20 Thou sittest *and* speakest a-
> gainst thy brother; thou slanderest
> thine own mother's son.
> 21 These *things* hast thou done,
> and I kept silence; thou thought-
> est that I was altogether *such an*
> *one* as thyself: *but* I will reprove
> thee, and set *them* in order before
> thine eyes.

> 22 Now consider this, ye that forget God, lest I tear *you* in pieces, and *there be* none to deliver.
>
> (King James Version)

It will be noted that in this comprehensive list of sins and infractions of the moral code, the last—and the list appears to be in climactic order—is the sin of ascribing to God the characteristics of man—the sin which Caliban is indulging in as he speaks. The significance of the motto seems to be that Browning is showing the folly and viciousness of making God in the image of man—and in this instance a man without redeeming qualities, a humanoid in whom folly and knavery maintain a perfect equipoise. The really important lines, however, are those in which God threatens the Israelites with instant dismemberment, tearing them limb from limb, for Caliban repeatedly ascribes to Setebos precisely this hideous desire—to rend and maim and tear off extremities in fury. The conclusion is inescapable: the Old Testament God, as seen in Psalm 50, and Setebos are much alike, so much alike, indeed, that the satire upon Setebos becomes satire on the jealous God of wrath and cruelty upbraiding his erring children.

Caliban, in postulating the character of God, looks into his own sadistic soul to find him. If he were Setebos, he would fashion a creature of clay and send him straightway on a mission to delight the gods: to "nip me off the horns/ Of grigs high up that make the merry din." And if in so doing, the bird fashioned of clay for the sport of rending grigs should fall and snap a brittle leg (a consequence of poor design and engineering)

> And he lay stupid-like,—why, I should laugh;
> And if he, spying me, should fall to weep,
> Beseech me to be good, repair his wrong,
> Bid his poor leg smart less or grow again,—
> Well, as the chance were, this might take or else
> Not take my fancy: I might hear his cry,
> And give the mankin three sound legs for one,
> Or pluck the other off, leave him like an egg,
> And lessoned he was mine and merely clay.
> Were this no pleasure, lying in the thyme,
> Drinking the mash, with brain become alive,
> Making and marring clay at will? So He.
>
> (ll. 86-97)

He loves to catch the jay and "from her wing . . . twitch the feathers blue." The pipe he uses to catch birds—if it boasted that it was "the crafty thing" and in truth caught the birds— "would not I smash it with my foot? So He." He kills wantonly two butterflies basking on the pompion bell, for the simple reason that cruelty is a natural part of godhead, and the butterflies were demonstrably happy and thus richly deserving their fate. But his most cherished pleasure is not in crushing to death such erring creatures, but in rending them and letting them live, the better to contemplate the nature of god and the extent of their miseries:

> 'Am strong myself compared to yonder crabs
> That march now from the mountain to the sea;
> 'Let twenty pass, and stone the twenty-first,
> Loving not, hating not, just choosing so.
> 'Say, the first straggler that boasts purple spots
> Shall join the file, one pincer twisted off. . . .
> (ll. 100-05)

The effect of the motto becomes painfully clear in the light of these fearful threats: the irony is that the penalty for ascribing to God the cruelty that prompts Caliban to tear his fellow creatures to pieces is to have God prove the accuracy of the charge by tearing the guilty ones to pieces, for such is God's promise in Psalm 50. Such substantiation of Caliban's charge in no way is intended to prove that God *is* Setebos, but rather it is a satiric indictment of the hosts of Calibans, from the beginning until this hour, who have seen God as a vindictive, implacable tormentor, whether or not they sprang from the loins of Calvin. Browning repudiated the concept of hell as a slander on the character of God, and this poem is a repudiation of the cruel Old Testament God and all those who yet believe in him, for their name is Caliban.

In the light of Browning's bold theme, it is dismaying to discover that the poem is widely held to reflect a normal state in man's religious thinking and even more, to find that it supposedly squares very largely with Browning's own religious views. One simple reflection should serve to disabuse one of this belief: the extraordinary repulsiveness—moral, intellectual, and esthetic—of Caliban. It is dubious that Browning would elect to show a natural state, one through which man had to pass, in the person of the most perverted sadist among all his twisted characters, and it is inconceivable that he would imply his own essential identity with such a moral and intellectual dwarf. Moreover, it is in the highest degree unlikely that, if Browning were intent upon revealing beliefs that he largely accepted, he would have placed his spokesman "in the pit's much mire" wherein to philosophize on the nature of God. The scene is the very stuff of satire, especially when Caliban is pictured as drooling with imbecilic delight in the sensations of the mire:

['Will sprawl, now that the heat of day is best,
Flat on his belly in the pit's much mire,
With elbows wide, fists clenched to prop his chin.
And, while he kicks both feet in the cool slush,
And feels about his spine small eft-things course,
Run in and out each arm, and make him laugh:
And while above his head a pompion-plant,
Coating the cave-top as a brow its eye,
Creeps down to touch and tickle hair and beard,
And now a flower drops with a bee inside,
And now a fruit to snap at, catch and crunch,—
He looks out o'er yon sea which sunbeams cross
And recross till they weave a spider-web
(Meshes of fire, some great fish breaks at times)
And talks to his own self, howe'er he please,
Touching that other, whom his dam called God.]
(ll. 1-16)

It must not be forgotten that, although Caliban does not specifically say that God also loves to wallow in the muck of the hog lot and giggle with sensuous delight as the worms and efts crawl up his flesh, it is perfectly implicit that he can conceive of God in no other terms. If Caliban lives on the level of sensation, however revolting, God must also, just as both love cruelty and caprice. Browning knew that his age was rampant with the fundamentalist faith in the Old Testament rigor, gore, and genocide—the spirit of Setebos, not of the God of love—and Browning in the poem is speaking to all such men of his age and to all who should come after.

It is sometimes forgotten that "Caliban upon Setebos" is a poem of fear as well as of cruelty. Caliban is mortally afraid of Setebos and takes elaborate precautions to be well hidden from him when discoursing on godhead. Fear and cruelty are but successive phases of the same thing, the one leading to the other in endless succession, and this Browning knew well. Both fear and cruelty are alien from love, and without love there is no God and no religion. Victorian religion was pungent with the stench of brimstone, which became thicker as the freethinkers—George Jacob Holyoake, Charles Bradlaugh, Annie Besant, David F. Strauss, John Robert Seeley, Bishop John W. Colenso, and the "Septem contra Christum," who contributed to the upsetting *Essays and Reviews*—became more vocal and as the scientists became more compelling. Fear and terror became the ultimate resource of the besieged fundamentalists, and the character of God was illumined by the lurid hues of hell as the Calibans fought their rearguard action.

St. John in "A Death in the Desert" recounts the history of the Church, and predictably he finds that change and growth are the law of spiritual life. What once was held as essential to belief, when no longer needed, is put by. The one thing needful and beyond change is to trust in God as love:

> "Then, as new lessons shall be learned in these
> Till earth's work stop and useless time run out,
> So duly, daily, needs provision be
> For keeping the soul's prowess possible,
> Building new barriers as the old decay,
> Saving us from evasion of life's proof,
> Putting the question ever, 'Does God love,
> And will ye hold that truth against the world?' "
> (ll. 266-73)

In St. John's account of the spiritual history of man, he says no word of the need to pass through or beyond the state in which he fears God and ascribes to him raw and naked brutality. Other states are outlined. At one time man required a belief in miracles, but now he has passed beyond the need for such childish supports for faith, for "That help, he needed once, and needs no more,/ Having grown but an inch by, is withdrawn. . . ." He asks

> Was man made a wheelwork to wind up,
> And be discharged, and straight wound up anew?
> No!—grown, his growth lasts; taught, he ne'er forgets:
> May learn a thousand things, not twice the same.
> (ll. 448-51)

Again, nothing here suggests that there was a time or circumstance when man had to be terrified into religion or perforce was constrained to see God as a brute who would rend him limb from limb either for cause or not for cause. To Browning any religion that was based on terror instead of love was vicious, and any religion that used the threat of hell to enforce obedience was the great enemy of God and man.

Caliban, it will be noted, intuitively hates joy in others, and he cannot abide indifference in others to his power to inflict misery wantonly upon them. He has unlimited contempt for consistency, principle, or simple kindliness. What is the point of being God, he asks, unless he can abuse his power? Half the fun of being a sadist is to be unpredictable, to act on impulse, to rend in unmeaning wrath. He knows that the finest instrument of torment in the sadist's kit is unpredictability: to build up hope one moment and to pull the fingernails off the next—and all for no reason, other than "I am God."

Caliban knows that Setebos must dwell in the "cold o' the moon"—a likely place, since he himself is wretched on cold nights and finds God the malignant source of woe. Thus, Setebos is chronically cold and is powerless to find warmth in body or in spirit. He compares Setebos to a fish who yearns for the "Green-dense and dim-delicious" of the sun-warmed sea, but who cannot live in the kinder element and so must return to the bone-racking cold, "Hating and loving warmth alike: so He." Setebos is clearly of exacerbated frustration, hating all creatures who can live in the warmth of the sea.

Setebos, Caliban believes, "Made all we see, and us, in spite: how else?" But fate played an ironic trick on Setebos, for his creatures, in spite of the malevolence of their God, are happier than their maker, having mates, and so are a standing affront to him and a renewed target for retribution. In words that seem a clear parody of the syllogistic method of argumentation habitual among the Higher Critics, Caliban says:

> He could not, Himself, make a second self
> To be His mate; as well have made Himself:
> He would not make what he mislikes or slights,
> An eyesore to Him and not worth His pains.
>
> (ll. 57-60)

Caliban discovers that man's bodily frailty was specifically designed the better to allow Setebos to vex with ease. While creating, Setebos could have made man with horny eyes, proof against the thorn, or conferred scales like an orc's armor against all mischief: "Ay—so spoil his sport!" Newts which had incurred the wrath of Setebos he turned to stone—a rare reference in Browning to the popular subject of fossils. The grand secret of life's cruel game is to guess God's ways and mood and to never repeat too often what once allayed his wrath:

> There is the sport: discover how or die!
> All need not die, for of the things o' the isle
> Some flee afar, some dive, some run up trees;
> Those at His mercy,—why, they please Him most
> When . . . when . . . well, never try the same way twice!
> Repeat what act has pleased, He may grow wroth.
> You must not know His ways, and play Him off,
> Sure of the issue.
>
> (ll. 218-25)

The only hope of change lies in the remote possibility that Setebos may (1) die, (2) grow ill or senile, (3) create a new world to draw his interest and attention away from us, or (4) grow into the Quiet, "As grubs grow butterflies." Until one of these happy events takes place, the wise creature follows the Puritanical injunction, "not to seem too happy," as the best way of escaping his ire. Caliban rejects the concept of hell (one of the few views he shares with Browning)—not on humanitarian grounds—but on the utilitarian consideration that if additional torments could be invented, they would surely be used here and now.

The conclusion is an obvious travesty of Calvinism and fundamentalism. Caliban summarizes his religious feelings:

> Even so, 'would have Him misconceive, suppose
> This Caliban strives hard and ails no less,
> And always, above all else, envies Him;
> Wherefore he mainly dances on dark nights,
> Moans in the sun, gets under holes to laugh,
> And never speaks his mind save housed as now:
> Outside, 'groans, curses. If He caught me here,
> O'erheard this speech, and asked "What chucklest at"
> 'Would, to appease Him, cut a finger off,
> Or of my three kid yearlings burn the best,
> Or let the toothsome apples rot on tree,
> Or push my tame beast for the orc to taste. . . .
> (ll. 263-74)

It is certain that Browning has in mind God's reproof of the Israelites in Psalm 50, whence the motto of the poem comes, for their substitution of sacrifice for obedience of the law. It is significant that God specifically assures the Israelites that He is not reproving them for their sacrifices, as such:

> 8 I will not reprove thee for thy
> Sacrifices or thy burnt offerings, *to*
> *have been* continually before me
> 9 I will take no bullock out of thy
> house, *nor* he goats out of thy folds.
> 10 For every beast of the forest *is*
> mine, *and* the cattle upon a thousand hills.
> 11 I know all the fowls of the
> mountains: and the wild beasts of
> the field *are* mine.
> 12 If I were hungry, I would not
> tell thee: for the world *is* mine,
> and the fulness thereof.
> 13 Will I eat the flesh of bulls, or
> drink the blood of goats?

This discourse on sacrificial offerings immediately precedes the recital of the sins of the children of Israel and the threat to dismember them as a reminder of his wrath. Caliban has no great faith in the efficacy of sacrifice, but he has a sturdy faith in the sure and ready woe that will attend his failure to sacrifice if Setebos finds him out. All in all, the best hope lies in the remote possibility that

> . . . will either the Quiet catch
> And conquer Setebos, or likelier He
> Decrepit may doze, doze, as good as die.
> (ll. 281-83)

It should be noted that he places greater hope in senility than in insurrection in overcoming Setebos. It seems clear that, although the Quiet is to be preferred to Setebos, Caliban places no trust in his incorruptibility, for he has demonstrated throughout his monologue that the essence of godhead is sadism, and political platforms, he knows, are the very fount of lies and deception.

A particular objection to the belief that Browning substantially embraced Caliban's primitive views of God is that Browning always held that progress is the law of life—and insofar as Caliban holds this view Browning concurred—but to force upon Browning Caliban's stricture, however imperfectly, is to force him at the same time back into the green ooze of the primordial swamp, side by side with this rudimentary organism of limitless superstition and heartless brutality. Browning wrote the poem to reveal dramatically his detestation of such primitive perversion, which unfortunately has survived and battened from the time of the antediluvian swamp until now. Nothing could be more certain than that Browning believed in the inevitability of man's spiritual and religious growth and outlook, but this does not imply that man must have passed through all bypaths of perversion and aberration on the way.

Browning's concept of a God of love stood in perfect opposition to the pair of bare-fanged deities who, Caliban assumes, may someday war to the death for dominion over a world of hate and fear. Caliban, unlike David in "Saul," could never experience a revelation of the Incarnation or see God as Love.

The conclusion, in which Caliban fears that the scudding raven, Setebos's spy, has informed his malevolent master of all that Caliban has said, perfectly shows Browning's loathing of Old Testament maceration of the flesh as atonement. Caliban, in terror, bites through his lip and promises to eschew quails and whelks from his diet if he may escape. The poem begins and ends in a reign of superstitious terror.

John Howard says: "But the poem is part of Browning's way of showing that God reveals to each creature only what he is capable of understanding." It is unquestionably true that Caliban concludes, from the blind workings of his twisted mind, that God is Setebos, but to say that God deliberately "revealed" himself to Caliban so is to place upon God the guilt of Caliban in both thought and deed. This was not Browning's intent. His satire is leveled not against the God of love, but against the god of hate and the men who fall down and worship him, while modeling their lives on his supposed conduct. To believe that Browning thought that God could purposely mislead men into perverse and evil beliefs and deeds will simply not serve. Man, it is true, always grows in concept and enlightenment with the passage of time, but he does the growing, without being deluded by false and misleading revelations by God. If it is argued that God may help his struggling children up the ladder toward truth by helpful flashes of insight, it may be asked in what manner the revelation granted to Caliban was a help or an aid toward growth. Caliban's picture of Setebos represents the absolute nadir in religious belief. Surely God did not give him that revelation. One should recall the unequivocal statement Browning made in the letter to Mrs. Thomas Fitzgerald, quoted earlier, that he would never think God "capable of punishing what Himself was the agent in producing."

SUGGESTED READINGS

Ames, C. G., "Caliban upon Setebos," *Boston Browning Society Papers* (New York, 1897), p. 69.

Brown, E. K., "The First Person in *Caliban upon Setebos*," *Modern Language Notes*, LXVI (1951), 392-95.

A penetrating commentary on the psychological and artistic purpose in Caliban's shifts between first and third persons in his monologue: "The passages in the first person can be accounted for as expressions of those elements in Caliban's character that are struggling against his fear of Setebos, and the shifts from one person to another then serve to show the heightening of tension within the speaker. Caliban moves into the first person plural at line 56 in an outburst of impudent resentment, "Made all we see and us in spite: how else?" (p. 393).

Brown points out that when Caliban uses the first person singular he is talking about what excites him: "the pleasures of intoxication and then the pleasure of arbitrary power with its opportunity for cruelty. He feels he is a god, and talks like one." Caliban returns to use of the third person when he makes a "dangerous generalization about Setebos."

Burrows, Leonard, *Browning the Poet: An Introductory Study* (Nedlands, Western Australia, 1969), pp. 202-20.

Caliban is the missing link, positioned in the Great Chain of Being below man but above the animals, a rudimentary creature "lacking reason and grace." He is primitive man, a slave to his gross sensuality, capable of "rudimentary reasoning." "Caliban's meditations upon God are those of some legendary 'early man' laboriously groping his way to a conception of deity, a conception directly and crudely derived from his own nature. . . . He is neither a realistic nor a 'noble' savage: he is a fanciful grotesque" (p. 207).

" 'Caliban' has satirical implications, though it would be wrong to call it simply a satire. What is being satirized? Man's ineradicable anthropomorphism. The theologian, amateur or professional, contemplating the admirable thoroughness of Caliban's analogizing must surely have borne in upon him that this *modus operandi*, delineated with the dismaying bite and sharpened significance of precise imaginative distortion, is essentially his own. In this respect Caliban is the satirist's dreadful warning to all who shape a likeness of their god" (pp. 219).

DeVane, William C., *A Browning Handbook*, 2nd ed. (1955), pp. 299-302.

DeVane believes that "Caliban upon Setebos" owes much to Theodore Parker, the American Unitarian, whom Browning met in Florence: "Parker strongly believed that at every stage of human development man has produced a theology to express the highest reaches of his spiritual life; and he saw the need for humanizing the deity to suit the mind of men, that is, he saw the necessity for anthropomorphism in religion. His ideas were close to Browning's" (p. 299).

Honan, Park, "Belial upon Setebos," *Tennessee Studies in Literature*, IX (1964), 87-98.

———, *Browning's Characters, A Study in Poetic Technique* (New Haven, 1961), passim.

Howard, John, "Caliban's Mind," *Victorian Poetry*, I (1963), 249-57. Denies that "Caliban upon Setebos" is a satire. A representative modern statement of the belief that Browning is not attacking Calvinism.

Kenmare, Dallas, *An End to Darkness* (London, 1962), pp. 202-06.

"From such obviously Christian poems to *Caliban upon Setebos* is perhaps a long journey, yet *Caliban* is also a poem of great importance from the Christian point of view. The meditations and speculations of the savage, scarcely human Caliban actually differ very little from much contemporary speculation, which means that modernistic agnostic thought has, philosophically speaking, led us back to the status of the savage. Such a result is inevitable when the human mind seeks to reduce eternal concepts to its own measure of understanding. Caliban is the typical egocentric agnostic. . . ." (p. 202).

Melchiori, Barbara, *Browning's Poetry of Reticence* (New York, 1968), pp. 140-57 and passim.

Mrs. Melchiori believes the theme of "Caliban upon Setebos" concerns the verbal tabu: "The point of Browning's poem, both at the beginning and the end, is that it is Caliban's *speech*, rather than his actions, which vexes Setebos. At the beginning Caliban goes into hiding, in his grotto, for the express purpose of saying what he thinks" (p. 145). At the end of the poem, Caliban in fear and penance says he will make his teeth meet in his upper lip: "So the *sin* of Caliban against Setebos, as Browning sees it (and he finds support for this interpretation both in *The Tempest* and in Psalm L) lies in his speech. To this extent Browning is dealing with a personal problem. As a writer he was concerned with speech, and he must often have asked himself whether he was not offending God by some of the ideas he expressed. In Caliban's case the offense is followed by swift punishment, showing that what Browning unconsciously feared was divine wrath and the punishment of Hell" (p. 146). Mrs. Melchiori supplies no evidence to support this interesting discovery, a significant pity.

Perrine, Laurence, "Browning's 'Caliban upon Setebos': A Reply," *Victorian Poetry*, II (1964), 124-27.

A sound and well-argued refutation of those who believe the poem is not a satire, but rather a dispassionate account of a natural and inevitable state in man's religious thinking: ". . . the poem is not satirizing Caliban, nor Caliban's ideas in so far as they are *his* ideas. We do not satirize a 'primitive subhuman' for thinking like a primitive subhuman. Caliban 'contemplates God in the only way he can!' " (p. 125). Perrine argues that it is the survival of Caliban's crude and sadistic ideas of God into the nineteenth century—and beyond—that is being satirized. Browning's poem is directed against all the people of his age—and of all ages—who embrace substantially the blind and cruel views of Caliban.

Tracy, C. R., "Caliban upon Setebos," *Studies in Philology*, XXXV (1938) 487-99.

An influential essay in support of the thesis that the poem is not a satire but rather is a sympathetic account of a natural and inevitable stage in man's development.

Whitla, William, *The Central Truth: The Incarnation in Robert Browning's Poetry* (Toronto, 1963), pp. 42-43 and passim.

"*Caliban upon Setebos* presents an anthology of pre-Christian theology, and Browning goes to great length to show that such theologies are not equivalent to the Christian essentials (as against the deists) and that all theologies are not natural as the projections of men's minds. . . . To Browning the concept of a God of wrath is pagan. He puts so much emphasis on the importance of divine love that he eliminates divine wrath, and almost all of divine judgment" (p. 42).

23

"Epilogue" to *Dramatis Personae*

Browning's "Epilogue" is a summary of the volume *Dramatis Personae* (1864), which includes some of his most powerfully conceived poems on love and the spiritual life. In the "Epilogue" he has two dramatic monologues, one by David and the other by Ernest Renan, representing on the one hand, the doctrinaire, fundamentalist, ritualistic, sacerdotal position, and on the other hand, the liberal, rationalistic, skeptic position.

The first speaker, David, speaks of the solemn, ritualistic dedication of Solomon's Temple, when "the thousands, rear and van,/ Swarming with one accord/ Became as a single man" in response to the singing and the ritual. The individual became as naught, and all sang as one man in unison. Then, under the impetus of such mass hypnotism,

> . . . the Temple filled with a cloud,
> Even the House of the Lord;
> Porch bent and pillar bowed:
> For the presence of the Lord,
> In the glory of His cloud,
> Had filled the House of the Lord.

This is David's view of God and religion, but it is to be understood that Browning, through David, is talking, not of a religious view held a millennium before Christ, but a view still held in 1864—and later. Watson Kirkconnell is correct in believing that Browning was talking of religious views of his own day:

> There seems no doubt to my mind that in this first section of the *Epilogue* Browning has set forth, symbolically, a point of view which was finding acute expression in England at the time he wrote this poem, namely, the intense sacerdotalism of the Oxford Movement and the Church of Rome. To such superlatively orthodox Christians, our knowledge of the Divine is gained through special revelation;

> God's will is manifested in His church; and in the 'sacred' edifices, with their priestly services and sanctified ceremonial, we come into the Holy of Holies, into the presence of the glory of the Lord.[1]

Browning was repelled by the trend toward ritual, the ornate service, the "good strong thick stupefying incense smoke" of the Catholic Church, toward which the leaders of the Oxford Movement were tending. In "Christmas-Eve" he made unequivocally clear the repugnance he felt in seeing the unreasoning, sensuous, conformist ritual of the Catholic Mass:

> The whole Basilica alive!
> Men in the chancel, body and nave,
> Men on the pillars' architrave,
> Men on the statues, men on the tombs
> With popes and kings in their porphyry wombs,
> All famishing in expectation
> Of the main-altar's consummation.
> For see, for see, the rapturous moment
> Approaches, and earth's best endowment
> Blends with heaven's; the taper-fires
> Pant up, the winding brazen spires
> Heave loftier yet the baldachin;
> The incense-gasping's, long kept in,
> Suspire in clouds; the organ blatant
> Holds his breath and grovels latent,
> As if God's hushing finger grazed him. . . .
>
> (ll. 562-71)

Here the sensuous Mass is heavily freighted with sexual symbolism, in such words as *wombs, consummation, rapturous moment, pant up,* and others. The scene and the tone are strikingly reminiscent of David's speech—with the exception of the disapproval Browning registers in the earlier poem—even to the seizures of religious rapture, the presence of God in the cloud, and the pillar of fire. Mr. Kirkconnell very properly says:

> Browning, too, often enunciates the gradual development of man's religious conceptions as a perfectly natural process, in which the highest conceptions of any age are right for that age. . . . The poet hardly wasted time in 1864 A.D. condemning David for holding in 1000 B.C. views which he himself had often declared to be justified in that day.[2]

---

1. "The *Epilogue to Dramatis Personae,*" *Modern Language Notes,* XLI (1926), 217.
2. Ibid., p. 217.

The perceptive phrase "the highest conceptions" is important, for this and nothing less is what Browning believed. For example, the vicious and degrading views of Caliban are by no means "the highest conceptions" of his age, but are rather the lowest conceptions of any age—including Browning's own. But David's views are clearly not to be compared with Caliban's.

Renan, the second speaker, the French rationalist who electrified England with his *Vie de Jésus* in 1863, speaks in the cold, depressed tone of the skeptic who has cleared away superstition, only to find that he has created a vacuum. He is strikingly like the bulbous-headed rationalistic professor in "Christmas Eve" who lectures without love or hope and who leaves the air "mephitic," incapable of supporting the life of the spirit. Indeed, the whole poem reflects substantially the position taken in the earlier poem.

Renan finds that the age of faith has gone and with it the direct awareness and perception of a personal God, symbolized in the Star of Bethlehem. Once men saw in the star a loving, intimate heavenly father:

We gazed our fill
With upturned faces on as real a Face
That, stooping from grave music and mild fire,
Took in our homage, made a visible place
Through many a depth of glory, gyre on gyre,
For the dim human tribute.

"Why did it end?" he asks. Why did the star, symbolizing a companionable God, address "Itself to motion" and disappear from man's view? The face that man fancied he saw for a time thereafter was the cold visage of the deistic God, unmoved by supplication, joy, or pain:

. . . awhile transpired
Some vestige of a Face no pangs convulse,
No prayers retard; then even this was gone,
Lost in the night at last.

Since that time man, "lone and left/ Silent through centuries," has found in the night sky only lesser lights, shining cold and distant in alien space. Where is the star that for a moment "chose to stoop and stay for us?"

Today the stars are objects of interest only to astronomers, who smile indulgently at the myths that gave comfort to primitive shepherds. But man needs the comfort of faith and the friendly face of a loving God. Without them the music in man's soul has fallen dumb, and a "Ghastly dethronement" has robbed man's life of joy and meaning.

The third speaker, who speaks for Browning, faults both David and Renan for their views:

> Witless alike of will and way divine,
> How heaven's high with earth's low should intertwine!
> Friends, I have seen through your eyes: now use mine!

There is no question that if Browning were forced to choose between the two views, he would unhesitatingly take that of David, for in "Christmas Eve" he made the same decision. It is certain that Browning is not condemning David of a millennium before Christ, but rather is condemning Edward Pusey, John H. Newman, Hurrell Froude, and all others associated with the Oxford Movement, together with all believers in ritualistic religion, Roman Catholic or Anglo-Catholic. In "Christmas-Eve," similarly, he placed the little dissenting chapel, with all of its ugliness and unwashed humanity, ahead of the Roman Catholic Church and far ahead of the Professor's cold and loveless lecture hall in Göttingen.

The "Epilogue" is Browning's most direct and succinct statement of Protestant faith. The ornate, sensuous, ritualistic religion, with its primitive belief in the actual presence of an anthropomorphic God, Browning believed, belonged to an earlier era, when men needed such beliefs to sustain their childish minds. A splendid parallel is expressed in "A Death in the Desert," where St. John explains that God does not perform miracles today, for men no longer need such a display of his power. Contemporary rationalism, which demanded that God be found in the laboratory, perhaps certified by the Society for the Diffusion of Useful Knowledge, or that his existence be proved by syllogistic processes, Browning thought was wholly destructive.

God may best be found in the diversity of mankind, the miracle of individual personality, the ceaseless growth of man toward perfection in spite of evil, frustration, and failure, for in man one can see best "How heaven's high with earth's low" intertwines. The surest way to find God is not to look up to the stars with or without a telescope in the hope of finding once again the friendly Face in a star, but rather to look at "the least man of all mankind" and to "find how and why/ He differs from his fellows utterly." Of all the poets of his age, Browning was the spokesman for the sanctity of difference among men, and his lifelong suspicion of institutions, particularly of the Roman Catholic Church, was rooted in his hatred of sameness, enforced conformity, witless affirmations by rote.

To God each man is of supreme importance and is different from his fellows, and Browning spent his poetic life in fascinated study of how each man differs from his brother and how the unique soul under stress might express itself freely. Browning employs an obscure myth of the instinct of the Arctic seas to rush toward one "elected point of central rock" as if of all rocks on earth it is of sole importance for a moment, and after paying homage to that one rock, "mimic monarch of the whirlpool, king/ O' the current for a minute," the waves "wring/ Up by the roots and oversweep the thing" and rush off to seek another "peak as bare,/ They find and flatter, feast and finish there." Each life, then, for a moment is the focal point of God and His creation; no life is forgotten; each for an instant has its supreme moment in the fourfold process that marks each life. The alliteration ("find and flatter, feast and finish there") he uses to name the four steps is designed (with dubious success) to suggest the sameness of the process, though unique in detail, controlling the lives of infinite difference.

Since the essence of life is the sacredness of difference

> Why, where's the need of Temple, when the walls
> O' the world are that? What use of swells and falls
> From Levites' choir, Priests' cries, and trumpet-calls?

Browning, it will be remembered, was not by any means a regular church goer, and in these lines may be seen the reason. Only in the Dissenting Chapel could he find the encouragement of diversity that he required. Religion to him was not a matter of credal or ritualistic conformity but was a kind of reverence for life and individuailty that found each man of supreme worth precisely because of his uniqueness. Men are not tested by life in groups or congregations, but as individuals. Childe Roland is alone in his journey through life, for this is the law of life. One may find love and friendship and song and joy, but for all that he is alone in his journey. The fact that imperfect man—incomplete in knowledge and in love—strives toward completion is to Browning the supreme earnest of the sacredness of each life and God's purpose and love.

SUGGESTED READINGS

Fotheringham, James, *Studies of the Mind and Art of Robert Browning* (London, 1898), p. 346.

"The Epilogue to 'Dramatis Personae,' with its fine suggestion of a spiritual religion—a religion that does not wait for any future state to find God and grasp life—suggests, by that very conception, the depth and spirituality of life, and thus its range and possibilities."

Bibliography of Works Published on Browning, 1945-69

The serious student of Browning will be aware of the indispensable *Robert Browning: A Bibliography, 1930-1950,* compiled by Leslie Nathan Broughton, Clark Sutherland Northrup, and Robert Pearsall, and published by the Cornell University Press, 1953; the annual *Victorian Bibliography*, beginning in 1932, included in *Modern Philology* until 1957 and since that date included in *Victorian Studies;* and the annual bibliography in *PMLA*.

In spite of these valuable scholarly tools, it seems advisable to supply a bibliography of post-war scholarship on Browning. Since 1945 the studies devoted to him have been increasing steadily, reflecting a marked revival of interest in the poet, after a generation of relative neglect. This bibliography of critical and biographical works on Browning includes almost all the significant publications, exclusive of reviews and commentary included in books only incidentally connected with Browning.

ABBREVIATIONS OF TITLES USED IN BIBLIOGRAPHY

AL	American Literature
AM	Atlantic Monthly
AN&Q	American Notes and Queries
BJRL	Bulletin of the John Rylands Library
BNYPL	Bulletin of the New York Public Library
BPLQ	Boston Public Library Quarterly
BUS	Boston University Studies in English
CE	College English
CEA	CEA CRITIC
CJ	Classical Journal
CL	Comparative Literature
CLAJ	College Language Association Journal
CLQ	Colby Library Quarterly
ContR	Contemporary Review
CP	Concerning Poetry
CritQ	Critical Quarterly
CW	Classical Weekly
DA	Dissertation Abstracts
EA	Études Anglaises
EIC	Essays in Criticism
EJ	English Journal
ELH	Journal of English Literary History

ELN	English Language Notes
EM	English Miscellany
ES	English Studies
EUQ	Emory University Quarterly
Expl	Explicator
HJ	Hibbert Journal
HLQ	Huntington Library Quarterly
IEY	Iowa English Yearbook
JAAC	Journal of Aesthetics and Art Criticism
JEGP	Journal of English and Germanic Philology
KM	Kansas Magazine
L&P	Literature and Psychology
LCUT	Library Chronicle of the University of Texas
LQHR	London Quarterly and Holborn Review
MLN	Modern Language Notes
MLQ	Modern Language Quarterly
MLR	Modern Language Review
MP	Modern Philology
NQ	Notes and Queries
NEQ	New England Quarterly
NwMSCS	Northwest Missouri State College Studies
PBSA	Papers of the Bibliographical Society of America
PLL	Papers of Language and Literature
PMLA	Publications of the Modern Language Association of America
PQ	Philological Quarterly
QR	Quarterly Review
RdP	Revue de Paris
REL	Review of English Literature
RES	Review of English Studies
RL	Revista de Literatura
RLC	Revue de Littérature Comparée
RS	Research Studies
SAQ	South Atlantic Quarterly
SEL	Studies in English Literature, 1500-1900
SLitI	Studies in the Literary Imagination
SP	Studies in Philology
SR	Sewanee Review
SUS	Susquehanna University Studies
TLS	[London] Times Literary Supplement
TQ	Texas Quarterly
TSE	Tulane Studies in English
TSL	Tennessee Studies in Literature
TSLL	Texas Studies in Literature and Language
UMSE	University of Mississippi Studies in English
UTQ	University of Toronto Quarterly
UWR	University of Windsor Review
VNL	Victorian Newsletter
VP	Victorian Poetry
VS	Victorian Studies
WVUPP	West Virginia University Philological Papers
XUS	Xavier University Studies
YR	Yale Review

1945

Arms, George. " 'Childe Roland' and 'Sir Galahad.' " *CE*, VI (1945), 258-61.

Basler, Roy P., Dudley Fitts, and DeLancey Ferguson. "Browning's 'The Statue and the Bust.' " *Expl*, III (1945), Item 62.

Holmes, Stewart Walker. "Browning: Semantic Stutterer." *PMLA*, LX (1945), 231-55.
McPeek, James A. S. "The Shaping of 'Saul.'" *JEGP*, XLIV (1945), 360-66.
Underhill, Frank. "The Young Browning." *TLS*, Oct. 6, 1945, p. 475 (a letter to the editor). See also Oct. 13, p. 487.
Wenger, C. N. "Clio's Rights in Poetry: Browning's *Cristina and Monaldeschi*." *PMLA*, LX (1945), 256-70.
———. "Sources of Mill's Criticism of *Pauline*." *MLN*, LX (1945), 338.

1946

Alington, C. A. "Browning and Beauty." *TLS*, April 13, 1946, p. 175.
Crosse, G., and N. Orsini. "Casa Guidi." *NQ*, CXC (June 1, 1946), 237; (Sept. 21), 129.
Curle, Richard. "The Brownings." *TLS*, Nov. 2, 1946, p. 535.
Dodds, M. H. "Anne Brontë and Robert Browning." *NQ*, CXC (1946), 81-82.
Duncan, Edgar H. "Browning's 'A Toccata of Galuppi's.'" *Expl*, V (1946), Item 5.
Dunsany, Lord. "Browning Is Blougram." *Nineteenth Century and After*, CXXXIX (1946), 175-77.
French, Hannah D. "The Two Brownings." *TLS*, Nov. 16, 1946, p. 563.
French, W. H. "The Sinai-Forehead's Cloven Brilliance." *MLN*, LXI (1946), 188.
Hood, Thurman L. "My Last Duchess and Cervantes." *Trinity Review*, I (1946), 3-4.
Kenmare, Dallas. "Robert Browning and Elizabeth Barrett, The Inner Drama." Sept. 1946. A paper written for the Poetry Society of England and the Boston Browning Society in commemoration of the marriage of Robert Browning and Elizabeth Barrett, Sept. 1846.
Laird, John. "Some Facets in Browning's Poetry." *Philosophical Incursions into English Literature*. Cambridge, Mass., 1946.
Memorabilist. [A commentary on a portion of *The Ring and the Book*], *NQ*, CXC (1946), 1.
Priestley, F. E. L. "Blougram's Apologetics." *UTQ*, XV (1946), 139-47.
Reese, Gertrude. "Robert Browning and his Son." *PMLA*, LXI (1946), 784-803.
Smith, G. "The Tennis-Ball of Fortune." *NQ*, CXC (1946), 202-03.
Tracy, C. R. "Browning and Goldsmith." *PMLA*, LXI (1946), 600-01.
Watt, Margaret. "A Famous Elopement." *National Review*, CLVII (1946), 499-505.

1947

Baker, Joseph E. *"Pippa Passes" and Shorter Poems*. New York, 1947.
Battenhouse, H. M. *Poets of Christian Thought: Evaluations*. New York, 1947.
Brooks, Cleanth. *The Well Wrought Urn*. New York, 1947.
DeVane, William C. "The Virgin and the Dragon." *YR*, NS, XXXVII (1947), 33-46.
Greene, Herbert E. "Browning's Knowledge of Music." *PMLA*, LXII (1947), 1095-99.
Hess, M. Whitcomb. "Margaret Fuller and Browning's Childe Roland." *Personalist*, XXVIII (1947), 376-83.
Lord Kennet of the Dene. "The Browning Marriage." *Poetry Review*, XXXVIII (1947), 13-16.
King, Roma A., Jr., ed. *Robert Browning's Finances from His Own Account Book*. Baylor Browning Interests Series, No. 15, 1947.
Knickerbocker, Kenneth L. "Browning and Swinburne: An Episode." *MLN*, LXII (1947), 240-44.
Long, Mason. "The Tennysons and the Brownings." *CE*, IX (1947), 131-39.
R. R. "Browning's 'How They Brought the Good News.'" *Expl*, VI (1947), Item 10.
Reese, Gertrude. "Isaac Casaubon and 'A Grammarian's Funeral.'" *NQ*, CXCII (1947), 470-72.

Sessions, Ina B. "The Dramatic Monologue." *PMLA*, LXII (1947), 503-16.
Tracy, C. R. "Browning and Goldsmith." *PMLA*, LXI (1947), 600-01.
Werry, Richard R. "Samuel Rogers's Approach to the Blank-Verse Dramatic Monologue." *MLN*, LXII (1947), 127-29.

1948

Armstrong, A. Joseph. "An Imaginary Conversation with Browning, With Apologies to Walter S. Landor." *The Baylor Line* (Baylor Ex-students Association publication), X (August 1948), 18-20.
Bayford, E. G. "Poem by Browning." *NQ*, CXCIII (1948), 248-49.
Chew, Samuel C. "The Victorian Period." *A Literary History of England*, 1948.
Cohen, J. M. "The Young Robert Browning." *Cornhill Magazine*, No. 975 (1948), pp. 234-48.
Cundiff, Paul A. "The Clarity of Browning's Ring Metaphor." *PMLA*, LXIII (1948), 1276-82.
Fuson, B. W. "Browning and His English Predecessors in the Dramatic Monologue." *State University of Iowa Humanistic Studies*, V (1948), 8.
Gide, A. *Journal, 1889-1939*, Paris, 1948, passim.
Harrod, Hazel. "Correspondence of Harriet Beecher Stowe and Elizabeth Barrett Browning." *U Tex St in Engl*, XXVII (1948), 28-34.
Lloyd, Francis V., Jr. "Browning's 'How They Brought the Good News from Ghent to Aix.' " *Expl*, VI (1948), Item 35.
Page, Frederick. "Browning: A Conversation." *Essays Mainly on the Nineteenth Century Presented to Sir Humphrey Milford*. Oxford U. Press, pp. 14-28.
Reese, Gertrude. "Robert Browning and 'A Blot on the 'Scutcheon.' " *MLN*, LXIII (1948), 237-40.
Smalley, Donald, ed. *Browning's Essay on Chatterton*. Cambridge, Mass., 1948.

1949

Bowers, R. H. "Santayana and Browning: A Postscript." *NQ*, CXCIV (1949), 433-34.
Fairchild, Hoxie N. "Browning the Simple-hearted Casuist." *TQ*, XVIII, 234-40.
———. "Browning's Heaven." *Review of Religion*, XIV (1949), 30-37.
Mabbott, T. O. "Browning's *A Serenade at the Villa*." *Expl*, VIII (1949), Q. 6.
Miller, Betty. "The Child of Casa Guidi." *Cornhill Magazine*, No. 978 (1949), pp. 415-28.
R. B. "Browning: 'A Grammarian's Funeral.' " *NQ*, CXCIV (1949), 284.
Ratcliffe, S. K. "Robert Browning's Early Friends." *Cornhill Magazine*, No. 979 (1949), pp. 81-89.
Thomson, Peggy. "For E. B. B. and E. D." *American Scholar*, XVIII (1949), 67.
Williams, Arnold. "Browning's 'Great Text in Galatians.' " *MLQ*, X (1949), 89-90.

1950

Altick, Richard D. "Robert Browning Rides the Chicago and Alton." *New Colophon*, III (1950), 78-81.
Attwater, Rachel, C. A. Alington, and Dallas Kenmare. "Versions of Browning." *TLS*, Jan. 13, 1950, p. 25; Jan. 27, 1950, p. 57.
Boyce, George K. "From Paris to Pisa with the Brownings." *New Colophon*, III (1950), 110-19.
DeVane, W. C., and K. L. Knickerbocker, eds. *New Letters of Robert Browning*. New Haven, 1950.
Fairchild, Hoxie N. "*La Saisiaz* and *The Nineteenth Century*." *MP*, XLVIII (1950), 104-11.

Gierasch, Walter. "Browning's A Serenade at the Villa." *Expl*, VIII (1950), Item 37.
Raymond, William O., *The Infinite Moment and Other Essays in Robert Browning*. Toronto, 1950.
Thompson, W. L. "Greek Wisdom and Browning." *CJ*, XLV (1950), 246-48.
Willy, Margaret. "The Indomitable Optimist," in *Life Was Their Cry*. Evan Bros., London, 1950, 153-96.
Winwar, Frances (pseud. of Francesca Vinciguerra). *The Immortal Lovers*. London, 1950.

1951

Altick, Richard D. "The Private Life of Robert Browning." *YR*, XLI (December 1951), 247-62.
Armytage, W. H. G. "Some New Letters of Robert Browning, 1871-1889." *MLQ*, XII (1951), 155-58.
Brown, E. K. "The First Person in 'Caliban upon Setebos.'" *MLN*, LXVI (1951), 392-95.
Buckley, Jerome Hamilton. *The Victorian Temper: A Study in Literary Culture*. Cambridge, Mass., 1951.
Dickson, Arthur. "Browning's 'Serenade at the Villa.'" *Expl*, IX (1951), Item 57.
Fairchild, Hoxie Neale. "Browning's Pomegranate Heart." *MLN*, LXVI (1951), 265-66.
———. "Browning's 'Whatever Is, Is Right.'" *CE*, XII (1951), 377-82.
Foster, J. T. "Browning's 'The Inn Album.'" *Expl*, X (1951), Item 18.
Himelick, Raymond. "Bayard Taylor and Browning's 'Holy Vitus.'" *SAQ*, L (1951), 542-51.
Howling, Robert Tunis. "Browning's Theory of the Purpose of Art." *SUS*, IV (1951), 215-28.
Knickerbocker, Kenneth L., ed. *Selected Poetry of Robert Browning*. New York, 1951.
Lewis, Naomi. "Browning's Poetry." *N Statesman & Nation*, XLI (1951), 161.
Lind, Sidney E. "James's 'The Private Life' and Browning." *AL*, XXIII (1951), 315-22.
McAleer, Edward C., ed. *Dearest Isa: Robert Browning's Letter to Isabella Blagden*. Austin, Texas, 1951.
———. "Isa Blagden to Kate Field." *BPLQ*, III (1951), 210-20.
Nowell-Smith, S., ed. *Browning: Poetry and Prose*. Cambridge, Mass., 1951.
"Poetry and Crime." *TLS*, Feb. 23, 1951, p. 117.
Rundle, James Urvin. "Burns' 'Holy Willie's Prayer' and Browning's 'Soliloquy of the Spanish Cloister.'" *NQ*, CXCVI (1951), 252.
Super, R. H. "Review of New Letters of Robert Browning." *MP*, XLIX (1951), 136-42.
Thaler, Alwin. "Whittier and the English Poets." *NEQ*, XXIV (1951), 53-68.
Tillotson, Geoffrey, *Criticism and the Nineteenth Century*. London, 1951.
Wallace, Sarah A. "Robert Browning in London Society." *MLN*, LXVI (1951), 322-24.
Weber, Carl J. "Much Ado about Browning." *CLQ*, III (1951), 44-45.

1952

Armytage, W. H. G. "Robert Browning and Mrs. Pattison: Some Unpublished Browning Letters." *UTQ*, XXI (1952), 179-92.
Bowman, W. P. "Browning Anecdote." *MLN*, LXVII (1952), 473-74.
Burrows, Leonard. *Browning: An Introductory Essay*. Perth, Australia, 1952.
Burtis, Mary Elizabeth. *Moncure Conway, 1832-1907*. New Brunswick, N.J., 1952.
Cohen, J. M. *Robert Browning*. London, 1952.
———. "Seeing Browning Plain." *Spectator*, CLXXXIX (1952), 637-38.
Corrigan, Beatrice. "New Documents on Browning's Roman Murder Case." *SP*, XLIX (1952), 520-33.

Coyle, William. "Molinos: 'The Subject of the Day' in *The Ring and the Book*." *PMLA*, LXVII (1952), 308-14.

Greer, Louise. *Browning and America*. Chapel Hill, N.C., 1952.

Harding, Joan O. H. "Charles Morgan and Browning." *HJ*, LI (1952), 55-62.

Jacobs, Willis D., "Browning's 'Porphyria's Lover,'" *Rocky Mountain Modern Language Association Bulletin*, V (1952), 8.

Jamieson, Paul F., "Browning's 'Pictor Ignotus, Florence, 15—.'" *Expl*, XI (1952), Item 8.

Johnson, Edward D. H. *The Alien Vision of Victorian Poetry: Sources of the Poetic Imagination in Tennyson, Browning, and Arnold*. Princeton, N.J., 1952.

Kenmare, Dallas. *Ever a Fighter: A Modern Approach to the Work of Robert Browning*. London, 1952.

Lowe, Robert L. "Scott, Browning, and Kipling." *NQ*, CXCVII (1952), 103-04.

McLachlan, H. John. "A Browning Letter." *TLS*, Feb. 8, 1952, p. 109.

Miller, Betty. "Elizabeth Barrett and Her Brother." *Cornhill Magazine*, VIII (1952), 221-28.

———. *Robert Browning: A Portrait*. New York, 1952.

Morgan, Charles. *Rapporto tra arte e genio Considerazioni sull' Andrea del Sarto di Browning*. Rome, 1952.

Osgood, Charles G. *The Voice of England: A History of English Literature*. New York, 1952.

Pearsall, Robert B. "Browning's Texts in Galatians and Deuteronomy." *MLQ*, XIII (1952), 256-58.

Purves, John. "New Letters of Robert Browning." *TLS*, June 6, 1952, p. 377.

Stevenson, Lionel. "The Pertinacious Victorian Poets." *UTQ*, XXI (1952), 232-45.

Super, R. H. "A Grain of Truth about Wordsworth and Browning, Landor and Swinburne." *MLN*, LXXVII (1952), 419-21.

Weaver, Bennett. "A Primer Study in Browning's Satire." *CE*, XIV (1952), 76-81.

Willey, Dale H. "Moral Meanings in *The Ring and the Book:* Three Symbols and an Allegory." *RS*, XX (1952), 93-111.

1953

Boulton, J. A. "Browning: A Potential Revolutionary." *EIC*, III (1953), 165-76.

Bowra, C. M. "Dante and Sordello." *CL*, V (1953), 1-15.

Broughton, Leslie N., Clark S. Northup, and Robert Pearsall, comps. *Robert Browning: A Bibliography, 1830-1950*. Cornell Studies in English Series, Vol. XXXIX (1953).

Charlton, H. B. "The Making of the Dramatic Lyric." *BJRL*, XXXV (1953), 349-84.

Chesterton, G. K. "Browning and His Ideal." *A Handful of Authors*. Ed. Dorothy Collins. New York, 1953.

Coombes, Henry. *Literature and Criticism*. London, 1953.

Duncan, Joseph E. "The Intellectual Kinship of John Donne and Robert Browning." *SP*, L (1953), 81-100.

Furnivall, F. J., ed. "Acquisitions." *HLQ*, XVI (1953), 437.

Gwynn, Frederic L. "Browning's 'Home-Thoughts from the Sea.'" *Expl*, XII (1953), Item 12.

Hogarth, Henry. "The Mystery of Molinos." *LQHR*, 6th ser., XXII (1953), 6-10.

Horsman, E. A., ed. *The Diary of Alfred Domett, 1872-1885*. New York, 1953.

Joseph, D. C. "A Browning Book." *TLS*, April 3, 1953, p. 221.

Kaiser, Leo M. " 'Urbs Roma' and Some English Poets." *CJ*, XLVIII (1953), 179-83.

———. " 'Urbs Roma' and Some English Poets." *CJ*, XLIX (1953), 181-85.

Kenmare, Dallas. "Robert Browning." *ContR*, CLXXXIV (1953), 355-59.

King, Roma A., Jr. "Some Studies in the Shorter Poems of Robert Browning: Stylistic Interpretations." *DA*, XIII (1953), 810.

Kirby, Thomas A. "Browning on Chaucer." *MLN* (1953), pp. 552-53.

Klomp, Henry. "The Idea of Aspiration in Early and Mid-Victorian Literature." *DA*, XIII (1953), 389.

Lovelace, Robert E. "A Note on Arnold's 'Growing Old.'" *MLN*, LXVIII (1953), 20-23.
———. "Wordsworth and the Early Victorians: A Study of His Influence and Reputation, 1830-1860." *Summary of Doctoral Dissertations, University of Wisconsin*, XIII (1953), 382-83.
Lowe, Robert L. "Browning and Donne." *NQ*, CXCVIII (1953), 491-92.
Mauer, Joseph A. "The Clitumnus." *CW*, XLVI (1953), 113-18.
Maurois, André. "Les Browning." *RdP*, LX (1953), 7-27.
McCormick, James P. "Robert Browning and the Experimental Drama." *PMLA*, *LXVIII* (1953), 982-91.
Metzdorf, Robert F. "The Full Text of Rossetti's Sonnet on *Sordello*." *Harvard Lib Bull*, VII (1953), 239-43.
Miller, Betty. " 'This Happy Evening.' " *Twentieth Cent*, CLIV (1953), 53-61.
Nitchie, Elizabeth. "Browning's 'Duchess.' " *EIC*, III (1953), 475-76.
Parr, Johnstone. "The Date of Composition of Browning's 'Love among the Ruins.' " *PQ*, XXXII (1953), 443-46.
———. "The Site and the Ancient City of Browning's 'Love among the Ruins.' " *PMLA*, LXVIII (1953), 128-37.
Pearsall, Robert B. "The Forthcoming Bibliography of Browning." *VNL*, No. 3 (1953), pp. 5-6.
Perrine, Laurence. "Browning's 'Respectability.' " *CE*, XIV (1953), 347-48.
Short, Clarice. "John Keats and 'Childe Roland.' " *NQ*, II (1953), 218-19.
Smith, Charles D. " Browning's 'How They Brought the Good News from Ghent to Aix.' " *Expl*, XI (1953), Item 42.
Stone, Wilfred H. "Browning and 'Mark Rutherford.' " *RES*, NS, IV (1953), 249-59.
Treves, Guiliana Artom. *Anglo-Fiorentine de cento anni fa*. Florence, 1953.
Worthington, Mabel Parker." Don Juan: Theme and Development in the Nineteenth Century." *DA*, XIII (1953), 399.
Wright, Maureen. " 'Karshish.' " *TLS*, May 1, 1953, p. 285.

1954

Akamine, Yoyoi. " 'Robert Browning, you writer of plays.' " *Athenaeum*, I (1954), 33-39.
Archibald, R. C. "Musical Settings of Robert Browning's Poetry and Drama." *NQ*, I 1954), 270.
Brundidge, Harry T. "Browning in Texas." *American Mercury*, LXXXIX (1954), 45-47.
Condee, Ralph W. "On Browning's 'Meeting at Night' and 'Parting at Morning.' " *Expl*, XII (1954), Item 23.
Dahl, Curtis. "A Note on Browning's 'Ben Karshook's Wisdom.' " *MLN*, LXIX (1954), 569-72.
Daniel, Robert N. "Robert Browning, Poet of Affirmation." *Furman Studies*, NS, I (1954), 1-14.
Du Bos, Charles. "Pauline de Browning. Extraits d'un cours inedit." *EA*, VII (1954), 161-64.
Federle, Walter. *Robert Brownings dramatisches Experiment*. Zurich, 1954.
Greer, Louise. "Browning in America: A Study of Browning Criticism and of Browning Reputation in the United States, 1839-1890." *DA*, XIV (1954), 1073-74.
Hartung, Charles V. "Browning and Impressionism." *DA*, XIV (1954), 358.
Hilton, Earl. "Browning's *Sordello* as a Study of the Will." *PMLA*, LXIX (1954), 1127-34.
Hood, Thurman L. "Browning's Hellenism." *Trinity Col Lib Gaz*, I (1954), 13-15.
Lloyd, Francis V., Jr. "On 'How They Brought the Good News from Ghent to Aix.' " *Expl*, XII (1954), Item 31.
Stange, G. Robert. "Browning and Modern Poetry." *Pacific Spec*, VIII (1954), 218-28.
"The Stature of Browning," *TLS*, June 4, 1954, p. 361.
Trevelyan, G. M. *A Layman's Love of Letters*. London, 1954.

Williams, W. E., ed. *Browning: A Selection*. Harmodsworth, 1954.

1955

Badger, Kingsbury. " 'See the Christ Stand!': Browning's Religion." *BUS*, I (1955), 53-73.
Dahl, Curtis. "The Victorian Wasteland." *CE*, XVI (1955), 341-47.
DeVane, William C. *A Browning Handbook*. 2nd ed. New York, 1955.
Duffin, Henry Charles. "Mysticism in Browning." *HJ*, LIII (1955), 372-75.
Glen, Margaret E. "The Meaning and Structure of *Pippa Passes*." *UTQ*, XXIV (1955), 410-26.
Katope, Christopher G. "Patterns of Imagery in Robert Browning's *The Ring and the Book*." *DA*, XV (1955), 403-04.
Maurois, André. *Robert et Elizabeth Browning*. Paris, 1955.
Parrott, Thomas M., and Robert B. Martin. *A Companion to Victorian Literature*. New York, 1955.
Priestley, F. E. L. "A Reading of *La Saisiaz*." *UTQ*, XXV (1955), 47-59.
Pucelle, Jean. *L'Idealisme en Angleterre, de Coleridge à Bradley: Être et Penser. Neuchâtel*, 1955.
Raymond, William O. " 'The Jewelled Bow': A Study in Browning's Imagery and Humanism." *PMLA*, LXX (1955), 115-31.
Ruffin, D. "Browning's 'Childe Roland' and Chaucer's *House of Fame*," in *Essays in Honor of Walter Clyde Curry*. Nashville, Tenn., 1955, pp. 51-60.
Sanders, Charles Richard. "Carlyle's Letters." *BJRL*, XXXVIII (1955), 199-224.
Thale, Jerome. "Browning's 'Popularity' and the Spasmodic Poets." *JEGP*, LIV (1955), 348-54.

1956

Beal, Chandler B. "A Dantean Simile in Browning." *MLN*, LXXI (1956), 492-93.
Corrigan, Beatrice, trans. and ed. *Curious Annals: New Documents Relating to Browning's Roman Murder Story*. Toronto, 1956.
Davison, Edward. "The Line of Caponsacchi," in *Great Moral Dilemmas in Literature, Past and Present*. New York, 1956, pp. 61-72.
De Selincourt, Aubrey. *Six Great Poets*. London, 1956.
Dietrichson, Jan W. "Obscurity in the Poetry of Robert Browning." *Edda*, LV (1956), 173-91.
Duffin, Henry Charles. *Amphibian: A Reconsideration of Browning*. London, 1956.
Faverty, Frederic E., ed. *The Victorian Poets: A Guide to Research*. Cambridge, Mass., 1956.
Going, William T. "The Ring and the Brownings." *MLN*, LXXI (1956), 493-95.
Hardy, Barbara. "Mr. Browning and George Eliot." *EIC*, VI (1956), 121-23.
Harrison, Thomas P. "Birds in the Poetry of Browning." *RES*, NS, VIII (1956), 393-405.
Hill, Archibald A. "Pippa's Song: Two Attempts at Structural Criticism." *U Tex St in Engl*, XXXV (1956), 51-56.
Jeffrey, Lloyd N. "Browning as Psychologist: Three Notes." *CE*, XVII (1956), 345-48.
Keller, J. C. *Literature and Religion*. Rindge, N.H., 1956.
Knickerbocker, Kenneth L. "A Tentative Apology for Browning." *TSL*, I (1956),75-82.
Langbaum, Robert. "*The Ring and the Book*: A Relativist Poem." *PMLA*, LXXI (1956), 131-54. (Included in *The Poetry of Experience*, pp. 109-36.
Lloyd-Jones, Richard. "Common Speech—A Poetic Effect for Hopkins, Browning, and Arnold." *DA*, XVI (1956), 957.
Lowe, Robert L. "Robert Browning to Percy William Bunting: An Unpublished Letter." *NQ*, III (1956), 539-41.
McAleer, Edward C. "Browning's 'Cleon' and Auguste Comte." *CL*, VIII (1956), 142-45.
McNeir, Waldo F. "Lucrezia's 'Cousin' in Browning's 'Andrea del Sarto.' " *NQ*, III 1956), 500-02.

Raymond, William O. "Truth in *The Ring and the Book*." *VNL*, No. 10 (1956), pp. 12-13.
Roppen, George. *Evolution and Poetic Belief: A Study in Some Victorian and Modern Writers. Oslo Studies in English Series*, No. 5. Oslo, 1956.
Schneck, Jerome M. "Robert Browning and Mesmerism." *Bulletin of the Medical Library Association*, XLIV (1956), 443-51.
Schweik, Robert C. "Bishop Blougram's Miracles." *MLN*, LXXI (1956), 416-18.
Singer, Armand E. "Supplement to a Bibliography of the Don Juan Theme: Versions and Criticism." *WVUPP*, X (1956), 1-36.
Smalley, Donald, ed. *Poems of Robert Browning*. New York, 1956.
Tillotson, Geoffrey. "Victorian Novelists and Near-Novelists." *SR*, LXIV (1956), 663-75.
Williams, Luster J. "Figurative Imagery in *The Ring and the Book*: A Study in Browning's Poetic Technique." *DA*, XVI (1956), 2153-54.
Windolph, Francis L. *Reflections of the Law in Literature*. Philadelphia, 1956.

1957

Altick, Richard D. "Browning's 'Karshish' and St. Paul." *MLN*, LXXII (1957), 494-96.
Baker, Joseph E. "Religious Implications in Browning's Poetry." *PQ*, XXXVI (1957), 436-52.
Dahl, Curtis. "*Neblaretai* and *Rattei* in Browning's 'Aristophanes Apology.' " *MLN*, LXXII (1957), 271-73.
De Courten, M. L. Giartosio. "Pen, il figlio dei Browning." *EM*, VIII (1957), 125-42.
Dudley, Fred A. " 'Hy, Zy, Hine.' " *RS*, XXV (1957), 63-68.
Erdman, David V. "Browning's Industrial Nightmare," *PQ*, XXXVI (1957), 417-35.
Fairchild, Hoxie Neale. *Religious Trends in English Poetry. Vol. IV: 1830-1880, Christianity and Romanticism in the Victorian Era*. New York, 1957.
Gray, Donald Joseph. "Victorian Verse Humor: 1830-1870." *DA*, XVII (1957), 1083.
Halliburton, M. "Browning's Other Romance." *American Merc*, LXXXV (1957), 46-57.
Henry, Marjorie Ruth. "The Pope in *The Ring and the Book*." *DA*, XVII (1957), 2010.
Houghton, Walter E. *The Victorian Frame of Mind, 1830-1870*. New Haven, 1957.
Jerman, B. R. "Browning's Witless Duke." *PMLA*, LXXII (1957), 488-93.
Kenmare, Dallas. *The Browning Love Story*. London, 1957.
King, Roma A., Jr. *The Bow and the Lyre: The Art of Robert Browning*. Ann Arbor, Mich., 1957.
Langbaum, Robert. *The Poetry of Experience: The Dramatic Monologue in Modern Literary Tradition*. London, 1957.
Lewis, Naomi. *A Visit to Mrs. Wilcox*. London, 1957.
Litzinger, Boyd. "A Note on 'Master Hugues of Saxe-Gotha.' " *NQ*, IV (1957), 266.
———. "Robert Browning's Reputation as a Thinker, 1889-1955." *DA*, XVII (1957), 123.
McAleer, Edward C. "Pasquale Villari and the Brownings." *BPLQ*, IX (1957), 40-47.
Miller, Betty. "The Seance at Ealing: A Study in Memory and Imagination." *Cornhill Magazine*, CLXIX (1957), 312-24.
Pepperdene, Margaret W. "Browning's 'Fra Lippo Lippi,' 70-75." *Expl*, XV (1957), Item 34.
Perrine, Laurence, and Edwin M. Everett. "Browning's 'Fra Lippo Lippi,' 70-75," *Expl*, XVI (1957), Item 18.
Praz, Mario. "Browning's 'A Grammarian's Funeral.' " *TLS*, Dec. 6, 1957, p. 739.
Reeves, James, ed. *Selected Poems*. London, 1957.
Slatin, Myles. " 'Mesmerism' A Study of Ezra Pound's Use of the Poetry of Robert Browning." *DA*, XVII (1957), 125.

Szladits, Lola L. "Browning's French Night-Cap." *BNYPL,* LXI (1957), 458-67.
Wain, John. *Preliminary Essays.* London, 1957.
Wishmeyer, William Hood. "The Myth in *The Ring and the Book.*" *DA,* XVII (1957), 3026.

1958

Adrian, Arthur A. "The Browning-Rossetti Friendship: Some Unpublished Letters." *PMLA,* LXXIII (1958), 538-44.
Arnold, Marian. *The Two Brownings.* London, 1958.
Cutts, John P. "Browning's 'Soliloquy of the Spanish Cloister.'" NQ, V (1958), 17-18.
DeVane, William Clyde. "Robert Browning." *VNL,* No. 13 (1958), p. 22.
Fiorini, Natale. *Robert Browning.* Torino, 1958.
Foakes, Reginald A. *The Romantic Assertion: A Study in the Language of Nineteenth Century Poetry.* New Haven, 1958.
Ford, Boris, ed. *Pelican Guide to English Literature. Vol. VI: From Dickens to Hardy.* Baltimore, 1958.
Herring, Jack W. "Critical Attitudes toward Browning since His Death." *DA,* XIX (1958), 798.
Hill, A. G. "Three Modes in Poetry." *TLS,* Sept. 12, 1958, p. 512.
Johnson, Agnes Boswell. "The Faust Motif in Browning's *Paracelsus.*" *DA,* XIX (1958), 319.
Kano, Hideo. *Crisis and Imagination.* Tokyo, 1958.
Landis, Paul, and Ronald E. Freeman, eds. *Letters of the Brownings to George Barrett.* Urbana, Ill., 1958.
Litzinger, Boyd. "Browning on Immortality." *NQ,* V (1958), 446-47.
Marks, Emerson R. "Browning's Abt Vogler,' 43-56." *Expl.* XVI (1958), Item 29.
McCrory, Thomas E. "Browning and Dante." *DA,* XIX (1958), 813.
Morse, J. Mitchell. "Browning's Grammarian, Warts and All." *CEA,* XX (1958), 1, 5.
Page, David. "Split in Wain." *EIC,* VIII (1958), 447-50.
Porter, Katherine A. *Through a Glass Darkly: Spiritualism in the Browning Circle.* Lawrence, Kans., 1958.
Rivers, Charles Leo. "Browning's Theory of the Poet, 1833-1841." *Abstracts of Dissertations, The University of Southern California,* 1958, pp. 52-53.
Shackford, Martha Hale. "Browning Selected Four Poems." *Talks on Ten Poets: Wordsworth to Moody.* New York, 1958.
Tanzy, C. E. "Browning, Emerson, and Bishop Blougram." *VS,* I (1958), 255-66.
Watkins, C. C. "Browning's 'Fame Within These Four Years.'" *MLR,* LIII (1958), 492-500.
———. "Browning's *Men and Women* and the Spasmodic School." *JEGP,* LVII (1958), 57-59.
Zamwalt, Eugene B. "Christian Symbolism in 'My Last Duchess,'" *NQ,* V (1958), 446.

1959

Alberich, Jose. "El obispo Blougram y San Manuel Bueno." *RL,* XV (1959), 90-94.
Albrecht, Sister Mary Catherine de Ricci. "Robert Browning's Classification of His Monologues in 1868." *DA,* XIX (1959), 104.
Altick, Richard D. "Browning's 'Transcendentalism.'" *JEGP,* LVIII (1959), 24-28.
Bell, Martha S. "Special Women's Collections in the United States Libraries." *College and Research Library,* XX (1959), 235-42.
Bevan, Bryan. "Poet's Novel." *Poetry Review,* L (1959), 29-31.
Britton, John. "Browning's 'Bishop Blougram's Apology,' 702-709." *Expl,* XVII (1959), Item 50.
"A Browning Exhibit in the Treasure Room." *BPLQ,* XI (1959), 50-52.
Bryson, John. *Browning. Writers and Their Work Series,* No. 106. London, 1959.

Cundiff, Paul A. "Robert Browning: 'Our Human Speech.' " *VNL*, No. 15 (1959), pp. 1-9.
Goldsmith, Richard W. "The Relation of Browning's Poetry to Religious Controversy 1833-1868." *DA*, XIX (1959), 2612.
Honan, Park. "Browning's Poetic Laboratory: The Use of *Sordello*." *MP*, LVI (1959), 162-66.
Hughes, R. E. "Browning's 'Childe Roland' and the Broken Taboo." *L&P*, IX (1959), 18-19.
Johnson, Charles E., Jr. "The Dramatic Career of Robert Browning: A Survey and Analysis." *DA*, XIX (1959), 2601.
Knickerbocker, Kenneth L. "Robert Browning: A Modern Appraisal." *TSL*, IV (1959), 1-11.
Lindberg, John. "Grail-themes in Browning's 'Childe Roland.' "*VNL*, No. 16 (1959), pp. 27-30.
Lindsay, Norman. 'The Mask of Robert Browning." *Southerly*, XX (1959), 182-200.
Litzinger, Boyd. "Browning's Reputation as a Thinker, 1889-1900." *TSL*, IV (1959), 43-50.
Maxwell, J. C. "Browning and Christopher Smart." *NQ*, VI (1959), 157-59.
Perrine, Laurence. "Browning's Shrewd Duke." *PMLA*, LXXIV (1959), 157-59.
Preyer, Robert. "Robert Browning: A Reading of the Early Narratives." *ELH*, XXVI (1959), 531-48.
Ransom, H. H. "The Hanley Library." *LCUT*, VI (1959), 33-35.
Raymond, William O. "Browning's 'The Statue and the Bust,' " *UTQ*, XXVIII (1959), 233-49.
Singer, Armand E. "Third Supplement to a Bibliography of the Don Juan Theme: Versions and Criticism." *WVUPP*, XIII (1959), 44-68.
Smalley, Donald. "Browning's View of Fact in *The Ring and the Book*." *VNL*, No. 16 (1959), pp. 1-9.
Smidt, Kristian. "The Intellectual Quest of the Victorian Poets." *ES*, XL (1959), 90-102.
Stange, G. Robert. "Browning's 'James Lee's Wife.' " *Expl*, XVII (1959), Item 32.
Stevenson, Lionel, " 'My Last Duchess' and Parisina." *MLN*, LXXIV (1959), 489-92.
Trawick, Buckner B. "The Moon Metaphor in Browning's 'One Word More.' " *NQ*, VI (1959), 448.
Vanson, Frederic. "Robert Browning—Christian Optimist." *LQHR*, CLXXXIV (1959), 331-35.
Watkins, Charlotte C. "The 'Abstruser Themes' of Browning's *Fifine at the Fair*." *PMLA*, LXXIV (1959), 426-37.

1960

Assad, Thomas J. "Browning's 'My Last Duchess.' " *TSE*, X (1960), 117-28.
Barbery, Y. "La critique moderne face à Elizabeth et Robert Browning." *EA*, XIII (1960), 444-51.
Barnett, Howard A. "Robert Browning and the Drama: Browning's Plays Viewed in the Context of the Victorian Theatre: 1830-1850." *DA*, XX (1960), 4097.
Bevington, Merle M. "Three Letters of Robert Browning to the Editor of the *Pall Mall Gazette*." *MLN*, LXXV (1960), 304-09.
Bodkin, Maud. "A Note on Browning's 'Childe Roland,' " *L&P*, X (1960), 37.
Brown, T. J. "English Literary Autographs XXXV: Elizabeth Barrett Browning, 1806-1861, and Robert Browning, 1812-1889." *Book Collector*, IX (1960), 317.
Corrigan, Beatrice. "Browning's Roman Murder Story." *EM*, XI (1960), 333-400.
———. "Vernon Lee and the Old Yellow Book." *CLQ*, V (1960), 116-22.
Cowan, James. "Literary Criticism and Projection." *KM*, 1960, pp. 84-87.
Cundiff, Paul A. "Robert Browning: 'Indisputable Fact.' " *VNL*, No. 17 (1960), pp. 7-11.
Dougherty, Charles T. "Browning's Letters in the Vatican Library." *Manuscripta*, IV (1960), 164-69.

Garriot, Harold M. "Characterization through Metaphor in *The Ring and the Book*, with Special Reference to the Guido Monologues." *DA*, XXI (1960), 892-93.

Honan, Park. "Browning's Pauline: The Artistic Safety Device." *VNL*, No. 18 (1960), pp. 23-24.

Jones, T. H. "The Disposition of Images in Browning's *The Ring and the Book*." *Journal of the Australasian Universities Language and Literature Association*, XIII (1960), 55-69.

Kendall, J. L. "Lippo's Vision." *VNL*, No. 18 (1960), pp. 18-21.

Langbaum, Robert. "The Importance of Fact in *The Ring and the Book*." *VNL*, No. 17 (1960), pp. 11-17.

Litzinger, Boyd. "Did Cardinal Wiseman Review *Men and Women?*" *VNL*, No. 18 (1960), pp. 22-23.

Millet, Stanton. "Art and Reality in 'My Last Duchess.' " *VNL*, No. 17 (1960), pp. 25-27.

Palmer, Rupert E., Jr. "The Uses of Character in 'Bishop Blougram's Apology.' " *MP*, LVIII (1960), 108-18.

Pipes, B. N., Jr. "The Portrait of 'My Last Duchess.' " *VS*, III (1960), 381-86.

Porter, Jenny Lind. "Physical Locale in *The Ring and the Book*." *Personalist*, XL (1960), 48-59.

Poston, Lawrence, III. "Ritual in 'The Bishop Orders His Tomb.' " *VNL*, No. 17 (1960), pp. 27-28.

Reed, Joseph W., Jr. "Browning and Macready: The Final Quarrel." *PMLA*, LXXV (1960), 597-603.

Sanders, Charles R. "Carlyle, Browning, and the Nature of a Poet." *EUQ*, XVI (1960), 197-209.

Smalley, Donald. "Browning's View of Fact in *The Ring and the Book*." *VNL*, No. 16 (1960), pp. 1-9.

Starkman, Miriam K. "The Manichee in the Cloister: A Reading of Browning's 'Soliloquy of the Spanish Cloister.' " *MLN*, LXXV (1960), 399-405.

Stevenson, Lionel. " 'My Last Duchess' and Parisina." *MLN*, LXXIV (1960), 489-92.

Waters, D. Douglas, Jr. "Does Browning's 'Great Text in Galatians' Entail 'Twenty-Nine Distinct Damnations'?" *MLR*, LV (1960), 243-44.

Wilkinson, D. C. "The Need for Disbelief: A Comment on *Pippa Passes*." *UTQ*, XXIX (1960), 139-51.

Willoughby, John W. "Browning's Familiarity with the Bible." *NQ*, VII (1960), 459.

1961

Austin, James C. "The Hawthorne and Browning Acquaintance: Including an Unpublished Browning Letter." *VNL*, No. 20 (1961), pp. 13-18.

Bevington, Merle M. "Browning and Wordsworth: The Argument for Immortality in 'Saul.' " *VNL*, No. 20 (1961), pp. 19-21.

Blair, Carolyn L. "Robert Browning as a Literary Critic." *DA*, XXII (1961), 1974.

Buhl, Pauline E. "A Historical and Critical Study of Browning's *Asolando* Volume." *DA*, XXII (1961), 562.

Chiarenza, Frank J. "Browning's 'The Bishop Orders His Tomb at St. Praxed's Church,' 73-79; 99-100" *Expl*, XIX (1961), Item 22.

Cox, Mary Elizabeth. "With Bernard de Mandeville." *WVUPP*, XIII (1961), 31-36.

Docherty, H. A. "Browning's Use of History: Its Effect on Meaning and Structure in His Poetry." *DA*, XXII (1961), 3659.

Gray, Donald J. "Arthur, Roland, Empedocles, Sigurd, and the Despair of Heroes in Victorian Poetry." *BUS*, V (1961), 1-17.

Hagopian, John V. "The Mask of Browning's Countess Gismond." *PQ*, XL (1961), 153-55.

Harper, James W. "Browning and the Evangelical Tradition." *DA*, XXI (1961), 3089-90.

Harrison, Thomas P. "Browning's 'Childe Roland' and Wordsworth." *TSL*, VI (1961), 119-23.

Hess, M. Whitcomb. "Graham Greene's Travesty on *The Ring and the Book*." *Catholic World*, CXCIV (1961), 37-42.

Honan, Park. *Browning's Characters: A Study in Poetic Technique*. New Haven, 1961.

Johnson, E. D. H. "Robert Browning's Pluralistic Universe: A Reading of *The Ring and the Book*." *UTQ*, XXXI (1961), 20-41.

Kelley, Lachlan P. "Robert Browning and George Smith." *QR*, CCXCIX (1961), 323-35.

Kilburn, Patrick E. "Browning's 'My Last Duchess.'" *Expl*, XIX (1961), Item 31.

King, Roma A., Jr. "Browning: 'Mage' and 'Maker'—A Study in Poetic Purpose and Method." *VNL*, No. 20 (1961), pp. 22-25.

Litzinger, Boyd A. "Incident as Microcosm: The Prior's Niece in 'Fra Lippo Lippi.'" *CE*, XXII (1961), 409-10.

———. "A Note on Browning's Defense of Chatterton." *VNL*, No. 19 (1961), pp. 17-19.

———. "The Prior's Niece in 'Fra Lippo Lippi.'" *NQ*, VIII (1961), 344-45.

———. "Browning's 'The Statue and the Bust' Once More." *Studies in Honor of John C. Hodges and Alwin Thaler*. Knoxville, Tenn., 1961, pp. 87-92.

McAleer, Edward C. "Browning's 'Nationality in Drinks.'" *Expl*, XX (1961), Item 34.

McNally, James J., Jr. "The Political Thought of Robert Browning." *DA*, XXII (1961), 142-50.

Mendl, R. W. S. "Robert Browning, the Poet-Musician." *Music and Letters*, XLII (1961), 142-50.

Nathanson, Leonard. "Browning's 'My Last Duchess.'" *Expl*, XIX (1961), Item 68.

Orenstein, Irving. "A Fresh Interpretation of 'The Last Ride Together,'" in Baylor Browning Interests Series, No. 18, Waco, Texas, 1961, pp. 3-10.

Peattie, D., and L. Peattie. "Immortal Romance." *Reader's Digest*, LXXIX (1961), 304-09.

Poisson, Jean, "Georges Connes: le livre et l'anneau de Browning." *EA*, XIV (1961), 354-55.

Puckett, W. M. "The Nineteenth Century Foundations of Robert Browning-Ezra Pound Bridge to Modernity in Poetry." *DA*, XXII (1961), 3205.

Rivers, Charles. *Three Essays on Robert Browning's Theory of the Poet*. *NwMSCS*, XXV, No. 3 (1961).

Rosenbaum, Robert A. *Earnest Victorians*. New York, 1961.

Sanders, Mrs. Steven. *A Supplementary Calendar of Letters*. Baylor Browning Interests Series, No. 18. Waco, Texas, 1961, pp. 11-20.

Schweik, Robert C. "The Structure of 'A Grammarian's Funeral.'" *CE*, XXII (1961), 411-12.

Shanks, Edward, ed. *Poems of Robert Browning*. London, 1961.

Sypher, Wylie, ed. *The Ring and the Book*. New York, 1961.

Thane, Adele. "'Pied Piper of Hamelin,' Dramatization of the Poem by Robert Browning." *Plays*, XXI (1961), 37-47.

Wasserman, George R. "The Meaning of Browning's Ring-Figure." *MLN*, LXXVI (1961), 420-26.

Woodard, Charles R. "The Road to the Dark Tower: An Interpretation of Browning's 'Childe Roland.'" *Studies in Honor of John C. Hodges and Alwin Thaler*. Knoxville, Tenn., 1961, pp. 93-99.

1962

Benziger, James. *Images of Eternity: Studies in the Poetry of Religious Vision, from Wordsworth to T. S. Eliot*. Carbondale, Ill., 1962.

Clarke, C. C. "Humor and Wit in 'Childe Roland.'" *MLQ*, XXIII (1962), 323-36.

Curran, E. M. "Browning: Tallow and Brown Sugar?" *CLQ*, Ser. VI (1962), 169-75.

Davies, Hugh Sykes. *Browning and the Modern Novel.* Hull University. Given as an address at St. John's College, Cambridge, England, 1961-62.

De Laura, David J. "The Religious Imagery in Browning's 'The Patriot.' " *VNL,* No. 21 (1962), pp. 16-18.

Dougherty, Charles T. "Three Browning Letters to His Son." *Manuscripta,* VI (1962), 98-103.

Fletcher, Richard M. "English Romantic Drama: 1795-1843. A Critical and Historical Study." *DA,* XXIII (1962), 1364.

Hess, M. Whitcomb. "Browning: An English Kierkegaard." *Christian Century,* LXXIX (1962), 569-71.

———. "Browning Sesquicentennial." *ContR,* CCI (1962), 268-70.

Kemper, Frances C. "Irony and Browning's *Fifine at the Fair.*" *DA,* XXIII (1962), 1351-52.

Kendall, J. L. "Browning's *Fifine at the Fair*: Meaning and Method." *VNL,* No. 22 (1962), pp. 16-18.

Kendall, Lyle H., Jr. "A New Browning Letter." *NQ,* IX (1962), 298-99.

Kenmare, Dallas. *An End to Darkness: A New Approach to Robert Browning and His Work.* London, 1962.

"Letters from the Brownings." *Listener* (1962), p. 842.

Litzinger, Boyd. "Browning's Reputation as a Thinker, 1900-1910." *Cithara* (1962), pp. 8-23.

———. "Robert Browning and the Babylonian Woman," in Baylor Browning Interests Series, No. 19, Waco, Texas, 1962.

Orel, Harold. "Browning's Use of Historical Sources in *Strafford,*" in *Six Studies in Nineteenth-Century Literature and Thought.* Eds. Harold Orel and George J. Worth. *University of Kansas Publications. Humanistic Studies, No. 35.* Lawrence, Kan., 1962, pp. 23-27.

Pietch, Frances. "The Relationship between Music and Literature in the Victorian Period: Studies in Browning, Hardy, and Shaw." *DA,* XXII (1962), 2386.

Ryals, Clyde De L. "The Poet as Critic: Appraisals of Tennyson by His Contemporaries." *TSL,* VII (1962), 113-25.

Seturaman, V. S. "Browning's 'By the Fireside': 'The Path Grey Heads Abhor.' " *NQ,* IX (1962), 297-98.

Stevenson, Lionel. "The Hawthorne and Browning Acquaintance: An Addendum." *VNL,* No. 21 (1962), p. 16.

Tilton, John W., and R. Dale Tuttle. "A New Reading of 'Count Gismond.' " *SP,* LIX (1962), 83-95.

Willoughby, John W. "Browning's 'Johannes Agricola in Meditation.' " *Expl,* XXI (1962), Item 5.

1963

Adair, Virginia H. "Browning's 'Soliloquy of the Spanish Cloister,' 65-72." *Expl,* XXII (1963), Item 24.

Altick, Richard D. " 'A Grammarian's Funeral': Browning's Praise of Folly?" *SEL,* III (1963), 449-60.

———. "Memo to the Next Annotator of Browning." *VP,* I (1963), 61-68.

Balliet, Conrad A. " 'Growing Old' Along with 'Rabbi Ben Ezra.' " *VP,* I (1963), 300-01.

Barnes, Warner. "The Browning Collection." *LCUT,* VII (1963), 12-13.

Cary, Richard. "Robinson on Browning." *VNL,* No. 23 (1963), pp. 19-21.

Columbus, Robert R. "A Critical Explication of Robert Browning's Parleyings with Certain People of Importance in Their Day." *DA,* XXIII (1963), 3370.

Crowell, Norton B. *The Triple Soul: Browning's Theory of Knowledge.* Albuquerque, N.M., 1963.

Drew, Philip. "Browning's *Essay on Shelley.*" VP, I (1963), 1-6.

Fleisher, David. " 'Rabbi Ben Ezra,' 49-72: A New Key to an Old Crux." *VP,* I (1963), 46-52.

Fryxell, Lucy Dickinson. "Browning's 'Soliloquy of the Spanish Cloister,' 65-72." *Expl*, XXII (1963), Item 24.
Gainer, Patrick W. "Hy, Zy, Hine.' " *VP*, I (1963), 158-60.
Graves, Robert. "Pretense on Parnassus." *Horizon*, V (1963), 81-85.
Guerin, Wilfred L. "Irony and Tension in Browning's 'Karshish.' " *VP*, I (1963), 132-39.
Holloway, Sister Marcella M. "A Further Reading of 'Count Gismond.' " *SP*, LX (1963), 549-53.
Howard, John. "Caliban's Mind." *VP*, I (1963), 249-57.
Johnson, Wendell Stacy. "Browning's Music." *JAAC*, XXII (1963), 203-07.
Kelley, Philip, and Ronald Hudson. "The Letters of the Brownings." *VP*, I (1963), 238-39.
Kishler, Thomas C. "A Note on Browning's 'Soliloquy of the Spanish Cloister.' " *VP*, I (1963), 70-71.
Leary, Lewis. "An American in Florence Meets the Brownings." *Columbia Library Columns*, XII (1963), 7-16.
Martin, Hugh. *The Faith of Robert Browning*. London, 1963.
Maxwell, J. C. "Browning's Concept of the Poet: A Revision in *Pauline*." *VP*, I (1963), 237-38.
McCall, John. "Browning's Uncloseted Dramas." *IEY*, No. 8 (1963), pp. 51-55.
Miles, Josephine. "Toward a Theory of Style and Change." *JAAC*, XXII (1963), 63-68.
Miller, J. Hillis. *The Disappearance of God: Five Nineteenth-Century Writers*. Cambridge, Mass., 1963.
Monteiro, George. "Browning's 'My Last Duchess.' " *VP*, I (1963), 234-37.
Paganelli, Eliosa. "Il teatro di Robert Browning." *Convivium*, XXXI (1963), 191-210.
Page, David. "And so Is Browning." *EIC*, XIII (1963), 146-54.
Raymond, William O. "Browning and the Harriet Westbrook Shelley Letters." *UTQ*, XXXII (1963), 184-92.
Ridenour, George M. "Browning's Music Poems: Fancy and Fact." *PMLA*, LXXVIII (1963), 369-77.
Ryan, William M. "The Classifications of Browning's 'Difficult' Vocabulary." *SP*, LX (1963), 542-48.
Sanders, Charles R. "Some Lost and Unpublished Carlyle-Browning Correspondence." *JEGP*, LXII (1963), 322-35.
Slakey, Roger L. "Browning's 'Soliloquy of the Spanish Cloister.' " *Expl*, XXI (1963), Item 42.
Stevens, Lewis Robert. "Robert Browning as a Myth-Maker in *The Ring and the Book*." *DA*, XXIV (1963), 1164.
Tobias, R. C. "The Year's Work in Victorian Poetry: 1962." *VP*, I (1963), 223-30.
Truss, Tom J., Jr. "Browning's 'Childe Roland' in Light of Ruskin's *Modern Painters*." *UMSE*, II (1963), 13-21.
Whitla, William. *The Central Truth: The Incarnation in Browning's Poetry*. Toronto, 1963.
Willoughby, John. "Browning's 'Childe Roland to the Dark Tower Came.' " *VP*, I (1963), 291-99.

1964

Armstrong, Isobel. "Browning's Mr. Sludge, 'The Medium.' " *VP*, II (1964), 1-9.
Bachem, Rose M. "Musset's and Browning's 'Andrea del Sarto.' " *RLC*, XXXVIII (1964), 248-54.
Bonner, Francis W. "Browning's 'The Bishop Orders His Tomb at Saint Praxed's Church.' " *Expl*, XXII (1964), Item 57.
Cadbury, William. "Lyric and Anti-Lyric Forms: A Method for Judging Browning." *UTQ*, XXXIV (1964), 49-67.
Collins, Thomas J. "Browning's Essay on Shelley: In Context." *VP*, II (1964), 119-24.
Columbus, Robert R., and Claudette Kemper. "Sordello and the Speaker: A Problem in Identity." *VP*, II (1964), 251-67.

Combecher, Hans. "Drei victorianische Gedichte." *Neuren Sprachen*, XIII (1964), 257-67.

Drew, Philip. "Henry Jones on Browning's Optimism." *VP*, II (1964), 29-41.

Fleming, John V. "Browning's Yankee Medium." *American Speech*, XXXIX (1964), 26-32.

Friend, Joseph H. "Euripides Browningized: The Meaning of *Balaustion's Adventure.*" *VP*, II (1964), 179-86.

Honan, Park. "Belial upon Setebos." *TSL*, IX (1964), 87-98.

———. "Browning's Testimony on His Essay on Shelley in 'Shepherd V. Francis.'" ELN, II (1964), 27-31.

Hooreman, Paul. "Promenades romaines. La recontre inopinée de Stendhal et de Robert Browning." *Stendhal Club*, VI (1964), 185-200.

Irvine, William. "Four Monologues in Browning's *Men and Women.*" *VP*, II (1964), 155-64.

Jennings, C. Wade. "Diderot: A Suggested Source of the Jules-Phene Episode in *Pippa Passes.*" *ELN*, II (1964), 32-36.

Kramer, Dale. "Character and Theme in *Pippa Passes.*" *VP*, II (1964), 241-49.

Litzinger, Boyd. *Time's Revenges: Browning's Reputation as a Thinker, 1889-1962.* Knoxville, Tenn., 1964.

Melchiori, Barbara. "Where the Bishop Ordered His Tomb." *REL*, V (1964), 7-26.

Mendel, Sydney. "Browning's 'Andrea del Sarto.'" *Expl*, XXII (1964), Item 77.

Nelson, Charles E. "Creative Consciousness in *The Ring and the Book.*" *DA*, XXIV (1964), 4179.

Perrine, Laurence. "Browning's 'Caliban upon Setebos': A Reply." *VP*, II (1964), 124-27.

Poston, Lawrence S., III. "Five Victorians on Italian Renaissance Culture: A Problem in Historical Perspective." *DA*, XXV (1964), 484.

———. "Ruskin and Browning's Artists." *EM*, XV (1964), 195-212.

Priestley, F. E. L. "The Ironic Pattern of Browning's *Paracelsus.*" *UTQ*, XXXIV (1964), 68-81.

Rivers, Charles. "The Twin Revealment: Subjective-Objective Polarity in the Poetry of Robert Browning." *NwMSCS*, XXVIII (1964), 3-31.

Shaw, W. David. "The Analogical Argument of Browning's 'Saul.'" *VP*, II (1964), 277-82.

———. "Character and Philosophy in 'Fra Lippo Lippi.'" *VP*, II (1964), 127-32.

Sullivan, Mary Rose. "Browning's Voices: A Study of the Speaker-Environment as a Primary Means of Control in the Dramatic Monologues of *The Ring and the Book.*" *DA*, XXV (1964), 2989.

Tamagnan, Jean. "Fenêtre ouverte sur Browning." *EA*, XVII (1964), 163-70.

Tillotson, Geoffrey. "A Word for Browning." *SR*, LXXII (1964), 389-97.

Triesch, Gisela. "Der dramatische Monolog in Robert Brownings *The Ring and the Book.*" *Neueren Sprache*, XIII (1964), 153-64.

Truss, Tom J., Jr. "Browning's Ambiguities and *The Ring and the Book.*" *UMSE*, V (1964), 1-7.

Watkins, Charlotte C. "Browning's *Red Cotton Night-Cap Country* and Carlyle." *VS*, VII (1964), 359-74.

1965

Altick, Richard D. "The Symbolism of Browning's 'Master Hugues of Saxe-Gotha.'" *VP*, III (1965), 1-7.

Ball, Patricia. "Browning's Godot." *VP*, III (1965), 245-53.

Bennett, James R. "Lazarus in Browning's 'Karshish.'" *VP*, III (1965), 189-91.

Berkey, John C. "*Sordello* by Robert Browning: A Variorum Text." *DA*, XXVI (1965), 3325.

Boo, Sister Mary Richard. "The Ordeal of Giuseppi Caponsacchi." *VP*, III (1965), 179-88.

Bose, A. "Browning's *Ring and the Book.*" *Essays Presented to Amy G. Stock*, pp. 78-94.
Chandler, Alice. " 'The Eve of St. Agnes' and 'Porphyria's Lover.' " *VP*, III (1965), 273-74.
Clements, Clyde C., Jr. "Browning's Poetry: Four Aesthetic Problems Answered." *McNeese Review*, XVI (1965), 3-15.
Collins, Thomas J. "Shelley and God in Browning's *Pauline*. Unresolved Problems." VP, III (1965), 151-60.
Dahl, Curtis. "Who Was Browning's Cleon?" *Cithara*, IV No. 2 (1965), 69-73.
Day, Robert A. "Browning's 'Soliloquy of the Spanish Cloister.' " 17-24, *Expl*, XXIV (1965), Item 33.
Dornberg, Curtis L. "Genial Humor, Comic Irony, and Satire in the Poetry of Robert Browning." *DA*, XXVI (1965), 1644-45.
Goldfarb, Russell M. "Sexual Meaning in 'The Last Ride Together.' " *VP*, III (1965), 255-61.
Gridley, Roy Elliott. "Browning's Monologuists: Self-Definition as Theme in *The Ring and the Book.*" *DA*, XXV (1965), 6624-25.
Hoar, Victor. "A Note on Browning's 'Childe Roland to the Dark Tower Came.' " *VNL*, No. 27 (1965), pp. 26-28.
Hudson, Gertrude R. *Browning to His American Friends: Letters between the Brownings, the Storys and James Russell Lowell, 1841-90*. New York, 1965.
Jerman, B. R. "The Death of Robert Browning." *UTQ*, XXXV (1965), 47-74.
Kroeber, Karl. "Touchstones for Browning's Victorian Complexity." *VP*, III (1965), 101-07.
Matthews, Jack. "Browning and Neoplatonism." *VNL*, No. 28 (1965), pp. 9-12.
Maxwell, J. C. "A Horatian Echo in Browning's 'Saul.' " *VP*, III (1965), 144.
Monteiro, George. "A Proposal for Settling the Grammarian's Estate." *VP*, III (1965), 266-70.
Perrine, Laurence. "Browning's 'The Bishop Orders His Tomb at Saint Praxed's Church.' " *Expl*, XXIV (1965), Item 12.
Preyer, Robert. "Two Styles in the Verse of Robert Browning." *ELH*, XXXII (1965), 62-84.
Puhvel, Martic. "Reminiscent Bells in The Waste Land." *ELN*, II (1965), 286-87.
Raymond, William O. *The Infinite Moment and Other Essays in Robert Browning*. Toronto, 1965.
Ricks, Christopher. "Two Letters by Browning." *TLS*, June 3, 1965, p. 464.
Rivers, Charles. "Robert Browning's *Pauline*: 'The Dim Orb of Self.' " *NwMSCS*, XXIX (1965), 3-19.
Smalley, Donald. "Joseph Arnould and Robert Browning: New Letters (1842-50) and a Verse Epistle." *PMLA*, LXXX (1965), 90-101.
Sprague, Rosemary. *Forever in Joy: The Life of Robert Browning*. Philadelphia, 1965.
Stempel, Daniel. "Browning's *Sordello*: The Art of the Makers-See." *PMLA*, LXXX (1965), 554-61.
Stevens, L. Robert. "Aestheticism in Browning's Early Renaissance Monologues." VP, III (1965), 19-24.
———. " 'My Last Duchess': A Possible Source." *VNL*, No. 28 (1965), pp. 25-26.
Timko, Michael. "Browning upon Butler; or, Natural Theology in the English Isle." *Criticism*, VII (1965), 141-50.

1966

Bishop, Morchard. "Towards a Biography of Flush." *TLS*, Dec. 15, 1966, p. 1180.
Camp, Dennis, "Browning's Pompilia and the Truth." *Personalist*, XLVII (1966), 350-64.
Collins, Thomas J. "The Development of Robert Browning's Moral Aesthetic Theory 1833-1855." *DA*, XXVII (1966), 454A.

———. "Shelley and God in Browning's *Pauline*: Unresolved Problems." *VP*, III (1966), 151-60.
DeLaura, David J. "A Robert Browning Letter: The Occasion of Mrs. Browning's 'A Curse for a Nation.' " *VP*, IV (1966), 210-12.
Drew, Philip, ed. *Robert Browning: A Collection of Critical Essays*. London, 1966.
Friedman, Barton R. "To Tell the Sun from the Druid Fire: Imagery of Good and Evil in *The Ring and the Book*." *SEL*, VI (1966), 693-708.
Gabbard, G. N. "Browning's Metamorphoses." *VP*, IV (1966), 29-31.
Govil, O. P. "An Echo of Tennyson in Browning." *NQ*, XIII (1966), 341.
———. "A Note on Mill and Browning's *Pauline*." *VP*, IV (1966), 287-91.
Guskin, Phyllis J. "Ambiguities in the Structure and Meaning of Browning's *Christmas-Eve*." *VP*, IV (1966), 21-28.
Hair, Donald S. "Genre in Browning's Poetry." *DA*, XXVII (1966), 774A (Toronto).
Hellstrom, Ward. "Time and Type in Browning's *Saul*." *ELH*, XXXIII (1966), 370-89.
Hitner, John M. "Browning's Grotesque Period." *VP*, IV (1966), 1-13.
Huebenthal, John. "The Dating of Browning's 'Love among the Ruins,' 'Women and Roses,' and 'Childe Roland.' " *VP*, IV (1966), 51-54.
Kintgen, Eugene R. "Childe Roland and the Perversity of the Mind." *VP*, IV (1966), 253-58.
Kvapil, Charline R. " 'How It Strikes a Contemporary': A Dramatic Monologue." *VP*, IV (1966), 279-83.
Langbaum, Robert. "Browning and the Question of Myth." *PMLA*, LXXXI (1966), 575-84.
Malbone, R. G. "Browning's 'Fra Lippo Lippi.' " *Expl*, XXV (1966), Item 20.
———. "That Blasted Rose-acacia: A Note on Browning's 'Soliloquy of the Spanish Cloister.' " *VP*, IV (1966), 218-21.
Marshall, George O. "Evelyn Hope's Lover." *VP*, IV (1966), 32-34.
McAleer, Edward C., ed. *Learned Lady: Letters from Robert Browning to Mrs. Thomas Fitzgerald, 1876-1889*. Cambridge, Mass., 1966.
Melchiori, Barbara. "Browning and the Bible: An Examination of 'Holy Cross Day.' " *REL*, VII (1966), 20-42.
———. "Browning's 'Andrea del Sarto': A French Source in De Musset," *VP*, IV (1966), 132-36.
———. "Browning's Don Juan." *EIC*, XVI (1966), 416-40.
———. "A 'Very Original Poem' by Robert Browning." *NQ*, XIII (1966), 340.
Nelson, Charles E. "Role-Playing in *The Ring and the Book*." *VP*, IV (1966), 91-98.
Nestrick, William V. "Robert Browning: The Maker-See." *EJ*, LV (1966), 682-89.
Parr, Johnstone. "Browning's *Fra Lippo Lippi*, Baldinucci, and the Milanese Edition of Vasari." *ELN*, III (1966), 197-201.
Penner, Allen R. "Judgment in *The Ring and the Book*." XUS, V (1966), 61-82.
Phipps, Charles T., S. J. "Browning's Clerical Characters." *DA*, XXVII (1966), 213A-14A.
Pitts, Gordon, "Browning's 'Soliloquy of the Spanish Cloister': 'Hy Zy, Hine.' " *NQ*, XIII (1966), 339-40.
Plunkett, P. M. "Browning's 'Abt Vogler,' Stanza IV." *Expl*, XXV (1966), Item 14.
Radner, Susan G. "Love and the Lover in Browning's 'Evelyn Hope.' " *L&P*, XVI (1966), 115-16.
Sandstrom, Glenn. " 'James Lee's Wife'—and Browning's." *VP*, IV (1966), 259-70.
Shaw, W. David. "Browning's Duke as Theatrical Producer." *VNL*, No. 29 (1966), pp. 18-22.
Shivers, Alfred S. "Nursery Stories for Adults. . . . The Real Story Behind Browning's 'My Last Duchess.' " *Amer Book Collector*, XVI (1966), 28-30.
Smith, John Henry. "Robert Browning to Lady Colville: An Unpublished Letter." *NQ*, XIII (1966), 67-68.
Thompson, Leslie M. "Browning's Theory of Success and Failure as Revealed in *The Ring and the Book*, *DA*, XXVI (1966), 2677-78.

Timko, Michael. "Ah, Did You Once See Browning Plain?" *SEL*, VI (1966), 731-42.

Vail, Margaret F. "Religious Symbolism as a Unifying Principle of Browning." *DA*, XXVII (1966), 487A-88A.

Wasserman, George. "Browning's 'Johannes Agricola in Meditation.'" *Expl*, XXIV (1966), Item 59.

1967

Altick, Richard D. "Lover's Finiteness: Browning's 'Two in the Campagna.'" *Papers on Language and Lit. III* (1967), pp. 75-80.

Barnes, Warner. *The Browning Collection at the University of Texas*. Austin, 1967.

Bisignano, Dominic J. "The Brownings and Their Italian Critics." *DA*, XXVII (1967), 4242A-43A.

Blackburn, Thomas. *Robert Browning: A Study of His Poetry*. London, 1967.

Collins, Thomas J. *Robert Browning's Moral-Aesthetic Theory, 1833-1855*. Lincoln, Nebr., 1967.

Columbus, Robert R., and Claudette Kemper. "Browning's Fuddling Apollo or the Perils of Parleying." *TSL*, XII (1967), 83-102.

Drew, Philip. "Another View of *Fifine at the Fair*." *EIC*, XVII (1967), 244-55.

Fleissner, R. F. "Browning's Last Lost Duchess: A Purview." *VP*, V (1967), 217-19.

Gridley, Roy. "Browning's Two Guidos." *UTQ*, XXXVII (1967), 51-68.

Grube, John. "Browning's 'The King.'" *UTQ*, XXXVII (1967), 69-74.

Honan, Park. "The Texts of Fifteen Fugitives by Robert Browning." *VP*, V (1967), 157-69.

Kelly, Robert L. "Dactyls and Curlews: Satire in 'A Grammarian's Funeral.'" *VP*, V (1967), 105-12.

Kemper, Claudette. "Irony Anew with Occasional Reference to Byron and Browning." *SEL*, VII (1967), 705-19.

Knickerbocker, Kenneth L. "A Critical Analysis of Robert Browning's *Pacchiarotto* Volume with a Study of the Background (1867-1876)." *DA* (1967), 233A.

Lamacchia, Grace A. "*The Ring and the Book*: Its Contemporary Reputation, Its Intellectual Background, and Its Internal Dynamics." *DA*, XXVII (1967), 2502A-03A.

Litzinger, Boyd. "Browning's Measure of Man." *Cithara*, VI, No. 2 (1967), 33-40.

Lucie-Smith, Edward, ed. *A Choice of Browning's Verse*. London, 1967.

McNally, James. "Suiting Sight and Sound to Sense in 'Meeting at Night' and 'Parting at Morning.'" *VP*, V (1967), 219-24.

Melchiori, Barbara. "Robert Browning's Courtship and the Mutilation of Monsieur Léonce Miranda." *VP*, V (1967), 503-04.

Nevins, Linda M. "The Theme of Death in the Poetry of Robert Browning: A Study of the Shift from Objective to Subjective Emphasis in the Late Period." *DA*, XXVIII (1967), 2216A.

Paananen, Victor N. "Byron and Browning: The Aesthetics of Skepticism." *DA*, XXVIII (1967), 639A-40A.

Patrick, Michael D. "The Dramatic Techniques of Robert Browning." *DA*, XXVII 1967), 2540A.

Ricks, Christopher. "An Echo of Tennyson in Browning." *NQ*, XIV (1967), 374.

Slakey, Roger L., "A Note on Browning's 'Rabbi Ben Ezra.'" *VP*, V (1967), 291-94.

Solimine, Joseph, Jr. "Browning's 'My Last Duchess.'" *Expl*, XXVI (1967), Item 11.

Sullivan, Ruth E. "Browning's 'Childe Roland' and Dante's *Inferno*." *VP*, V (1967), 296-302.

Svaglic, Martin J. "Browning's Grammarian: Apparent Failure or Real?" *VP*, V (1967), 93-104.

Tanzy, C. B. "Madness and Hope in Browning's 'Evelyn Hope.'" *L&P*, XVII (1967), 155-58.

Thompson, Leslie M. "Biblical Influence in 'Childe Roland to the Dark Tower Came.'" *PLL*, III (1967), 339-63.

———. "Regular and Irregular Deeds in *The Ring and the Book*." *PLL*, III (1967), 80-85.
Timko, Michael. "Ah, Did You Once See Browning Plain?" *SEL*, VI (1967), 731-42.
Ward, Maisie. *Robert Browning and His World, I: The Private Face, 1812-1861*. New York, 1967.
Williams, Ioan M. *Browning*. London, 1967.
Winter, J. L. "Browning's Piper." *NQ*, XIV (1967), 373.
Yetman, Michael G. "A Study of the Characterization of Caponsacchi in *The Ring and the Book*." *DA*, XXVIII (1967), 1801A-02A.

1968

Altick, Richard D., and James F. Loucks, II. *Browning's Roman Murder Story: A Reading of "The Ring and the Book."* Chicago, 1968.
Armstrong, Isobel. "A Note on the Conversion of Caponsacchi." *VP*, VI (1968), 271-79.
Baker, Ronald. "Collection: The University of Texas, Austin (Recent Acquisitions)." *Browning Newsletter*, I (1968), 7-8.
Brown, Bernadine. "Robert Browning's 'The Italian in England.'" *VP*, VI (1968), 179-83.
Brugière, Bernard. "Guido dans *The Ring and the Book* de Robert Browning." *EA*, XXI (1968), 19-34.
"A Checklist of Publications (June 1967—June 1968)." *Browning Newsletter*, I (1968), 44-46.
Collins, Thomas J. "Browning's Early Poetry: The Problem of Critical Sophistication." *Cithara*, XIII, i (1968), 47-53.
Cook, Margaret E. "Browning's Lyrics: An Exploration." *DA*, XXVIII (1968), 4624A-25A.
Cox, Ollie. "The 'Spot of Joy' in 'My Last Duchess.'" *CLAJ*, XII (1968), 70-76.
Crowell, Norton B. *The Convex Glass: The Mind of Robert Browning*. Albuquerque, N.M., 1968.
Cundiff, Paul A. "'Andrea del Sarto.'" *TSL*, XIII (1968), 27-38.
D'Avanzo, Mario L. "King Francis, Lucrezia, and the Figurative Language of 'Andrea del Sarto.'" *TSLL*, IX (1968), 523-36.
Donaghy, Henry J. "*The Ring and the Book*: Its Conception, Current Reputation, and Meaning." *SlitI*, I, No. 1 (1968), 47-66.
Drew, Philip. "A Note on the Lawyers." *VP*, VI (1968), 297-307.
Goyne, Grover C., Jr. "Browning and the Higher Criticism." *DA*, XXVIII (1968), 4128A.
Gridley, Roy E. "Browning's Caponsacchi: 'How the Priest Caponsacchi Said His Say.'" *VP*, VI (1968), 281-95.
———. "Browning's Pompilia." *JEGP*, LXVII (1968), 64-83.
Hancher, Charles M., Jr. "The London Browning Society, 1881-1892." *DA*, XXIX (1968), 601A.
Harrold, William E. "The Complementary Poems of Robert Browning." *DA*, XXVIII (1968), 3637A.
Herring, Jack. "The Baylor Browning Letters: Plans for a New Edition." *Browning Newsletter*, I (1968), 14-18.
Hoerner, Dennis R. "Giuseppe Caponsacchi: Man of God or Man of Flesh?" *Paunch*, XXXII (1968), 39-45.
Honan, Park. "The Murder Poem for Elizabeth." *VP*, VI (1968), 215-30.
Houghton, Esther R. "Reviewer of Browning's *Men and Women* in *The Rambler* Identified." *VNL*, XXXIII (1968), 46.
Isaacs, Neil D. "Browning's 'Laboratory.'" *AN&Q*, VII (1968), 21-23.
Jack, Ian. "Robert Browning." Warton Lecture, 1967, to the British Academy. *Proceedings of the British Academy*, LIII (1968), 219-41.

Jones, A. R. "Robert Browning and the Dramatic Monologue: The Impersonal Art." *CritQ*, IX (1968), 301-28.

Kendall, Lyle H., Jr. "The Not-So-Gentle Art of Puffing: William G. Kingsland and Thomas J. Wise." *PBSA*, LXII (1968), 25-37.

King, Roma A., Jr. "Karshish Encounters Himself: An Interpretation of Browning's Epistle." *CP*, I, No. 1 (1968), 23-33.

———. "The Ohio University Press Edition: *The Complete Works of Robert Browning with Variant Readings, Annotated.*" *Browning Newsletter*, I (1968), 9-13.

———. *The Focusing Artifice: The Poetry of Robert Browning*. Athens, Ohio, 1968.

Korg, Jacob. "A Reading of *Pippa Passes.*" *VP*, VI (1968), 5-19.

Lint, Robert G. "Syntax in Browning's 'Sordello.' " *DA*, XXVIII (1968), 4617A.

Loschky, Helen M. "Free Will Versus Determinism in *The Ring and the Book.*" *VP*, VI (1968), 333-52.

Loucks, James F., II. " 'Scripture for His Purpose': A Study of Robert Browning's Use of Biblical Allusions in *The Ring and the Book.*" *DA*, XXVIII (1968), 3676A-77A.

McCrory, J. V. "A Study of Robert Browning's Representative Personal Satires." *DA*, XXVIII (1968), 2650A.

Melchiori, Barbara. *Browning's Poetry of Reticence*. New York, 1968.

Millhauser, Milton. "Poet and Burgher: A Comic Variation on a Serious Theme." *VP*, VII (1968), 163-68.

Milosevich, Vincent M. "The Theme of Renunciation in Browning." *DA*, XXVIII (1968), 2652A.

Ortego, Philip D. "Robert Browning's 'Rabbi Ben Ezra.' " *CEA*, XXX, No. 6, (1968), 6-7.

Otten, Terry. "*A Blot in the 'Scutcheon* and the *Pièce Bien Faite*: An Artistic Dilemma." *RS*, XXXVI (1968), 214-23.

Parr, Johnstone. "Browning's 'Fra Lippo Lippi,' Vasari's Masaccio, and Mrs. Jameson." *ELN*, V (1968), 277-83.

Parsons, D. S. "Childe Roland and the Fool." *UWR*, IV, No. 1 (1968), 24-30.

Peckham, Morse. "Historiography and *The Ring and the Book.*" *VP*, VI (1968), 243-357.

Phipps, Charles T., S. J. "Adaptation from the Past, Creation for the Present: A Study of Browning's 'The Pope.' " *SP*, LXV (1968), 702-22.

Poston, Lawrence, III. " 'Baroque' as a Literary Term: An Early Victorian Example." *AN&Q*, VII (1968), 6.

Powell, David L. "Robert Browning's *Dramatis Personae*: A Variorum Text." *DA*, XXVIII (1968), 4185A.

Raymond, William O. "The Pope in *The Ring and the Book,*" *VP* (1968), 323-32.

Reid, Robert E. "A Variorum Edition of *Jocoseria* by Robert Browning." *DA*, XXVIII (1968), 3154A-55A.

"Research in Progress and Announcements of Forthcoming Publications." *Browning Newsletter*, I (1968), 19-22, 27.

Senescu, Betty C. "Another Pippa." *VNL*, No. 33 (1968), 8-12.

Shaw, W. David. *The Dialectical Temper: The Rhetorical Art of Robert Browning*. Ithaca, N.Y., 1968.

Short, Clarice. "Childe Roland, Pedestrian." *VP*, VI (1968), 175-77.

Sonstroem, David. "Animal and Vegetable in the Spanish Cloister." *VP*, VI (1968), 70-73.

Stasny, John F. "Selected Bibliography." *VP*, VI (1968), 374-75. A bibliography of *The Ring and the Book*.

Sullivan, Mary R. "The Function of Book I in *The Ring and the Book.*" *VP*, VI (1968), 231-41.

Swingle, L. J. "Truth and *The Ring and the Book*: A Negative View." *VP*, VI (1968), 259-69.

Talon, Henri A. "*The Ring and the Book*: Truth and Fiction in Character Painting." *VP*, VI (1968), 353-65.

Thornton, R. K. R. "A New Source for Browning's 'Love Among the Ruins.' " *NQ*, XV (1968), 178-79.

Tracy, Clarence, ed. *Browning's Mind and Art*. London, 1968.

Turner, Richard M. "A Study of Robert Browning's Blank Verse Technique." *DA*, XXVIII (1968), 4650A.

Werlich, Egon. "Robert Browning, Home Thoughts from Abroad: An Interpretation with Particular Emphasis on the Poem's Structural and Syntactical Symbolism." *Praxis*, XV (1968), 135-42.

Wyant, Jerome L. "The Legal Episodes in *The Ring and the Book*." *VP*, VI (1968), 309-21.

1969

Burrows, Leonard. *Browning the Poet: An Introductory Study*. Nedlands, Australia, 1969.

Carrington, C. E. " 'My Last Duchess.' " *TLS*, Nov. 6, 1969, p. 1288.

Collins, Thomas J. "The Sources of Browning's 'Clive': New Evidence." *Browning Newsletter*, III (1969), 3-8.

Culver, Rennie W. "The Dramatic Structure of Browning's *The Ring and the Book*." *DA*, XXIX (1969), 3093A-94A.

Eissenstat, Martha T. "Robert Browning's Use of Italian Renaissance Sources." *DA*, XXIX (1969), 2671A.

Greenberg, Robert A. "Ruskin, Pugin, and the Contemporary Context of 'The Bishop Orders His Tomb.' " *PMLA*, LXXXIV (1969), 1588-94.

Hart, Nathaniel I. "The Nature of the Grotesque in Robert Browning's Poetry." *DA*, XXIX (1969), 2212A.

Hitner, John M. *Browning's Analysis of a Murder: A Case for "The Inn Album."* Marquette, Mich., 1969.

Lee, Young G. "The Human Condition: Browning's 'Cleon.' " *VP*, VII (1969), 56-62.

Marshall, George O., Jr. "Tennyson's 'The Sisters' and 'Porphyria's Lover.' " *Browning Newsletter*, III (1969), 9-11.

McBride, Mary G. "The Idea of Joy: Robert Browning and the Nineteenth-Century Tradition." *DA*, XXIX (1969), 3148A.

Miller, Roy W. "Robert Browning as Poet-Prophet in *The Ring and the Book*." *DA*, XXIX (1969), 2269A-70A.

Milosevich, Vincent M. "Browning's 'The Bishop Orders His Tomb at Saint Praxed's Church.' " *Expl*, XXVII (1969), Item 67.

Mudford, P. G. "The Artistic Consistency of Browning's *In a Balcony*." *VP*, VII (1969), 31-40.

O'Malley, Myles. "Browning's Pope: 'The Last Personage of His Age.' " *XUS*, VIII (1969), 5-20.

Omans, Glen. "Browning's 'Fra Lippo Lippi': A Transcendentalist Monk." *VP*, VII (1969), 129-45.

Peckham, Morse. "Robert Browning: A Review of the Year's Research." *Browning Newsletter*, II (1969), 3-9.

Peterson, William S. "Interrogating the Oracle: A History of the London Browning Society, 1881-1892." *DA*, XXIX (1969), 2223A-24A.

———. "A Re-examination of Robert Browning's *Prose Life of Strafford*." *Browning Newsletter*, III (1969), 12-22.

———. "An Unpublished Memoir of Robert Browning." *VP*, VII (1969), 147-51.

Phipps, Charles T., S. J. "Browning's 'Soliloquy of the Spanish Cloister': Lines 71-72." *VP*, VII (1969), 158-59.

———. "The Monsignor in *Pippa Passes*: Browning's First Clerical Character." *VP*, VII (1969), 66-70.

Pinion, F. P., ed. *Dramatis Personae*. London, 1969.

Plotinsky, Melvin L. "The Kingdom of Infinite Space." *TSLL*, XI (1969), 837-49.

Rich, Nancy B. "New Perspective on the Companion Poems of Robert Browning." *VNL*, XXXIV (1969), 5-9.

Ryals, Clyde De L. "Browning's Amphibian: *Don Juan at Home.*" *EIC*, XIX (1969), 210-17.

———. "Browning's *Fifine at the Fair*: Some Further Sources and Influences." *ELN*, VII (1969), 46-51.

Shapiro, Arnold. " 'Participate in Sludgehood': Browning's 'Mr. Sludge,' the Critics, and the Problem of Morality." *PLL*, V (1969), 145-55.

Stack, V. E., ed. *How Do I Love Thee? The Love-Letters of Robert Browning and Elizabeth Barrett*. New York, 1969.

Sullivan, Mary R. *Browning's Voices in "The Ring and the Book": A Study in Method and Meaning*. Toronto, 1969.

Sutton, Max Keith. "Language as Defense in 'Porphyria's Lover.' " *CE*, XXXI (1969), 280-89.

Thompson, Leslie M. "A Ring of Criticism: The Search for Truth in *The Ring and the Book*." *PLL*, V (1969), 322-35.

Trammell, Jerry P. "La Saisiaz: The Two Poets of Croisic by Robert Browning. An Edition with Variants, Annotated." *DA*, XXIX (1969), 3111A.

Ward, Maisie. *Robert Browning and His World: Two Robert Brownings? 1861-1889*. London, 1969.

Wolfe, Edward L. "Browning's 'Dramatic Idyls, First and Second Series': A Critical Text with Annotations and Introduction." *DA*, XXIX (1969), 2287A-88A.

Index